Nonprofit Organizations

Foundations of Social Work Knowledge
Frederic G. Reamer, Series Editor

Social work has a unique history, purpose, perspective, and method. The primary purpose of this series is to articulate these distinct qualities and to define and explore the ideas, concepts, and skills that together constitute social work's intellectual foundations and boundaries and its emerging issues and concerns.

To accomplish this goal, the series will publish a cohesive collection of books that address both the core knowledge of the profession and its newly emerging topics. The core is defined by the evolving consensus, as primarily reflected in the Council of Social Work Education's Curriculum Policy Statement, concerning what courses accredited social work education programs must include in their curricula. The series will be characterized by an emphasis on the widely embraced ecological perspective; attention to issues concerning direct and indirect practice; and emphasis on cultural diversity and multiculturalism, social justice, oppression, populations at risk, and social work values and ethics. The series will have a dual focus on practice traditions and emerging issues and concepts.

Complete series list follows the index.

Thomas P. Holland
Roger A. Ritvo

Nonprofit Organizations:
Principles and Practices

COLUMBIA UNIVERSITY PRESS NEW YORK

Columbia University Press
Publishers Since 1893
New York   Chichester, West Sussex
Copyright © 2008 Columbia University Press
All rights reserved

Library of Congress Cataloging-in-Publication Data
Holland, Thomas P.
Nonprofit organizations : principles and practices / Thomas P. Holland and Roger A. Ritvo.
p.   cm. — (Foundations of social work knowledge)
Includes bibliographical references and index.
ISBN 978-0-231-13974-8 (cloth : alk. paper) — ISBN 978-0-231-13975-5 (pbk. : alk. paper)
1. Nonprofit organizations. 2. Nonprofit organizations—Management.
I. Ritvo, Roger A., 1944– II. Title. III. Series.
HD62.6.H65   2008
658'.048—dc22   2007053052

This work is dedicated to my wife, Myra,
who has been the ideal partner in working to strengthen
the effectiveness of so many nonprofit organizations.
(TPH)

To my wife, Lynn, whose career reflects the values
of this volume by helping improve the lives
of children and students.
(RAR)

Contents

Figures

Tables

Preface

This book is an introduction to nonprofit organizations, the fastest-growing sector of the American economy. The number of nonprofit organizations has expanded dramatically over the past two decades, building on the American tradition noted long ago by Alexis de Tocqueville of volunteers working together to address community issues. Recent estimates count approximately 2 million nonprofit organizations in the United States plus countless others outside this country. These organizations employ about 12 million workers, or almost 8 percent of the domestic workforce, plus another 6 million volunteers.[1]

Nonprofit organizations may be divided into *service providers* (such as health care providers, nursing homes, educational institutions, day care centers), *advocacy* (civil rights, environmental issues, women's issues, gay rights, progressive and conservative movements), *expressive* (artistic, social, religious), and *community building* (associations, charitable foundations).

Pressures on nonprofits are growing rapidly. Whereas federal financial support of nonprofit organizations outdistanced private charitable contributions by two to one in the late 1970s, public support then declined rapidly in the 1980s and 1990s, and the projected national deficits promise a continuation of this downward trend. Most public support for nonprofits is now in the form of consumer subsidies, such as the Medicare and Medicaid programs. In recent decades, private giving has risen by only small amounts and now stands just under 2 percent of personal income, with declines in giving by the wealthy, albeit with the noteworthy exceptions of Bill Gates, Warren Buffett, and Ted Turner. Indeed, nonprofits are facing an increasingly competitive marketplace for funding, complicated by demands that they develop complex billing and reimbursement systems and learn how to market their services to potential customers. Scarce funds squeeze budgets and make it hard to sustain activities that are critical to the organization's mission but difficult to support.

This concern extends beyond nonprofit organizations. As the importance of philanthropy grows, the business community has responded through its own charitable giving and by providing others with useful information about nonprofit organizations ranging from major universities to local homeless shelters, from the multimillion-dollar foundations to the local art museum. To help in this regard, the Better Business Bureau established its Wise Giving Alliance to help donors make decisions about their philanthropic contributions (www.give.org).

As competition for scarce resources grows and public expectations rise, nonprofit leaders have come to appreciate capable managers. Educational and technical assistance centers for nonprofits have opened in larger cities across the United States, and supportive services to member units are the major concerns of numerous national associations. Colleges and universities across the country have established more than one hundred academic programs in the nonprofit field, with more planned, and the preparation of effective leaders for nonprofit organizations is supported by recent studies of the U.S. Department of Labor, which project a growth of more than 50 percent in positions in this field in the coming decade. Adding to the workforce demand is the retirement of many of those who led nonprofits in the past.

Despite the many books addressing particular aspects of this rapidly growing field, few of them cover the range of topics needed by those entering nonprofit organizations and those emerging as their leaders. Accordingly, most teachers have to piece together their course readings from a variety of sources. This volume is intended to fill this gap with its examination of many of the most important current aspects of the nonprofit field. It is an introductory textbook to help prepare the next generation of leaders for the field; for the faculty in schools of social work, public administration, business, law, public health, adult education, and other fields; as well as instructors in resource centers serving nonprofits.

Figure 0.1
David Kolb's Model and Process of Learning

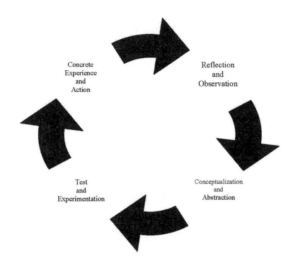

Using This Book

We learn in a variety of ways, both through planned structures and at unexpected moments. We, the authors of this book, believe that David Kolb's model and process of learning, depicted in the figure above, cites those categories useful to students.[2] The circular flow of this model shows that learning can begin at any point, although Kolb and others note that action, referred to here as *concrete experience*, is the most likely starting point, especially in Western cultures.

In some ways, concrete experience is life; we live through our actions, activities, choices, desires, aspirations, ambitions, and goals and reflect on them in a variety of ways. Some people are prolific journal writers, and many try to understand the patterns of their life. We try to understand what works for us and where we can change, improve, and grow, and these reflections lead to broader theories, ideas, and values that we deem important. Then as we grow and change, travel, marry, and have children, we test these theories and values in new situations. In order to maintain our own balance, we keep what works and change or discard those things that do not. The cycle of learning thus is having concrete experiences, reflecting on them, forming concepts and frameworks for understanding them, and testing conclusions in new situations.

For example, think about how you would try to learn a new card game. Some people want to watch others play the game (observation). Others might prefer just to sit at the table and deal the cards and learn by playing (experience). A third option is to read the rules and understand the broad concepts (poker is about cards and bluffing the opponent; bridge relies on communication through a bidding language of its own); this is the theoretical approach. A fourth group plays without keeping score but asks questions and replays the hands to test and learn. Eventually the entire learning process must include all four approaches; otherwise, even the most insightful observers will never play, and without reflection and testing, the person who says "deal me in" will never figure out what does and does not work in different situations.

Organizations have similar learning styles. With their bias toward action—one of John Kenneth Galbraith's axioms for excellence—organizations spend most of their time, energy, and resources in concrete experience; this is the work of the organization. Assessment, performance reviews, and evaluation programs represent observation and reflection. Strategic plans document the abstract concepts needed to lead the organization into the future. Pilot programs and demonstration projects illustrate testing in new situations. Finally, programs are evaluated for their effectiveness by means of systematic observation and reflection.

This textbook uses all four approaches to reinforce learning. Like Kolb, we believe that learning is most effective when the cycle goes through all four processes. Thus, we supplement the theories we cite in the text with alternative models so that the reader can develop multiple perspectives. The case studies encourage application, and the web assignments show how others practice these ideas, theories, and models. We hope that the class discussions, lectures, role plays, and other pedagogical techniques will help students decide what works best for them in accordance with their values, career goals, and work experiences.

Anne Frank, a victim of the brutality and inhumanity of the Nazi regime in World War II, remained optimistic in the face of loss, death, and degradation: "How wonderful it is that nobody need wait a single minute before starting to improve the world." In a similar way, nonprofit organizations try to improve the world through their programs and services. To do this, nonprofits first must be managed most effectively, through professional development, licensure, certification, formal educational programs, accreditation reviews, insurance compliance programs, government regulation, financial audits, risk management assessments, and liability actions. This textbook provides information and action-oriented solutions for people at all levels of organizational responsibility to build on the competencies needed for effective practice.

Competencies

The increased interest in competency-based approaches can be traced back to the 1982 book entitled *The Competent Manager*. Of the many themes in that volume, those that stood out most to both practicing managers and educators in business schools across the country was the amalgamation of what had been distinct themes. Using the broad concept of competencies, Boyatzis argued that successful managers combine skills, knowledge, values, and social roles with a thorough understanding of the organization's culture and internal processes.[3] This was not just a conceptual model; his work was grounded in a large-scale research effort, and he developed a new approach focusing on managerial competencies.

Competency may be defined as using those skills, knowledge, information, and personal characteristics in ways that lead to the successful performance of a task, role, function, or job. Specifically, competencies must be practiced; hence "using" them is key. Conceptually, one might have a competency that is not used, in which case it is not part of being an effective manager. *Skills* are the techniques used to implement a competency. Thus, one may have good financial competencies, and the skill might be expertise on Excel spreadsheets. *Knowledge* comes from a variety of sources and is part of maintaining currency in one's field. *Information* refers to the data and their meaning for appropriate decisions. All these elements must be combined for successful performance. Poor decisions, incomplete actions, or low-quality services are not the result of competent actions.

Peter Vaill questioned whether competencies actually make a difference in results.[4] Although there are numerous intervening variables, we believe that without appropriate competencies and the skills to implement them, poor performance is a more likely outcome. Therefore, each chapter in this book uses competencies as an organizing principle and describes the skills needed to implement them.

Organization of the Book

Each chapter of this book covers the material needed for competent practices for board members, managers, supervisors, staff, and volunteers.

Chapter 1, "Nonprofit Organizations Today," examines the growth and trends in the nonprofit sector. As a result of mastering this material, the reader will be able to

1. Understand how gaps in public- and private-sector services and missions helped create the need for voluntary community-based action.
2. Trace the rise of social responsibility and stewardship as critical values for the nonprofit sector.
3. Explain how the consumer movement grew in the twentieth century.
4. Discuss the public policy issues related to nonprofit organizations' special tax status.

Chapter 2, "History and Theories of Nonprofit Organizations," explores the principal developments in the history of nonprofit organizations from the early colonial days to the current situations faced by these agencies. Using theories and models related to nonprofit systems, readers will be able, by the end of this chapter, to

1. Describe the growth of the nonprofit sector in the United States.
2. Use at least two different economic models to explain these changes.
3. Retrace a selected nonprofit organization's history.
4. Compare and contrast different types of nonprofit organizations.

Chapter 3, "Ethical Issues in Nonprofit Organizations," focuses on a challenging aspect of this sector. Ethical decision making has recently gained national attention in the corporate, governmental, and voluntary sectors. Examples include Enron, WorldCom, the American Red Cross, the United Way, and the United Nations' Oil-for-Food program. When they understand these issues, readers will be able to

1. Describe the major ethical frameworks.
2. Apply these frameworks to individual and organizational processes and decisions.
3. Deal with the ethical issues raised by the need to ration limited resources.
4. Learn how nonprofit organizations can develop and sustain an ethical culture.
5. Analyze the connected concepts of consumer rights and organizational responsibility.

Chapter 4, "Creating Effective Nonprofit Organizations," shows how ideas can become realities. When a community has needs, visionary leaders work to fill the gaps. The organizations they create require several basic components and must comply with the federal and state laws regulating nonprofits. The objectives of this chapter are to enable the reader to

1. Understand the basic steps in establishing a nonprofit organization.
2. Describe the federal and state regulations governing the required components of such an organization.
3. Explain and apply the basic legal duties of nonprofit leaders.

Chapter 5, "Understanding Organizations," is an overview of the major conceptual frameworks and principles used to examine and understand organizations. All the workers in organizations have specific responsibilities, and their supervisors and managers oversee them, are accountable for them, settle disputes, draw up budgets, and other such tasks. Understanding these components helps define each organization's particular characteristics and culture. This chapter traces the major developments in organization theory and management practice with applications for those who lead, manage, and supervise nonprofit systems. Its objectives are to enable the reader to

1. Describe the major conceptual frameworks for organizations.
2. Identify some of their strengths and limitations.
3. Describe their applicability to nonprofit organizations.

Chapter 6, "Leading and Managing Nonprofit Organizations," examines the core skills, abilities, and perspectives that supervisors, middle managers, and leaders of nonprofit organizations need to ensure their effectiveness. The objectives of the chapter enable the reader to

1. Describe an organization's culture.
2. Identify the important skills of leadership.
3. Understand how to improve staff performance.
4. Describe the characteristics of effective staff teams.
5. Identify steps to improve one's use of time.

Chapter 7, "Key Issues in Human Resources," addresses those aspects of dealing with the most important resource in any nonprofit organization: its people. Skills in relating to others inside and outside the organization are crucial to its overall effectiveness. Developing and sustaining work environments in which staff, consumers, volunteers, and others are comfortable and motivated toward the organization's mission are among the most important ingredients of success. This chapter helps readers

1. Identify some of the main purposes and components of personnel policies.
2. Understand the ingredients of a successful volunteer program.
3. Know how to diversify the staff.
4. Learn how to accommodate the needs of people with disabilities.
5. Help an organization create a more family-friendly work environment.
6. Prevent and deal with sexual harassment.

Chapter 8, "Governing Effectively," examines the boards of nonprofit organizations. Despite their being in positions of power, authority, responsibility, and visibility, the directors of many boards are not as effective as they can and must be. The problem lies not in the lack of good intentions. Based on research and analysis of best practices, effective boards must have and practice six competencies. The material in this chapter is designed to help the reader

1. Understand the most important responsibilities of nonprofit boards and its members.
2. Learn the competencies necessary for effective board-level decision making and functioning.
3. Explore how different sources of power can be used to achieve desired policy, program, and service goals.

Chapter 9, "Organizational Growth and Renewal," explores the typical stages of organizational growth and development, identifies common challenges to success, and discusses intervention strategies for changing problematic situations, dealing with crises, and restoring the health of the work environment. The chapter's objectives are enabling the reader to

1. Identify the phases of organizational life cycles and their typical features.
2. Describe "founder's syndrome" and its challenges to an organization.
3. Recognize and deal with mission drift.
4. Understand and apply some methods of organizational development and renewal.
5. Know the basic principles and procedures for dealing with conflicts in organizations.
6. Plan for and respond appropriately when changes are resisted.

Chapter 10, "Strategic Planning," explains how nonprofit organizations create strategic plans. Often the problem with strategic plans is that they appear only in an annual report or are kept in an executive's file cabinet. This means the plans are not guiding the organization's decision making, allocation of resources, or development of priorities. Such plans must form the basis for nonprofit organizations to make the most effective and efficient use of all resources. The material in this chapter enables the reader to

1. Understand the basic components and processes of developing a strategic plan.
2. Analyze an organization's internal strengths and weaknesses and its external opportunities and threats.
3. Recognize the principles of effective strategic planning.
4. Analyze and use mission statements to guide strategic planning.

Chapter 11, "Community Relations," discusses how to form and sustain strong and positive relationships with an organization's multiple stakeholders, that is, those people who have an interest in the organization, its mission, and its effectiveness in pursuing it. This chapter enables readers to

1. Connect the concept of social responsibility to a nonprofit organization's community relations initiatives.
2. Use sound marketing principles to increase a nonprofit's visibility and reputation in the community.
3. Use proven techniques to develop and maintain a media relations program.
4. Know how to use advocacy and lobbying efforts.
5. Understand the broad concepts and skills needed to form mutually beneficial partnerships with other organizations.

Chapter 12, "Principles and Practices of Effective Fund-Raising," takes up the crucial matter of obtaining the money needed to sustain the organization. Although some people would prefer not to discuss financial matters outside the privacy of their home, money is the driving force of nonprofit organizations. This chapter shows how to get the results needed to continue offering quality programs and services. Readers learn how to

1. Identify different revenue and income streams.
2. Write grant proposals for public and private organizations.
3. Ask individual donors to increase their philanthropic generosity.
4. Run a successful annual campaign.

5. Use all resources effectively, no matter what their source.

6. Use the ten keys to successful fund-raising programs.

Chapter 13, "Program Evaluation," describes the components and steps of assessing the impacts of nonprofit programs on their users. The continuing public outcry for greater transparency and accountability means that nonprofits must conduct more open and rigorous self-evaluations or outsiders will do it for them. The thesis of this chapter is that nonprofit organizations should take the initiative in program evaluation and work cooperatively and collaboratively with others. The objectives of this chapter are to enable readers to

1. Understand the uses and benefits of program evaluations in nonprofit organizations.

2. Identify the components and steps of a sound evaluation.

3. Specify a program's goals and ways of measuring them.

4. Understand the basic designs used in evaluations.

5. Apply principles and skills of leadership in planning, conducting, reporting, and using findings to improve an organization's performance.

Chapter 14, "Accountability," takes up the increasingly important matter of nonprofit organizations' accountability. Criticism of their performance and demands for their greater accountability are growing rapidly. Since nonprofits are dependent on public trust and credibility, they must make their policies and practices as transparent and open as possible. This chapter looks at the issues related to accountability and the steps that nonprofit organizations and their leadership must take to meet these challenges. Understanding the material in this chapter will help readers

1. Describe the steps that individual employees, departments, organizations, and boards should take to demonstrate their accountability.

2. Differentiate process accountability from structural accountability.

3. Discuss important federal legislation designed to increase accountability.

4. Understand when public advocacy (acceptable) becomes political lobbying (problematic).

5. Be aware of the consequences of failing to meet these rising expectations for greater accountability.

Chapter 15, "Financial Accountability," examines the basic financial accounting documents used in nonprofit organizations. In order to sustain their trust and support, organizations owe their supporters accurate information about how their contributions were used. The objectives of this chapter are to enable readers to

1. Explain the relationships between income and expenses, and priorities and cost controls.
2. Understand the principles of accountability to donors regarding the organization's income.
3. Understand the importance of setting and following the organization's priorities.
4. Use the basic financial documents of organizations, including budgets and financial reports to sponsors and the public.

Chapter 16, "Nonprofit Organizations Tomorrow," discusses trends that we believe will affect most nonprofit organizations in the future. Leaders who anticipate future developments must deal with change; those who overlook these changes will have to adapt later. Effective leadership requires environmental scanning, reliable information, innovation, and creativity in addressing new circumstances. In many ways this chapter is a synthesis of the material covered in previous chapters. By thinking about these issues, readers will be able to

1. Identify those political, professional, and policy issues that will affect nonprofit organizations and their programs.
2. Design appropriate responses to meet these challenges.
3. Formulate their ideas of what the future might hold and how to prepare for it.

Each chapter contains features intended to help both instructors and students learn. The web assignments encourage students to search for current information and can be used as out-of-class projects and examples of salient points during the class. Case studies challenge readers to assume the role of someone confronting a specific problem or concern in a nonprofit. They provide opportunities to apply concepts and principles from the text. Readers will encounter questions that require critical thinking—not just opinions but reflective analysis and defendable positions.

In the old television show *Dragnet*, Sergeant Joe Friday used a phrase that has become common today: "Just the facts, ma'am." Even though there always are more facts to discover, working with limited information is often the reality in most organizational decisions. We can always conduct another study, appoint a committee, gather more data, and search for alternatives or best practices. But we have to make many decisions in less time than ideal. Dealing with the thought-provoking cases and discussion exercises should include attention to such questions as

1. What are the major issues in this situation?
2. What are the central themes or principles that should be used to analyze it?
3. Rather than discuss the situation case as an objective observer, assume a role. Perhaps you are one of the people mentioned in the case. Or maybe you are a newspaper reporter covering this situation or a prospective donor trying to understand what is going on.
4. Clarify the assumptions needed to reach a conclusion. Since there are never enough facts, knowing how to make assumptions and fill in the gaps can help others understand our conclusions.
5. Sometimes it helps to frame the issues as a question. For instance, if the issue is about the allocation of financial resources, we could ask, "Which clients need what services first?" We would likely reach a very different conclusion than if we asked, "Which services cost the least to provide?"

Finally, the most important aspect is the discussion, not the conclusions. No views are totally right or totally wrong. Equally important as any answers to a case are the assumptions that people make about their roles, constraints, options, and opportunities. It is important to examine each person's role and how it affects the situation, the assumptions made, and the principles chosen for action.

Acknowledgments

The entire staff at Columbia University Press has made the process, from idea to final proofs, enjoyable, productive, and timely. We say, "Thank you, one and all."

In conclusion, we are indebted to all those who have written about, done research on, and examined nonprofit organizations. The field is growing rapidly, and it is likely that new ideas, insights, and good practices will emerge in the coming years. Future editions of this volume will likely show many changes in the principles and practices useful for those entering the field and those emerging as leaders in it. We encourage our readers to share their experiences widely and offer their learning to others. We accept responsibility for the limitations of the current volume and welcome suggestions to improve it.

Nonprofit Organizations

Nonprofit Organizations Today

We begin with an overview of some of the major themes and influences shaping the contemporary nonprofit field. The purpose of this chapter is to help readers

1. Understand the importance of voluntary, community-based action.
2. Trace the rise of social responsibility and stewardship as critical values for the nonprofit sector.
3. Explain how the consumer movement grew in the twentieth century.
4. Discuss the public policy issues related to nonprofit organizations' special tax status.

The nonprofit sector has a long and distinguished history of contributing to the health, well-being, education, culture, artistic diversity, philanthropic, and community services offered throughout the United States. Many thousands of such organizations have been established in recent years, building on the American tradition noted by Alexis de Tocqueville in the 1830s of volunteers working together to address community issues. Americans' idea and ideal to make a difference in the lives of others and their communities have deep roots in this country. The sociologist Max Weber observed that "voluntary associations" were critical to the fabric of our culture, and prominent historians have developed this theme further. Max Lerner's scholarly book entitled *America as a Civilization* stresses that residents are "intense joiners"[1] and notes that previous generations established a pattern of service by forming organizations to promote services (hospitals), expand cultural activities (museums), reflect on mutual experiences (Veterans of Foreign Wars, American Legion), and fight for individual rights through concerted actions (unions and professional associations). Churches were the first nonprofit organizations in the early American colonies, and Harvard University was the first educational nonprofit in the country and, according to its Web site, "the oldest in the Western hemisphere."[2] Harvard was established in the colony of Massachusetts in 1636. That year, twelve overseers formed a governing board composed of six public representatives and six clergy to offer educational programs, and in 1650, this entity became what is now known as Harvard University, in Cambridge, Massachusetts.

Recent estimates indicate there are more than 2 million nonprofit organizations in the United States plus countless others in other countries. These organizations employ about 12 million workers, or almost 8 percent of the U.S. workforce, plus another 6 million volunteers. Combining paid and volunteer staff, employment in nonprofits approaches that of all forms of manufacturing combined. Most of these employees work in one of three fields: health (43%), education (22%), and social services (18%). The civic, social, fraternal, and cultural organizations are smaller categories, but when volunteers are included, this distribution changes, with religious organizations rising to 23 percent and health dropping to 34 percent.[3]

The nonprofit sector is broad and diverse. Salamon divides such organizations into four functional categories:

1. *Service providers*: health care, nursing homes, educational institutions, and day care centers.
2. *Advocacy* organizations: civil rights, environmental issues, women's issues, gay rights, and progressive and conservative movements.
3. *Expressive* organizations: artistic, social, and religious systems.
4. *Community-building* groups: associations and charitable foundations.

In a major recent study, the Corporation for National and Community Service documented the extensive impact of volunteerism in the United States. Its report, entitled *Volunteering in America, 2002–2005: State Trends and Rankings*, shows that 65.4 million people volunteered in some way in 2005, the latest year for which data are available.[4] This figure exceeds the 59.8 million who were recorded as volunteering in 2002, an increase of 9.3 percent. The report echoes one of the themes of this book: "This upward trend in volunteering represents a once-in-a-generation opportunity to tap into Americans' ingenuity, civic mindedness and generosity to build powerful new solutions to old problems in our communities." When challenged, people in this country rise to fulfill needs.

The biggest group of volunteers is married women. Males are slightly less likely to volunteer than women, and being single does not translate into more volunteer activities. People between the ages of thirty-five and forty-four are the most likely to volunteer, and more than one-third of volunteers choose to work in religious organizations, consistent with the Bush administration's faith-based initiatives.

People serve as teachers, fund-raisers, mentors, tutors, advocates, and workers in food banks and soup kitchens. When people decide to volunteer, they do so with noteworthy commitment and energy: on average, volunteers spend more than fifty hours per year, or almost one full hour each week. *Volunteering in America 2002–2005* provides an extensive state-by-state database and is available free to the public through the Internet at http://www.nationalservice.gov/pdf/VIA/VIA_fullreport.pdf.

As described in the preface, the extent of the recent turbulence in the external environment of nonprofit organizations is illustrated by the Lockheed Martin Corporation's recent bid to manage welfare contracts. The executives of this internationally renowned aircraft manufacturer believe that the firm's project management skills could be adapted to the nonprofit sector,[5] an approach that may well represent the leading edge of a major shift from welfare as a public program to a publicly funded competitive program. The United States' health and medical delivery systems already have undergone changes brought about by competition and by the entry of for-profit corporations.

These changes in the community environment can be found prominently in health care, a field that has made substantial differences in the organizational form providing services. In the 1970s, nonprofit hospitals dominated the U.S. health system, and for-profit organizations were criticized for skimming off the easy-to-treat patients and dumping others, thereby putting profits and dividends to stockholders ahead of medical care. Although at that time, nonprofits dominated this field, for-profit hospitals now are making a comeback. Even for-profit schools and correctional facilities are being tried.

Accordingly, the competition for external funds from for-profit corporations and smaller businesses seeking to take on some of the services traditionally offered by nonprofits and governmental entities has resumed. These competitors can build on years of successful projects, demonstrated abilities to manage complex projects, and reputations for quality. These transferable institutional assets offer intense competition for those segments of the population served by nonprofit organizations.

What distinguishes the for-profit from the nonprofit organization? One answer is money and what the organization does with its surplus. Profit motives and publicly traded firms pay out their surplus in dividends to stockholders, whereas nonprofits put their surplus, if any, into expanding services, upgrading equipment, training staff, and other activities to support their mission. Other differences are that manufacturing requires efficient production, whereas human service systems help individuals and families change their situations or provide information, recreation opportunities, or cultural activities. As such, most of the nonprofits' work is intangible. While we may derive direct benefits from a nonprofit organization's work, its emphasis is not on a tangible product that we can buy, store, dust off, and use later. The formal distinction between profit and nonprofit systems comes from the United States' federal tax code and its supporting laws, regulations, and reporting requirements. Nonprofits do not have to pay taxes on their revenues, and donors can take a tax deduction for their gifts.

This text uses the term *nonprofit* for organizations that meet section 501c of the U.S. Internal Revenue Service's tax code, as well as for other not-for-profit systems, such as government departments and quasi-public boards and agencies. The determining factors for this definition are taken from the federal tax code (see box 1.1).

The IRS Tax Code's Definition of Charitable Organizations

To be tax-exempt as an organization described in IRC Section 501(c)(3) of the Code, an organization must be organized and operated exclusively for one or more of the purposes set forth in IRC Section 501(c)(3) and none of the earnings of the organization may inure to any private shareholder or individual. In addition, it may not attempt to influence legislation as a substantial part of its activities and it may not participate at all in campaign activity for or against political candidates. These organizations are commonly referred to under the general heading of "charitable organizations."

The exempt purposes set forth in IRC Section 501(c)(3) are charitable, religious, educational, scientific, literary, testing for public safety, fostering national or international amateur sports competition, and the prevention of cruelty to children or animals. The term charitable ... includes relief of the poor, the distressed, or the underprivileged; advancement of religion; advancement of education or science; erection or maintenance of public buildings, monuments, or works; lessening the burdens of government; lessening of neighborhood tensions; elimination of prejudice and discrimination; defense of human and civil rights secured by law; and combating community deterioration and juvenile delinquency.

The articles of organization must limit the organization's purposes to one or more of the exempt purposes set forth in IRC Section 501(c)(3). In addition, assets of an organization must be permanently dedicated to an exempt purpose. The organization must not be organized or operated for the benefit of private interest. . . . No part of the net earnings may inure to the benefit of any private shareholder or individual.

Excerpts from http://www.irs.gov/charities/charitable/article/0,,id = 96099,00.html (accessed December 31, 2005).

This tax code directly affects nonprofit organizations' governance, management, and service delivery. Events like the federal investigation of the congressionally chartered American Red Cross and the passage of the Sarbanes–Oxley Act of 2002 have brought attention to conflicts of interest and poor governance in large corporations and nonprofits. The IRS tax code specifies that no individuals (private interests) should benefit financially from their role in nonprofit governance. In addition, detailed sections of the tax code refer to the bylaws, articles of incorporation, and basic practices of good governance, which also apply to the bylaws and policy manuals of nonprofit organizations.

Goods Versus Services

Goods versus services forms an important distinction between many nonprofit and for-profit organizations. *Goods* generally represent those items and products that are sold to consumers rather than to other manufacturers for processing. *Services* are processes, often individualized, such as education, training, counseling, the arts, civic clubs, advocacy programs, information gathering and dissemination, and health care. In basic economic terms, goods and services are often found in the same sentence, almost as if they were a single hyphenated word. For nonprofit organizations, however, this distinction forms the basis of their missions. Services are often less tangible and visible than goods and cannot be sold in bulk or inventoried. They may benefit both the recipients and the providers, but not in the same ways. Services often are tailored to the needs or interests of the people using them. For example, a college provides courses, but very few students graduate having taken exactly the same courses. Electives, majors, and internships or semesters abroad offer a range of ways for students to earn a college degree. Conversely, toy manufacturers seek standardization; each item should be exactly like the others using the same name. McDonald's has acquired an international reputation for offering food that tastes the same and is delivered in the same manner in almost all countries in which it has franchises. Table 1.1 summarizes the differences between goods and services.

At the staff level, providing services requires education, training, appropriate skills, and often licensure and continuing professional development. Organizations have other challenges. Whereas manufacturing systems produce approximately what they need and think they can sell in a reasonable period of time, the service sector must be prepared when the clients need or want its services. If a museum were unable to accommodate stu-

Table 1.1

Differences Between Goods and Services

Goods	Services
Manufactured	Delivered
Stockpiled	Used or not available
Customers	Clients
Can be shipped great distances	Generally used where offered
Marketing strategies	Public information strategies
Sold on basis of cost	Delivered on basis of need or interest
Accentuates features	Accentuates benefits
Tangible	Intangible
Efficiency in production	Effectiveness in delivery
Quantity	Quality
Can create demand	Responds when needed

dent field trips when requested, the school system would look elsewhere. But the museum cannot purchase art just for one field trip; it must have a collection of importance and interest to the whole community it serves. Similarly, docents must be hired, trained, and scheduled in advance of the students' arrival.

Determining quality is another distinction between nonprofit services and programs and for-profit goods, services, or products. Whereas the nonprofits want to change their customers, the for-profits want to please them. The goal for people who attend a seminar on the stock market is to convince them to invest with a certain company or broker. Compare this with the people who use a food co-op or eat their holiday dinner at a Salvation Army center. Providing food is a service that changes the people who eat there by satisfying their hunger. The stock seminar also satisfies a hunger, albeit one for a better financial return. Nonprofits often provide services, such as homeless shelters, that would not be profitable if offered by a corporation. Both approaches require different planning and evaluation techniques.

These differences often are found in organizations' mission statements. A *mission statement* is a public pronouncement of the reason for an organization's existence and what it wants to accomplish. The mission statement transcends long- and short-range plans, annual budgets, and quarterly reports. It should be broad enough to last for many years. The following are examples of some of the differences between a for-profit and a nonprofit mission statement:

> At IBM, we strive to lead in the invention, development and manufacture of the industry's most advanced information technologies, including computer systems, software, storage systems and microelectronics. We translate these advanced technologies into value for our customers through our professional solutions, services and consulting businesses worldwide.

The national United Way's Web site contains the following statements:[6]

UNITED WAY'S MISSION AND VISION

> The United Way Movement: United Ways across the country bring diverse people and resources together to address the most urgent issues their communities face. Through unique partnerships and approaches, United Ways mobilize resources beyond the dollars that are pledged through their fund-raising efforts. Community partners often include schools, government policy makers, businesses, organized labor, financial institutions, voluntary and neighborhood associations, community development corporations, and the faith community.

Mission: To improve lives by mobilizing the caring power of communities.

Vision: We will build a stronger America by mobilizing our communities to improve people's lives.

To do this we will:

- Energize and inspire people to make a difference
- Craft human care agendas within and across our communities
- Build coalitions around these agendas
- Increase investments in these agendas by expanding and diversifying our own development efforts and supporting those of others
- Measure, communicate, and learn from the impact of our efforts
- Reflect the diversity of the communities we serve

Web Assignment

Compare and contrast mission statements from a governmental agency, a non-profit organization, and a large corporation in your hometown.

Interview Exercise

An organization's mission statement provides clues to its importance to participants. Ask its leaders these questions:

1. Do the organization's strategic plans and goals clearly support its mission statement?

2. Does the mission statement create a sense of external involvement?

3. How well do employees know what is in the mission statement and understand its implications for their work?

4. Are the organization's resources targeted to key aspects of the mission statement?

5. Does the mission statement inspire people to perform as well as they can?

An important similarity has emerged between for-profit and nonprofit organizations, which is the idea that customers and consumers have rights, has changed the way in which firms conduct their business. The old adage "caveat emptor" (Let the buyer beware) means that a buyer should be aware of problems and defects before buying a product. The burden was clearly on the individual to be smart enough to spot the trick, to know when the scam was on, to find the flaws in the advertising. But public reaction to such practices led many companies to draw up various bills of rights for their customers. Through changes in laws and corporate practices, organizations now commonly have a bill of rights, a customer pledge, a patient's bill of rights, numerous privacy notices, and information sheets about the client's right to refuse services. In addition, the Association of Fundraising Professionals added to its code of ethics a section entitled The Donor Bill of Rights (www.apfnet.org/ethics).

Such statements define the rights of people who use an organization's products and services. Companies want their customers to enjoy the right to safe processes and products, and the consumers of corporate products and

Web Assignment

Go to www.afpnet.org/ethics and review The Donor Bill of Rights.

Discussion Exercise

Review and compare the following pledge with those cited earlier: "Consumers have the right to receive accurate, easily understood information and some require assistance in making informed health care decisions about their health plans, professionals, and facilities. Each consumer has the right to a choice of health care providers that is sufficient to ensure access to appropriate high-quality health care. Consumers have the right and responsibility to fully participate in all decisions related to their health care. Consumers who are unable to fully participate in treatment decisions have the right to be represented by parents, guardians, family members, or other conservators."[7]

Consider the following excerpt from the consumer statement offered by creditcard.com,[8] and compare it with the preceding pledge: "*Know Your Consumer Rights:* A good credit rating is very important. Businesses inspect your credit history when they evaluate your applications for credit, insurance, employment, and even leases. Based on your credit payment history, businesses can choose to grant or deny you credit provided you receive fair and equal treatment. Sometimes, things happen that can cause credit problems: a temporary loss of income, an illness, even a computer error. Solving credit problems may take time and patience, but it doesn't have to be an ordeal if you know your consumer rights."

Web Assignment

Find at least two consumer bills of rights, and compare their goals and appeals. *Hint:* Medicare's Part D Prescription Drug Plans have detailed statements.

clients of nonprofits have the right to relevant information about their services, goods, and products. They also have the right to appeal or complain in a timely manner and expect a fair hearing of their concerns. Customers and clients have the right to expect that personal information (health status, credit card and financial information) will be protected and treated as confidential. Customers and clients expect all staff to treat them professionally and courteously. Donors have rights, too, such as designating where their contributions are to be used.

It would be wonderful if the hundreds of millions of individual transactions each day went as smoothly as these bills of rights assume they will. A mission statement and a bill of rights are, however, only as effective as management wants them to be. Leadership defines a system's culture and shapes the organization's daily operations accordingly, including its relations with all its constituencies.

Social Responsibility

Social responsibility became a viable organizational force in the 1960s, during which social movements and changes affected many segments of U.S. culture, including how organizations responded to their external stakeholders. Over the past fifty years, this abstract notion of social responsibility has been reinforced in more tangible, legal ways.

An organization's stakeholders are all those individuals, governmental agencies, and other organizations and groups that have an interest, a stake, in what the organization does and does not do. Clients, vendors, contractors, donors, staff, referral sources, neighbors, employees and interns are some of a nonprofit organization's numerous stakeholders. Almost all organizations today have internalized the concept of responsibility to these outside groups. To date, there have been more than a million computer search hits for a description of this concept, and at least one Web site is devoted to its aspirations. A good resource is www.sociallyresponsible.org.

The public's expectations of greater corporate social responsibility emerged as a viable organizational force several decades ago and continue to rise. This concept of responsibility may include such goals as sustainability, the enforcement of child labor laws in international trade, fiscal prudence, environmental consciousness, and human well-being. Such general values must be expressed through specific actions, or the ways in which this organization will benefit the public.

An organization's core values provide the framework for its decisions and actions, plans and programs. These values provide the moral and ethical compass for all members of a nonprofit organization. As part of every organization's culture, core values must be practiced, reviewed, acknowledged, and transmitted from one generation to the next through words and deeds. Today, social responsibility is a core organizational value of most public, for-profit, and nonprofit organizations in the United States.

Social responsibility refers to the values an organization intends to follow in all its activities, services, and programs and its awareness of the consequences of its decisions and actions. For organizations serving individual and family needs, these values may pertain to diversity, empowerment of clients, acknowledgment of basic human rights, and fulfillment of an individual client's or participant's needs. For systems focused on community concerns, social responsibility may include support for religious activities, education, cultural awareness, environmental protection, workers' rights, and volunteerism. The following statements, from both profit and nonprofit organizations, indicate the range of these public declarations:

> Our corporate responsibility efforts are grounded in The Chevron Way, which outlines our commitment to "conduct business in a socially responsible and ethical manner . . . support universal human rights . . . protect the environment, benefit the communities where we work . . . learn from and respect cultures in which we work." At Chevron, we define corporate responsibility as:
>
> 1. Consistently applying our core values, set out in The Chevron Way;
>
> 2. Maximizing the positive impact of our operations on current and future generations.
>
> 3. Integrating social, environmental and economic considerations into our core practices and decision making.
>
> 4. Engaging with and balancing the needs of our key stakeholders.[9]

Do you need a cup of coffee as you read the following?

> At Starbucks, it's the way we do business: Contributing positively to our communities and environment is so important to Starbucks that it's a guiding principle of our mission statement. We jointly fulfill this commitment with partners (employees), at all levels of the company, by getting involved together to help build stronger communities and conserve natural resources.[10]

The following is a statement from Texas Nonprofits, which defines its mission as "Building Community Deep in the Hearts of Texans."

Texasnonprofits.org strengthens Texas communities by maximizing access to resources for nonprofits through leveraging internet technology to facilitate and encourage connections between charitable causes and potential contributors.

Web Assignment

Go the National Association of Socially Responsible Organizations, www.global-equality.org, or another organization's Web site to find values that are important to you. Identify the values in these organizations' statements. How do they realize their goals? If you see an advocacy position on current political issues, how do you react?

The social responsibility movement brings us to the next important concept: stewardship.

Stewardship

The concept of stewardship emerged from the history of nonprofit and nongovernmental organizations. When referring to an individual, *stewardship* refers to caring for others. In a societal framework, it implies a concern for everything from the environment to peaceful coexistence. In regard to nonprofit organizations, stewardship means the organization's responsibility to use all its resources as effectively and efficiently as possible in the pursuit of its mission, including using sponsors' contributed resources as intended. An effective stewardship begins with both the governing board as an entity and its individual members. Boards are "fiduciaries" of their organizations' resources, a legal term meaning that the board is obligated to ensure that the organization's resources are used to carry out the mission and comply with the donors' intentions. The next question then must be, "Stewardship of what?"

The most obvious answer is money, whether in the form of charitable donations, revenues from services, grants, contracts, endowment earnings, or investments. We offer a broader definition that includes how the organization manages its time, physical space, people, reputation, and connections to the greater community. Stewardship practices become tangible and transparent to the public through the organization's strategic plans, conflict-of-interest policies,[11] rigorous financial controls, open and collaborative decision making, and acknowledgment of their sponsors' intentions.

For many nonprofits, the concept of stewardship takes the form of servant leadership.[12] This term, coined by Robert Greenleaf, has evolved into a concept practiced around the world in many different types of nonprofit organizations, from educational and religious organizations, welfare systems and health care delivery facilities, art museums and fund-raising campaigns. At its heart, servant leadership expands the concept of stewardship by asking whether our efforts do indeed help others "become healthier, wiser, freer (or) more autonomous."[13]

Another theme is the commitments of the organization's leaders to its employees. *Covenant leadership* is related to the concept of servant leadership. For example, Admiral Vern Clark commanded more than 125,000 employees and subordinates as head of the U.S. Navy's Atlantic Fleet. He adopted the philosophy that "we make commitments to one another. Leaders promise and commit things to subordinates, and subordinates promise and commit things to the bosses."[14] This model has its roots in classical management literature, in the notion that an effective organization meets the needs of its employees and in return, the employees subordinate their individual interests for the greater good. Edgar Schein's concept of the "psychological contract" echoed these ideals in the late twentieth century. Even though covenant leadership has religious roots and applications, its concepts of reciprocity and contribution serve many managers and their organizations.

Conclusion

Around the world, nonprofit organizations have changed dramatically, and historians offer differing perspectives on how these changes came about. Some argue that the advent of Medicare and Medicare did much to extend the role of the public sector in health and welfare. Others cite President Ronald Reagan's social revolution, which encouraged local responsibility to meet local needs. In fact, both contribute to the situations that nonprofits face now and will in the future. Building on the traditions of philanthropy and community, the voluntary sector must be managed efficiently and effectively. The public demands it; the recipients of service deserve it; legislators exhort strong accountability from organizational leadership; laws require it; and donors expect it.

Discussion Questions for Chapter 1

1. How would you describe the state of nonprofit organizations in the United States today? Would this description apply to the organizations in your own community?

2. Select a population trend in your state. Consider its impacts on local nonprofit organizations. What effect do you envision? How should leaders respond to them, if at all? How else could they respond, and why?

3. Given the widespread belief that local problems should be addressed locally, how can you justify federal (versus state, county, or municipal) funding of nonprofit programs? What is the role of each level of government in delivering health and human services? How are these related to nonprofit organizations?

4. Should public funds be limited to only essential services (health, safety, mandatory educational support, highways, etc.), thereby leaving the performing, cultural, and fine arts to find their own support? If you were an art museum's coordinator of community programs, how would your reply differ from that of the director of the county health department?

5. Why do you think that certain nonprofit jobs are held mostly by women (such as nursing, teaching, and social services)? How has this situation changed in the past several decades?

6. What are the patterns in your local community of coordinating nonprofit organizations? What are the purposes of such efforts (effectiveness, reducing duplication, cost savings, etc.)?

2

History and Theories
of Nonprofit Organizations

This chapter explores the main developments in the history of nonprofit organizations, from the early colonial period to today. By the end of the chapter and using theories and models related to nonprofit systems, readers will be able to

1. Describe the growth of the nonprofit sector in the United States.
2. Use at least two different economic models to explain these changes.
3. Retrace the history of a local nonprofit organization.
4. Compare and contrast different types of nonprofit organizations.

Beginning with Many Roots

Nonprofit organizations enable people to work together to address a community's needs when multiple interests exist without widespread consensus on the best course of action.[1] This perspective is called *pluralistic theory* and refers to several agencies trying to fulfill a particular need. Sometimes coordinated, often not, each organization carves out a specific area of activity. From a micro perspective, the hope is that success comes to one organization at a time. From a macro-community perspective, the hope is that needs are addressed by all the activities together. The early history of nonprofit organizations documents this pluralism in action.

The United States has a long and diverse history of local groups of volunteers coming together to address social, cultural, educational, and human needs. The early colonists saw themselves as a self-organizing and self-governing nation. In reaction to the eighteenth-century European monarchies, state-established religions, and inherited status hierarchies, the newly arrived immigrants emphasized voluntary initiatives, local government, separation of church and state, and egalitarian relationships.[2]

Well before the United States' war for independence from Great Britain, Americans distrusted governmental involvement in many aspects of their lives, an attitude that continues to shape many of their political views. Americans believe that needs are best understood by the people in the community and that they are the best ones to address it. Furthermore, Americans see themselves as benevolent people who care for one another, especially the needy, and are ready to work as a community to take care of problems.

Organizations to help the needy originated in the early days of our colonies, in which less formal approaches were used to resolve civic concerns. The first English settlements in the New World emphasized the practice of charity; indeed, the Puritans in New England saw it as a religious duty. In a sermon in 1630, as a group of settlers set out for Massachusetts Bay, John Winthrop declared that their new community would become a "City upon a Hill," an exemplary model of mutual love and caring, inspired by divine grace. This compassion took many forms, but at its core was caring for one another. Inequalities were accepted as given parts of the natural order, driving people to depend on one another to thrive.

In every community that the Puritans founded, as well as those in other colonies, the residents understood that they had a moral duty to govern themselves and to care for all their community's inhabitants. Poverty therefore was seldom seen as a problem, as neighbors expected to help one another. The next line of support was to turn to relatives for help. If they were not available, people in need were understood to have a claim on the community for aid, which often was disbursed through local congregations. Since the communities were so small, their leaders often wore several hats in local government, business, and as "overseers of the poor."

Public, business, and nonprofit endeavors had few distinctions. The designated overseers sought gifts of food, clothes, firewood, and other necessities to enable those in need to get through their temporary distress. Most people lived in families, either with their own or in the houses of others, exchanging labor for food and shelter.

In those days, few people worried that aiding people in distress might lead to idleness and dependence. Rather, people saw the charitable support of those in need as a virtue to be cultivated. Those rare individuals who seemed to be exploiting or abusing such support were simply refused more help, a practice that later led to the distinction between the "worthy" and the "unworthy" poor. Moreover, there was a recognized distinction between neighbors and strangers. Strangers, or transients, had no claim on the community for help. If they had the temerity to ask for it, they could expect to be refused and "warned out," that is, given official notice that this town had no obligation to give anything to them. Sometimes transients were even forced to leave the community and move on or return to their place of origin.

Many churches designated a portion of their collections for local people in need, and some towns established funds from which the overseers could draw to purchase needed supplies. In other areas, pooled funds were used to establish programs that were widely seen as needed by the whole community. One of the first needs was for an educated clergy, which led groups of wealthy citizens to found Harvard and Yale Colleges, both of which soon received legislative grants. In New England, some larger towns levied taxes to support local schools, while education elsewhere in the colonies tended to be offered on a limited basis by churches and private tutors. Gifts from wealthy benefactors provided most of the financial resources for these early organizations, although a few began soliciting wider support. For example, in 1818 Yale College posted the following public notice:

> Being insufficient to found and support professorships and enlarge the library . . . an appeal is made to the liberality of the public in aid of the Institution, the undersigned committee . . . cherish the hope that, when the wants of the College are known, the public will not suffer its interests to languish.

Benjamin Franklin was an early advocate of mutual aid groups that would strengthen the capabilities of members to become hardworking, thrifty, and self-reliant. Indeed, Americans value local initiatives to address community concerns, believing that government at all levels is inefficient and ineffective as a means of meeting local needs or solving problems. The freedom to form voluntary associations is thus prized.

One view of nonprofits sees them as *mediating structures*, as smaller social agencies linking individuals to larger organizations and systems such as government and large businesses. Mediating structures include the family, religious organizations, civic clubs, and other such associations that contribute to positive social values and community engagement. They draw our attention beyond our own self-interests to the well-being of other people.

The Commons

Drawing on the old practice of having an open space in or near a village for everyone's use, the theory of the commons emphasizes our mutual responsibilities and shared values for life together. Beyond the individual market transactions of buying and selling, communities are held together by a shared language, culture, values, and resources that enrich the lives of everyone in them. The commons refers to practices of religious worship, artistic expression, recreation, and other forms of voluntary activity that contribute to the well-being of everyone in the community.

Lohmann identified several important dimensions of the commons: Every culture has forms of collective activity through which people demonstrate values beyond their individual interests.[3] These activities are grounded in shared, subjective meanings and are intended to produce something for the good of others, not for individual profit. Often they are led by people who have adequate provisions for their own basic needs, so they have the freedom to become engaged in efforts that are not primarily intended for self-interest or gauged on the basis of efficiency. In fact, actions that are perceived to be self-serving are regarded as inauthentic and sometimes lead to expulsion from the group. As altruistic activities become formally organized, they often acquire rituals that reinforce shared norms and link the past, present, and future.

The practice of having young men become apprentices to successful people in business or the trades struck Benjamin Franklin as forcing them to be dependent on the largess of the privileged. He therefore set up mutual aid groups that provided the knowledge, skills, and habits that its members needed to become successful in their own enterprises and, in so doing, would benefit the whole community and not just the members. Franklin applied similar reasoning to the problem of poverty. Rather than just giving poor people money, which they would soon spend, Franklin's approach was to form educational groups in which people would learn the basic skills they needed to become self-supporting.[4]

This emphasis on individual and community improvement through local initiatives was central to the values of those who formed the new nation of the United States. After a few decades of independence, several thousand associations had been established, designed to benefit their members and their communities, such as organizations for small business owners, orphanages, schools, and volunteer fire brigades. By the time Alexis de Tocqueville toured the country, many philanthropic programs were already in existence.

Churches had long been the main promoters of community service programs and had begun expanding their efforts well beyond the towns where they were located. Members created both associations to send missionaries into the frontier and Bible printing houses to supply the materials they needed for their work. Women were very active in these efforts, especially in large-scale projects to help widows and orphans. In several states, women succeeded in obtaining grants from the state legislatures to expand the reach of their services.

The Pre–Civil War Period

When the Frenchman Alexis de Tocqueville toured the United States in 1831, he documented its "immense assemblage of associations" and made this community development the highlight of his *Democracy in America*. Such organized, collaborative efforts illustrated how Americans expressed their freedom and democracy, a tradition that continues today.

> Americans of all ages, all conditions, and all dispositions constantly form associations. They have not only commercial and manufacturing companies, in which all take part, but associations of a thousand other kinds, religious, moral, serious, futile, general or restricted, enormous or diminutive. The Americans make associations to give entertainments, to found seminaries, to build inns, to construct churches, to diffuse books, to send missionaries to the antipodes; in this manner they found hospitals, prisons, and schools. If it is proposed to inculcate some truth or foster some feeling by the encouragement of a great example, they form a society. Wherever at the head of some new undertaking you see the government in France, or a man of rank in England, in the Unites States you will be sure to find an association.

Economic theory helps explain this early history. Weisbrod proposed that nonprofit associations and organizations formed because the government had failed to offer these services.[5] In democratic countries, governments tend to address the interests and needs of the average voter and to ignore those of people at the margins of society, such as the wealthy and the poor or members of a particular region. Those people may respond in several ways. For example, they may move in order to find a better school system or lower taxes. They may seek to satisfy their interests through a lower level of government, such as convincing a local government to increase its support of libraries or health care. Affluent people have the alternative of looking to the private sector for services that interest them, such as gated residential communities with hired security guards. Finally, citizens may choose to work together voluntarily to supply a resource that they value, such as establishing a museum or a shelter for the homeless. According to this perspective, a greater number of nonprofit organizations can be found in communities whose population is more diverse.

Nonetheless, the public sector and government still figure in this history, for the next step was obtaining legislative approval for such programs to incorporate and acquire the rights of other business organizations. These programs were permitted to own property, make contracts, and continue to exist beyond the participation of their current members. In some states, they were exempted from taxes and were allowed to raise money through such efforts as fairs and lotteries.

By the early to mid-1800s, organizations that provided similar services had begun forming associations across state lines. The American Bible Society established its national headquarters in New York in 1816 and coordinated the projects of its affiliate groups all over the country. To support the efforts of volunteers in local communities, the national office hired professional staff, instituted systematic accounting procedures, opened regional offices, and published national magazines.

Other associations followed similar patterns. Local abolition groups formed national alliances and then formal organizations. For example, in 1833 the American Anti-Slavery Society was founded in Boston, and in 1826, temperance groups joined to form a national organization, the American Temperance Society. In 1848 women's suffrage programs from several states convened at the Seneca Falls, New York, convention, and in 1869 Elizabeth Stanton and Susan Anthony formed the National Women's Suffrage Association.

The Reconstruction Period

After the Civil War, the federal government established the Freedmen's Bureau, which oversaw a variety of reconstruction programs intended to help newly freed slaves become established as full members of society.[6] Among these efforts was the establishment of schools, some funded publicly and many through the work of volunteer missionaries and educators from religious organizations in the northern states. Self-help groups made up of former slaves were numerous, including ones offering food, job skills, and help in finding employment. In the face of pervasive southern racism, however, these efforts fell far short of the needs. Land reform to enable people to establish their own small farms never worked out as promised, and subsistence tenant farming thus soon became the norm for freedmen.

In the next decades, nonprofit organizations in the northern states accelerated the pattern of coming together to form national associations that addressed a wide range of community needs. But the rapid growth of such national organizations was not welcomed by everyone, especially those in more rural areas. Critics saw them as bureaucracies that were undermining the traditional links of personal charity, in which givers and receivers knew each other. Because they had hired staff, larger associations were seen as self-serving, as raising money to support themselves as well as delegating impersonal services. Tension grew between those who valued individual acts of charity and those who preferred in large-scale, well-organized philanthropic programs.

Andrew Carnegie

Andrew Carnegie is a prime example of philanthropist with a focused goal. A Scottish weaver's son born in 1835, Carnegie became one of the wealthiest steel barons in American history, donating hundreds of millions of dollars to causes that he deemed worthy.

In his 1889 essay, *The Gospel of Wealth*, Carnegie addressed the challenge of how best to administer huge personal fortunes.[7] He believed that capital accumulation was a "natural state" and indicative of a healthy economy but unfortunately led to great disparities between owners and workers. The responsible disposal of surplus wealth warranted careful thought in order to optimize the benefits to society, since its economic structure led to the accumulation of wealth by the industrious. Some small portion should be willed to members of their immediate families for their ongoing support, but huge gifts of this sort would only promote indolence and prevent the next generation from dealing directly with the competitive challenges of the marketplace, which he saw as the proving ground for effective, continuing capitalism. Leaving wealth to governments to be used after one's death might benefit the society in some ways, but such acts were vulnerable to political pressures and demonstrated the individual's lack of attention to the responsible use of resources. Carnegie approved of governments taking substantial taxes from huge estates left at death, ensuring that a portion of the money would be directed to public purposes.

The prospects of wasteful children and unpredictable politicians should motivate wealthy people to plan for the best uses of their resources before they die. Since wealth came from the nation's wise path of capitalism, the nation should be the appropriate concern of the wealthy. Simply scattering small amounts of money among all the citizens would likely result in little lasting benefit for the whole, whereas directing all the wealth to one huge project might benefit a few but neglect of the many.

Rather, a more thoughtful and responsible approach would be to use the money for many smaller projects that benefited a large number of people in ways that enabled them to become successful. Examples receiving Carnegie's approval were schools, hospitals, observatories, parks, museums, swimming pools, research laboratories, libraries, and other resources that supported individual learning and well-being, particularly for those who took the initiative to use them. The founding benefactors of the nation's leading universities were granted Carnegie's strong praise.

Carnegie's own childhood experience of having been allowed to take books from a neighbor's library influenced his decision of how best to use his own estate: He made grants to communities all around the world to establish free public libraries. In return, the communities were to fill the libraries with books and maintain them. By the time Carnegie died, he had built more than 2,500 community libraries. This was his ideal way to use his enormous wealth to benefit the nation that had allowed him to accumulate it. Soon, other wealthy individuals were forming private foundations to administer their wealth and provide grants to projects that interested their founders.

Girl Scouts

Another example of a pioneering leader is Juliette Gordon Low, founder of the Girls Scouts of the United States. Low, born in 1860, believed that all girls should be given opportunities for physical, mental, and spiritual development. In 1912, she organized the first Girl Scout group in Savannah, Georgia, drawing on the ideas developed earlier by Sir Robert Baden-Powell, the English founder of the Boy Scouts. Low wanted to take girls out of isolated homes and into community service projects, sporting and camping programs, and other enrichment activities. Girls of all backgrounds were given opportunities to learn self-reliance and resourcefulness, building skills they would need for active citizenship. Low also welcomed girls with disabilities, even though they were ostracized from other programs. From her original group of eighteen, Low's dream has evolved into a worldwide movement that has attracted more than 50 million girls (see www.girlscouts.org).

The Post-Depression Era

Well into the twentieth century, private donations by wealthy individuals and grants from foundations provided the main sources of revenue for most nonprofit organizations. Then, when the nation entered the Great Depression in the 1930s, the federal government took several steps to help the needy, including the establishment of the Social Security system to benefit aged persons, Aid to Dependent Children, and public works programs to provide employment to the unemployed. Although such programs helped many people regain their independence, they brought criticism from those who believed that such expenditures undermined self-reliance.

Another economic perspective on the history of nonprofit organizations pertains to limitations in the free market. Although capitalism works well for those people who have the resources to purchase what they need, it does not work as well for those who do not have such resources. If demand is low, companies cannot make profits, and so they ignore the needs for these goods or services. Nonprofits, however, can provide a service at a lower cost, since they do not have to pay taxes, and they also have access to private donations that help offset the cost of providing it. Thus a nonprofit organization can offer a service—such as home-delivered meals for the elderly—that would not be economically feasible for a for-profit organization. Nonetheless, all these ideas collapsed when the Depression hit millions of people across the country, and the federal government had to step in both to help those in need and to impose controls on the market. As a result, nonprofits were overwhelmed by those needing their services just to survive.

After the Depression, the distinctions among the public, corporate, and nonprofit sectors were clarified, even though many programs still were administered by hybrid organizational forms, as they are now. Citizens often joined many different voluntary associations, with these overlapping memberships reaching across social boundaries and discouraging the emergence of dominating class structures.[8] Although these networks contributed to innovation and local experiments with community programs, at the same time they limited the development of comprehensive national programs of both social and health services and cultural and artistic support.

Another economic perspective stresses that all of the costs of transactions are not borne by people who do not purchase a product or service. These hidden costs are referred to as *externalities*. Examples of negative externalities are the pollution created by some manufacturing processes or the greater traffic congestion brought on by an industry. Positive externalities are the greater tax income from the business and the increased employment of those in the community who work there. For example, people buy paper that has been made from wood. Although the manufacturing process may pollute the local water supply, the downstream cleanup costs often are not included in the price of the paper. We get cheap paper, and somebody else has to worry about the effects that are "external" to the purchase price. Capitalism produces profits for shareholders, but unemployment also results. Shareholders do not have to pay for that negative externality (other than indirectly, through a small tax to provide a few benefits to the unemployed).

Some nonprofits are established to address such externalities. Addressing a negative externality may take the form of advocacy against locating a landfill near a neighborhood or efforts to require a power company to reduce its emissions. Promoting positive externalities may be establishing after-school programs for low-income children, with the long-term objective of improving the quality of life for both them and those around them as well as reducing delinquency rates in the community.

Private foundations have often been a source of funds to address these unexpected consequences, and they have enlarged and extended their efforts to improve particular aspects of the nation as a whole. But in the mid-twentieth century, questions were raised about these foundations' rapidly growing endowments, as well as questions about the nonprofit organizations that benefited from the gifts from those foundations and from wealthy benefactors. There was little public regulation of these organizations, and critics saw them as amassing enormous sums of money free from both taxes and public scrutiny. Congressional hearings led to the passage of the Tax Reform Act of 1969, which instituted two new regulations: Foundations were required to distribute at least 5 percent of their assets every year, and nonprofits were required to report their income and expenses annually, using the new 990 tax form.

The Children's Defense Fund

Marian Wright Edelman founded the Children's Defense Fund (CDF) in 1973, which today is recognized for its effective advocacy for children and families. Its mission is to ensure that every child has a healthy and well-prepared start in life (see www.childrensdefense.org/about). A private, nonprofit organization, the CDF accepts support from foundations, corporations, and individuals. It does not accept government funds. The fund adopted the popular slogan "Leave no child behind" and continues to advocate for children.

Edelman, a graduate of both Spelman College and Yale Law School, first directed the Jackson, Mississippi, Office of the NAACP Legal Defense and Educational Fund. In 1968, she moved to Washington, D.C., as the legal counsel for Dr. Martin Luther King Jr.'s Poor People's Campaign. Then, after serving for two years as the director of the Center for Law and Education at Harvard University, she started the CDF, which she still directs.

The Children's Defense Fund has had documented success in improving the lives of children through its research, public education programs, budget and policy advocacy, and coalition building. Edelman notes that "service was as much a part of my upbringing as eating breakfast." She is well on her way to fulfilling her desire that "the legacy I want to leave is a child-care system that says no kid is going to be left alone or feel unsafe."[9]

Public support for community services came to a peak with President Lyndon Johnson's "Great Society" legislation directing money to numerous local projects designed to help individuals gain greater skills and resources as well as to become more active participants in local governments.

The Filer Commission

A noteworthy contribution to the history of American philanthropy was the 1975 report of the Filer Commission. Entitled "Giving in America: Toward a Stronger Voluntary Sector," this report became popularly known by the name of the commission's chairman, John H. Filer. Initiated in 1973 through the support of John D. Rockefeller III, Congressman Wilbur D. Mills, and Undersecretary of the Treasury William E. Simon, the commission was composed of leading religious and labor leaders, former cabinet members, federal judges, executives of foundations and corporations, and representatives of several minority organizations.

The Filer Commission's findings built on its extensive examination of nonprofit organizations and foundations in this country, highlighting a number of important issues and research results regarding the challenges facing them. It brought national attention to, and respect for, the importance of nonprofit organizations, and it originated the concept of a distinct, third sector of the American economy. The commission stimulated the establishment of the Independent Sector, a national association of nonprofit organizations, and it also led to the development of university undergraduate, graduate, and continuing professional education programs concentrating on nonprofit organizations.

The Reagan Revolution

Despite these efforts, public dissatisfaction grew over the huge federal expenditures for local community services, especially when some of them included activities to increase the political influence of the poor. Accordingly, the Reagan administration (1981–1989) began withdrawing federal support from programs serving low-income people, thereby leaving them to local nonprofit organizations, which soon became overwhelmed with the widespread needs and the scarcity of resources. In response, these organizations began allocating more staff time to fund-raising, leading eventually to the creation of a new profession, that of nonprofit fund-raiser (for more information about this profession, see www.afpnet.org). Some nonprofits began charging or raising user fees for their services, and special events to attract local donors soon became common in most communities. Continuing to the present is this trend of declining federal support for social services and increasing efforts by nonprofits to raise the funds they need. The growing competition among nonprofits for contributions has led to turbulence in the field and to the rise of public demands for accountability regarding how the nonprofits raise and use their funds.

Another economic perspective can help explain the next part of this history. *Contract failure theory* notes that some products and services, such as education, health care, and art, are very difficult to evaluate for quality. When a for-profit organization offers such programs, many people question whether the company will try to cut costs by reducing quality in order to increase profits. Even though the actual costs of providing a service for profit may be less than the price charged to customers, the specific amount of the difference is not disclosed to the customer.

This asymmetry of information also occurs when the service is too complex or too difficult for the customer to evaluate (such as health care). Nonprofits are believed to be less likely to have incentives to take advantage in these situations and hence to offer better quality. Nonprofits also can reduce quality and increase prices, but they do not have incentives to do so, since any profits cannot be distributed to owners. Instead, nonprofits' leaders are assumed to be motivated to act in the public interest rather than seeking their own advantage or profits.

In summary, Bennett and DiLorenzo concluded that nonprofits exist because of

- Thin markets: the demand for services is too small for a business to make a profit.

- Public goods: the inefficiencies of the political process in developing and distributing services to those who need it.
- Contract failure: buyers unable to assess the quality of a service.
- Equity promotion: poorer consumers unable to buy needed services.[10]

The Contract for America

The challenges of assessing the quality, efficiency, and effectiveness of nonprofit and governmental services opened the door to conservatives' questions about the role of the federal government in funding these megaprograms. Dissatisfaction with federal expenditures for community programs led to political victories in the 1990s of candidates espousing two basic assumptions:

1. The federal government is wasteful and ineffective in producing results. Some candidates argued that President Johnson's Great Society programs were more rhetoric than accomplishment.
2. Social welfare programs are more harmful than helpful to the people they claim to be serving. A better approach would be one in which governmental policies emphasize self-sufficiency through individual responsibility rather than dependence on public support (see www.paytonpapers.org).

Often referred to as the Republican Party's Contract for America, these efforts led to steep reductions in both the federal bureaucracy and federal spending for public welfare programs, cultural, arts, humanities organizations, and research in all fields. If individuals or organizations want to support any of these endeavors, they should do so on their own.

As we have noted, the emphasis on individualism is a deeply held American value, and personal responsibility and self-help are matters of ethics as well as economics. We live in networks of memberships that provide mutual aid, starting with the family and extending to civic and religious organizations and professional associations. We have long assumed that some services should be public responsibilities, such as defense, police, highways, emergency disaster assistance, and foreign policy. This is communitarian ethics. Beyond those areas, though, we are unsure about the appropriate role of the federal government in meeting community needs.

The most visible target of reduced spending is welfare, especially when it seems to be supporting people who are able-bodied but unemployed, in other words, what some have called the "undeserving poor." Unfortunately, attacks on such expenditures also threaten children, the elderly, persons with disabilities, and other vulnerable populations. Nonetheless, many people expect private philanthropy to deal with such issues without public support. Nonprofit organizations are thus being asked to do more in absolute terms and to do so with private contributions.

Although some forms of private giving are increasing very slowly, the shift of demands to nonprofits promises extreme vulnerability in these organizations, as demands are increasing far more rapidly than are the resources with which to address them. Advocates for returning to more public support for community programs are opposed by those who continue to demand less such support and more individual initiatives. It remains unclear how the nation will resolve these tensions.

By the last decade of the twentieth century, those concerned with the credibility of nonprofit organizations began establishing several national programs to monitor their performance and to make their evaluations publicly available. The national Better Business Bureau instituted its Wise Giving Alliance, which formulates standards of accountability for nonprofits, periodically surveys nonprofits on key aspects of their performance, and then reports their findings on www.give.org. Another organization began collecting IRS 990 forms, which report the financial performance of all nonprofits, and making them publicly available at www.guidestar.org.

Web Assignment

Search the preceding two Web sites for information about several nonprofit organizations that interest you. Did you learn anything new about them? Did anything you learned influence your attitudes toward those organizations?

Reactions to intrusive telemarketers representing businesses and nonprofits led to two more changes. The federal government set up a national do-not-call list, through which citizens could have their telephone numbers removed from telemarketers' lists. In addition, many states began requiring nonprofits engaging in fund-raising campaigns to register with the state attorneys general or the secretary of state's office and then report annually on the amounts raised and the proportion of that sum spent on the fund-raising effort itself. The state office that controls this usually posts the annual fund-raising results, allowing the public to find out how much money a specific nonprofit raised and how much of that went to the nonprofit's programs and how much to the fund-raisers.

Web Assignment

Go to www.nasco.org/agencies, and click on your state to see how it regulates nonprofit organizational fund-raising. Search for reports on individual nonprofits' fund-raising costs, and compare them with similar reports from other states. In what ways does such information influence your interest in giving to any of them? What questions might you want to ask an organization that solicits you for a donation?

Paradigm Shifts

Both history and economic theory illustrate that nonprofit organizations have grown, developed, adapted, changed, altered, and adjusted their purposes, missions, and aspirations to meet emerging needs. Nonprofits help define the United States' ethos of caring and represent its effective response to shifting national political views and changing local needs.

Indeed, change, or *paradigm shift*, has become a constant idea in management circles, television talk shows, and educational seminars. What does change mean, and what does it mean to nonprofit organizations? The word *paradigm* comes from the Greek *paradeigma*, which means "model," "pattern" or "structure," especially in reference to language and linguistics. Paradigms within a system or a culture include theories, rituals, rules, customs, and traditions. When accepted patterns undergo a fundamental, usually irrevocable, change, it is called a *paradigm shift*. Imagine the paradigm shift resulting from a counseling agency that decided to hire social workers, educational counselors, and psychologists instead of psychiatrists! Some people would argue that this was an effective and efficient move, but others would regard it an unwarranted paradigm shift.

The next step in such an analysis is to consider the impact of existing paradigms on nonprofit systems. Most serve to reinforce the status quo; they provide stability in times of external change or threat. For example, nonprofit organizations' traditional client record has spawned a subindustry in which some professionals transcribe material from the handwritten notes to a formal, indexed record and others store, retrieve, and conduct research on these re-cords. But now this practice is undergoing a major shift. Instead of each or-ganization having its staff write, transcribe, review, and store its own client records, professionals summarize their record of the client's or patient's visit on a laptop computer, which sends the material to a work center for storage and later retrieval. Through the Internet, the office staff has immediate access to the full record, which is backed up for security purposes in a location other than the provider's office. A special advantage is that the record can be instantly transmitted to other providers, along with documentation of when it was sent and to whom it was delivered. Moreover, the transcribing center may be located in China, India, or anywhere else in the world. This change means that the medical records profession has undergone a shift in its roles, responsibilities, and, indeed, in its paradigm.

One way to persuade the staff of any organization to explore new options and opportunities is to ask, If money were not a constraint, what would we do that we are not able to do now? Answers will range from "give salary increases" to "start a new service center," from "hire more staff" to "upgrade technology." In some cases, the replies pertain to overcoming an existing deficit, but in other instances, the responses focus more on ways to meet or expand the nonprofit's mission.

The role of the federal government in the past fifty years has undergone two major paradigm shifts. The first occurred in the 1960s under President Lyndon Johnson and the Great Society. In this paradigm, the shift was away from the relaxed post–World War II society in which the government stayed out of its citizens' personal lives to one that wanted and supported federal, state, and local governments helping those in need. Medicare, Medicare, the Voting Rights Act, and the civil rights movements all were part of this effort.

The next big change came in the 1980s. Two decades after the Great So-ciety programs were enacted, the Reagan revolution began. The term *revolu-tion* itself is a clue that the shift was of major proportions. In the 1980s, the paradigm shifted power from the federal government to the state and local governments. The goal was to let local authorities assess local needs and use local funds to meet them. The federal government was the last resort for only rare cases and national emergencies. The results of this shift remain with us into the twenty-first century.

One of the paradigm shifts that may be occurring as this book is being written is the growing need for nonprofit partnerships. Partly in response to the declining funds and partly in response to a general feeling that nonprofit organizations should not compete because this leads to duplication, the num-ber of mergers and partnerships is increasing. Both of us formerly taught at

Case Western Reserve University, which once was two separate universities of distinction. But pressure from governmental funding agencies and community leaders helped set the stage forty years ago for the Case Institute of Technology and Western Reserve University to federate. The process of federation defined the new entity, for which the term *merger* was not seen as desirable because it means one university subsuming the other, whereas *federation* implied equals coming together. Both nonprofit universities benefited from this partnership, an unusual model in higher education. Their sum is now greater than that of the two parts.

As this chapter has shown, nonprofit organizations have a long and proud history. In summary, the private, nonprofit organization has the following characteristics: It has legal standing and a defined legal purpose. It has no stockholders, no investors, and no dividends. It has a board of trustees with specified fiduciary and other legal responsibilities. It does not generate a profit but can use any surplus to fulfill its mission. Although nonprofit organizations do not pay taxes on mission-related activities, they must file tax returns and other required public and private forms. And, of great interest, they may receive tax-deductible donations.

Nonprofit organizations fulfill five important roles in our society.[11]

1. They provide services to those in need or programs for those with a specific interest. *[Salvation Army]* *[Banjo Museum]*
2. They support innovation by testing new models of practice, service, and research. *[Aids cocktail, polio vaccine]*
3. They are effective advocates in their local communities and among wider constituencies. *[MADD, nature conservatives]*
4. They have enriched the fabric of every community since the earliest colonial days. *[Library, opera, church]*
5. Finally, they have become public resources for information and professionalization of their fields of practice. *[museum]*

The United States is estimated to have about two million nonprofit organizations. According to Peter Drucker, more than 70 percent of these were established since the mid-1960s.[12] Thus, this explosive growth occurred during the expansion of social change in the 1960s and later helped fill the gaps in health, human services, the arts, and other social concerns created by the Reagan revolution.

Although there is no single comprehensive directory of nongovernmental, nonprofit organizations, the National Center for Charitable Statistics compiles data for public access. As of January 2006, it noted that the Internal Revenue Service had registered 1,418,445 nonprofit organizations (many more are not registered). The gross receipts reported on the required IRS 990 forms exceeded $2.3 trillion, and the total assets of these organizations were more than $3 trillion.[13] Thus, the nongovernmental, nonprofit sector has gross revenues rivaling the size of the entire federal budget for FY 2007.[14]

In summary, there are a number of perspectives on why nonprofit organizations exist and why they act as they do, but none of them completely explains the sector, and none has become the standard or consensus view. Rather, each perspective offers an important insight into these organizations and suggests plausible reasons for their importance. Debates over the scope and limits of nonprofit organizations will continue, along with controversies about the issues they should and should not serve.

3

Ethical Issues
in Nonprofit Organizations

This chapter looks at ethical issues in nonprofit organizations, a topic that recently has gained national attention in the corporate, governmental, and voluntary sectors. When they understand these issues, readers will be able to

1. Describe some of the major ethical frameworks.
2. Apply these frameworks to individual and organizational processes and decisions.
3. Deal with the ethical issues raised by the need to ration limited resources.
4. Learn appropriate strategies for nonprofit organizations to develop and sustain an ethical culture.
5. Analyze the connected concepts of consumer rights and organizational responsibility.

Over the past few years, ethical violations by the leaders of several national and international corporations have grabbed the public's attention and concern. Sensing a change in public attitudes, Congress passed new laws, notably the Sarbanes-Oxley Act of 2002 (PL 107–204), in an effort to prevent these problems from happening again. Even though they have received less attention in the press, nonprofit organizations have not completely avoided such scandals and have been exposed to public scrutiny and distrust as well.

For example, the Allegheny Health, Education, and Research Foundation, a large nonprofit health care network in Pennsylvania, went through a $1.3 billion bankruptcy in 1998. As Burns and colleagues observed, the foundation's executive director and board exercised remarkably little fiscal responsibility and accountability, which led to several lawsuits, including one against board members individually for failing to meet their fiduciary responsibilities.[1] The CEO received a prison sentence of almost two years.

Congress also questioned the nonprofit status of several other hospitals, owing to charges that they provided little service to the poor, a commitment that was necessary to obtain their nonprofit status.[2] In early 2006, the Getty Museum in Los Angeles was under investigation for questionable expenditures, during which its executive director resigned and returned a substantial sum of money to the institution.[3] Events such as these erode public trust and compel closer scrutiny at the federal and state levels of government. Understandably, demands for greater accountability and for higher standards of ethical practice are growing, and tighter restrictions are almost inevitable.

Nonprofit organizations hold their resources in trust to serve the purposes that motivated their founders to establish them and their donors to sustain them. The people who originally established the nonprofit had detected a community need warranting attention and created the organization to carry out a particular mission. Rather than turn over their resources to the government, they entrusted them to a board and staff that were charged with serving the intended beneficiaries in the ways specified by the founders. The current board and staff members of any nonprofit are therefore morally obligated to continue the mission and purposes for which the organization was created.

The needs of communities for and the beneficiaries of a nonprofit organization's services may, however, change over time, necessitating a reinterpretation of the founders' intentions. The board then must decide how the organization should respond to the community's emerging needs and changing conditions. Because these needs and conditions may involve multiple, often divergent, demands, the board must adapt the organization's programs and services to circumstances that the founders could not have anticipated.

In accordance with the community values of promoting justice and integrity, the board has to make difficult decisions about what the organization will do with its limited resources and the directions it will and will not take. Trying to remain faithful to the founders' intentions while at the same time being responsive to current beneficiaries and community needs can divide a board by causing controversies over future goals and directions. It may try to stay with the founders' original purposes but, in so doing, risk having the organization become irrelevant to new conditions. The organization may try to respond to new interests but then faces the challenge of deciding on which of many interests it should focus. The board must work to reconcile all these demands as well as link the original intentions with some of the current interests, thereby bridging the old and the new ways to serve the community effectively.

Balancing multiple interests and setting clear priorities are difficult challenges for governance. The organization must periodically revisit its mission statement in light of present and emerging community needs. While honoring those who emphasize the founders' intentions, board members also must work with those who have a stake in the organization's current and future work. This includes staff, consumers, donors, and community leaders. Although the board must understand the interests of such groups, it also must maintain some objectivity and distance from them. During this time, it will hear the many concerns and preferences expressed by constituencies seeking common ground and priorities for using the organization's resources. Often there is competition among various interests and conflicts in meetings. Handling these effectively requires clarity regarding the values and ethical principles that ground the board's work.

Ethical Principles and Frameworks for Analysis

Much of the field of ethics pertains to decisions by individuals, but the basic principles also apply to organizations. The concerns of individual consumers, organizational staff, donors, and others must be balanced within the organization's limitations of resources, public policy, laws, and regulations. Nonprofits' staff, managers, and board members should understand that an ethical analysis of challenging situations is a primary component of their work, and so they should examine the ethical components of problems systematically and reach publicly defensible conclusions. A thoughtful analysis of ethical dilemmas is vital to maintaining public trust and accountability.

Fortunately, useful principles and frameworks for ethical analysis have been established, among the most widely recognized being the basic principles of respecting autonomy, doing good for people, avoiding doing them harm, and promoting social justice.[4] Respect for autonomy means that we should respect people's values and choices and also enable them to act as free, informed, and self-determining agents. Respect also means making sure that appropriate protections are in place when people have limited capacities for making free choices.

Doing good, referred to as *beneficence*, and *avoiding doing harm*, referred to as *nonmaleficence*, are related principles. The first is to do and promote good for people, and the second is to avoid doing them harm. *Promoting justice* is ensuring fairness in decisions, with equitable distributions of benefits and burdens. It means treating people in equal situations equally. When their situations are unequal, we may have to treat them differently in order to maintain overall fairness.

While these principles seem intuitively important, they may be difficult to apply, especially when acting on one of them puts us in conflict with another. For example, how far should a supervisor bend the rules and tolerate low performance for a staff member known to have severe family problems? Or what should staff do when a client in counseling makes threatening comments about an acquaintance? Should they respect the client's choices and privacy, or should they warn the person who was threatened?[5] Frameworks for weighing possible decisions in light of these principles can help apply them in difficult situations.

The first approach to making decisions in a difficult situation is to give priority to the results or outcomes of each possible choice in that situation. Known as *consequentialism*, this approach holds that the way to know whether an action is right is to determine its costs and benefits. Thus we weigh each choice and select the one with the most net benefits or the fewest net costs (or least amount of harm) for all those involved. We hear such thinking when someone says of a person in a permanent vegetative state that he and his family "would be better off if he were dead." Because none of us can predict the future, assessing costs and benefits can often be quite difficult. Likewise, many people object to a system that can so easily be translated into "the ends justify the means," however unjust the means may be. If you and many other people would enjoy some benefit if you were to lie rather than tell the truth about some situation, would that make it the right thing to do?

An alternative approach is examining one's duties and obligations to others. Known as *deontology*, this approach first identifies the various ethical obligations of a decision, such as keeping one's promise to another, treating others fairly, respecting their freedom, avoiding or preventing harm, and treating others in a caring way. Then the various duties are weighed to determine which one should take priority. In the counseling problem noted earlier, the staff member may conclude that the promise of confidentiality and client privacy is less important than the obligation to warn and prevent harm to the person threatened. In the case of the poorly performing employee, the supervisor may conclude that accepting that person's autonomy would mean compromising the organization's obligations to many others.

Jodi Picoult summarized these principles in her popular novel, *My Sister's Keeper*.

> There are six principles we try to follow. . . . *Autonomy*, or the idea that any patient over the age of 18 has the right to refuse treatment; *veracity*, which (leads to) informed consent; *fidelity*, that is, a health care provider fulfilling his duties; *beneficence*, or doing what's in the best interests of the patient; when you can no longer do good, you shouldn't do harm . . . like performing major surgery on a terminal patient who's 102 years old; and finally, *justice*—that no patient should be discriminated against in receiving treatments.[6]

These principles apply to almost all nonprofit organizations and provide a framework for offering programs, services, and activities. They also serve decision makers as a guide for making difficult choices.

Another contemporary framework, *feminist ethics*, also can be helpful to nonprofit organizations facing challenging situations. Feminist ethics starts with the premise that gender biases are a core component of our society. Related biases include discrimination on the basis of race, ethnicity, age, disability, or sexual orientation. Justice requires that imbalances of power that work against some people be corrected and overcome. Rather than starting with abstract principles and rational analysis of alternative choices, feminist ethicists point to the role of caring relationships and emotional attachments as the basis for our ethical views and the framework for our ethical choices.

Like everyone else, people in nonprofit organizations face socially entrenched power structures that shape decisions, policies, and programs. Some differences may be based on expert knowledge, which is appropriate to and useful for a program's effectiveness. But inappropriate power hierarchies may distort activities in ways that limit their benefits to some staff and consumers. Finding ways to redefine situations in terms of equality of input and worth are necessary to escape power-based hierarchies, in which some people win at the expense of others. Power-based hierarchies are characteristic of authoritarian organizational structures.

There are other frameworks for ethical decision making. Instead of just describing ways of making moral choices, we should actively use them in our lives. That is, we might decide to tell the truth because there would be bad consequences if our lying were to be discovered. Or we may decide to tell the truth because we conclude that keeping our word to another is more important. Or we may choose to do so because it would be the most caring and mutually respectful thing to do. People tend to examine any complex situation from different perspectives and to emphasize different aspects of it. Therefore, understanding how we and those around us apply ethical principles is important to our working together effectively and arriving at shared conclusions that protect the organization's integrity.

Applying the Frameworks

Let us consider how these frameworks may be used in practical decisions. Returning to the counseling client who was making threatening statements about an acquaintance, staff members may apply ethical principles and come to different conclusions. One may look at the costs and benefits of maintaining confidentiality with the client so the counseling relationship is not damaged, as it well might be if the client found out the staff member had warned the threatened acquaintance. Conversely, the credibility of the threat may lead to the conclusion that the likelihood of harm to another was comparatively small, so violating confidence was not worth the risk of damaging the client's trust.

Another person may approach that situation from a more duty-based framework. First, she would try to identify all the values present in the situation, including making promises to the client, respecting his autonomy and self-direction, promoting justice for everyone affected by a choice, and preventing harm. Then weighing all these factors might lead her to conclude that justice for the acquaintance and respect for her autonomy were more important than honoring the client's freedom of choice.

A third person may approach the situation by looking at the power imbalances in the relationship between the client and the acquaintance and decide what would be the most caring thing to do. In many interpersonal relationships, women and members of disenfranchised minority groups have far less power than do men and people in positions of authority. Finding ways to show caring to both the client and the acquaintance also may require some effort to address the balance the power. If the acquaintance were less powerful than the client, the counselor may decide to share information with the acquaintance about the threat from the client in order to balance their power. Or a counselor may conclude that this client may be best helped by working to help him find more caring ways of relating to others.

Case 3.1: Peeking Into the Files

Chris is an intake worker at a health clinic and knows many of the clients because they are her neighbors. Although this makes her job easier, since the clients trust her, at the same time, she has been tempted to look in the case files to learn something about those clients she does not like. On a recent coffee break, she peeked into John's file, since he is dating her niece Adrianna. She almost dropped the papers on the floor when she read the orders to test John for sexually transmitted diseases. She wants to tell Adrianna or her parents... after all, this is family. What should Chris do?

Because the family is a cornerstone of our society, would it be harmed if Adrianna did not know about this (potential) problem? From a different perspective, however, Chris is bound by the organization's rules regarding the confidentiality of client information. Sharing this information with anyone would violate those tenets. And if Chris wanted to tell someone, whom should she tell? And what would she say? Would sharing the information get Adrianna in trouble and result in additional harm? From a feminist ethics perspective, women may find out that their partners have sexually transmitted diseases too late to take preventive actions, thus perpetuating harms from hierarchical imbalances of power.

Case 3.2: Can Active Listening Be an Ethical Problem?

You are visiting a friend who is a resident at the Easy Acres Nursing Home. Since you are a regular visitor, you have met many of the staff and gotten to know them a bit. So on your friend's eightieth birthday, you arranged for a local caterer to send party trays for the residents and staff to have a joyful celebration.

During the festivities, you overhear three of the staff talking about other patients—not just the usual chatter about someone's room number or what their occupation was when they were working. Rather, you are almost positive they were discussing a medical prognosis, residents' diagnoses, medications, side effects, family histories, and who has visitors and who does not. At first, the conversation was interesting, since you also knew the patients. Then a little voice in your mind started to wonder whether this information was confidential.

How would you decide what you should do in this situation? What ethical principles would you use to decide? Should you speak directly to the staff members having this conversation in a public area? Are there other reporting options? What might happen if you did nothing?

Individuals face ethical choices each day, some so minor we may not even consider them as such. For example, should any employee be allowed to take a pad of paper or pen home for personal use? Most organizations have policies against such practices, and if asked, most people would say no. But you can hear them say, What if everyone did it? There would never be enough supplies at work. If such a practice were commonplace, management may have a budgetary issue, and the organization may have an ethical one.

Another kind of ethical problem that surfaces in nonprofit organizations is conflicts of interest. Interests may conflict when a person has two hats or roles in the organization, both of which may involve benefits to herself, her relatives, or her partners in an outside business. For example, a board member may also be an owner of a private company that supplies materials or contracts equipment to the nonprofit. Another example is a board or staff member who wants the organization to hire a relative for an open position. In such circumstances, the organization member generally is seen as using her insider position to get an additional benefit that is not equally available to everyone else.

Such conflicts of interest may be examined in accordance with any of the frameworks described earlier. Although an inside deal may benefit the individual, such practices, if they were to become known, would damage public trust in the nonprofit's fairness. So a consequentialist may see them as wrong. A deontologist may see them as not treating everyone fairly, and a feminist ethicist may see them as perpetuating imbalances of power in the organization.

Many nonprofits have adopted explicit policies on conflicts of interest, which are intended to prevent unethical practices and sustain public trust. Even the appearance of double interests or self-dealing can be damaging to an organization, so these policies require that everyone in the organization recognize and act responsibly when they come up. First, such policies should state explicitly that everyone in the organization must place the organization and its consumers above his or her own self-interest. Next, the policy should have provisions requiring the full disclosure of any situation in which a person might have an interest or might benefit from a decision the organization may be facing. In addition to such disclosures, that individual must not participate in or influence such a decision, keeping well away from any discussions of or votes on the matter. Failure to comply with such regulations is often sufficient grounds for dismissal from the organization.

Policies regarding how the organization will treat its employees are (or should be) based on ethical principles of fairness and justice. They are intended to create and sustain a work environment in which people are treated equally

Discussion Exercise

The Hintonville Children's Center has grown rapidly and now needs to find more spacious accommodations for its several programs. Jack Ronsil, a wealthy land developer in the community, serves on the center's board. In a board meeting, he tells the chairperson that the board doesn't need to waste its time on this matter, since he has some available space in a building across town and can lease to the center. Some of the other board members say this is a good, efficient solution, but another asks whether the board shouldn't also explore other possibilities.

1. Is there any conflict of interest in this situation?
2. How should the board respond to Jack?
3. What should the board do about the center's space issue?

and expectations are clear and understood. The evaluation criteria should be known in advance, and unfair discrimination should be prevented. Because any organization can be charged with unfair treatment, healthy ones are careful to set down and disseminate specific rules about how people will be treated, assessed, and rewarded or punished. Leaders, particularly, should be explicit in their commitment to integrity and fair practices and model them in all their work. Failing to have and follow clear personnel policies can lead to staff dissatisfaction, turnover, lawsuits, and public distrust of the organization. Good personnel policies contain elements of all these ethical frameworks, and incomplete ones can be improved by thoughtful examination of the principles and frameworks described.

Discussion Exercise

Jennifer recently joined the staff of the Piedmont Community Center. She soon concludes that seniority, not expertise, is the main consideration when problems arise. In several recent staff discussions, she was treated as a second-class citizen and is becoming increasingly unhappy with her coworkers.

1. What should Jennifer do about her concerns?
2. She tries to talk with her supervisor about them, who tells her that she shouldn't rock the boat when she hasn't been working at the center long enough to understand how decisions are made there. What else might she consider doing? Why?

Rationing Services

Whether or not a nonprofit wishes to acknowledge it, most have greater demands on them than they have resources to fulfill. This problem leads to rationing: decisions about how to allocate limited resources. Ideally, in a free-market economy, access to health care, human services, and the cultural and performing arts is available to all consumers or clients. This ideal is consistent with the principle of autonomy, the ability to make informed choices without coercion or constraint.

Unfortunately, this ideal is rarely found. Some of the approaches to rationing limited resources are as follows: *First come, first serve* is akin to the bakery store model. Individuals take a number and join the queue in the order in which they arrive or make a reservation. Most health clinics work in this manner, and general admissions to museums follow a similar approach. When the number of individuals who can access the desired service is limited, this model meets the needs of the "early birds." The fire marshal can set the limit on the number of people who can safely enter a museum or auditorium; the staff's skills and number of employees can effectively limit the number of patients in any one clinic. But when too many people show up, congestion results, and the system may shut down or become overwhelmed, so latecomers are turned away.

Serving those with the *greatest need* is an alternative to the first come, first served approach. Here, the nonprofit organization and/or its staff apply their established criteria to decide who is most needy, and these clients are served first. Inherent in this approach is the assumption that some people have the ability to decide who is most, or more, needy.

Triage is another model. From the French word for "sorting," *triage* decisions focus on who can benefit most from receiving the services. In this framework, sometimes the neediest clients are passed over in favor of others who are more likely to show positive outcomes from receiving the limited services. Imagine the typical emergency room. In some cases, the most severely injured person is beyond help. Taking professionals' limited time to help those with little or no hope could mean that others who would benefit do not get what they need. This is triage, and it is used every day.

Another form of rationing is *keeping benefits hidden or hard to access* so that only the most determined individuals will receive them. Some government programs are so complex that people who are eligible give up in frustration. In fact, if everyone eligible for Medicare's Part D drug coverage were to take full advantage of the system, Medicare's trust fund would be depleted sooner than currently projected.

Price itself becomes a rationing tool. Those with more resources often receive higher-quality or preferred benefits and services compared with the poor. For example, the United States now has a dual-track system for health care. Whether this is "good' or not depends on the criteria one chooses. By definition, Medicaid is for the poor and others who need governmental support. Compare this with the new boutique model of health care in which wealthy patients pay a fee for the right to see immediately and at any time a doctor of their choice. In return, the physician limits the number of patients in his or her practice, guarantees 24/7/365 service, and even makes house calls. One gets what one is willing and able to pay for.

These models describe the ways that many service organizations carry out their work, but the question remains of how they *should* work. How should we and our nonprofit organizations act fairly and responsibly is a challenge of ethics. Principles of ethics can be applied to rationing models, supervisory relationships, decisions about maintaining or breaking confidentiality, and many other aspects of nonprofit organizations. The ethically responsible organization pays careful attention to the principles to be used in complicated situations and to the ways that it wants participants to apply them in their work.

Discussion Exercise

Douglasville's Family Counseling Center has a branch that provides subsidized counseling services in a low-income area for clients who cannot afford the full price of counseling. The number of applications has grown rapidly and is outrunning the available staff time. Staff members are working overtime and becoming exhausted by trying to help everyone. While the board is working on raising the money for additional staff, the current staff members want to find some way to deal right now with the impossible demands for their time.

1. What are some approaches they might consider in deciding how to deal with the situation? What are the advantages and disadvantages of each?

2. What approach would be the fairest to the applicants and the staff? Why?

Developing an Ethical Culture in the Organization

One of the first steps to developing and maintaining an ethical culture in nonprofit organizations is to decide on the principles and practices that are to guide members in dealing with difficult decisions. This will require some thoughtful reflection, drawing on a wide range of resources to formulate a code of ethical behavior for the organization. Many professional associations have codes of ethics for their members, but these codes emphasize individual responsibilities, so further work is needed to clarify how they apply to entire organizations. The leaders of all nonprofits should prepare a code or statement of ethical principles by which the organization itself will operate and the steps to follow when differences arise about their applications.[7]

Exercise

Go to your profession's Web site, and examine its code of ethics. Use a search engine to look for other codes of ethics that apply at the organizational level. For example, look at the code for "An Accountable Nonprofit Organization" on the Web site of the Association of Fundraising Professionals (www.afpnet.org). Can you find others? Try to identify common themes across several codes as well as some differences between the codes for professions and those for organizations. What are some of the principles that you think should be emphasized in a nonprofit with which you are familiar?

Codes of ethics cannot cover every possible situation. In a specific ethical dilemma, members of an organization may well understand their moral responsibilities differently, sometimes leading to disputes about what should be done. Intentionally or not, some people tend to emphasize weighing the likely consequences of choices, and others may want to act according to multiple principles, weighed in the light of the current situation. While respect for everyone's viewpoint is important, healthy organizations take the time to examine the different perspectives and work toward a process that everyone can use in unusual situations. The following are actions that can help participants develop such a shared system:

First, *it is important that everyone involved with a problem (or potential problem) has a full understanding of the facts.* Relevant information about the organization, the people, and the problem should be available and known by those looking for a solution. Often, some information is not available because of a lost consent form, test results, inability to contact a family member, history from a previous provider. In these instances, educated guesses may be needed. If the missing data are critical to a decision, then doing nothing is an option, since that will reinforce the status quo.

The next step is to *identify what is at stake for everyone affected by the situation.* The claims, interests, and values of the organization, the member, and anyone else legitimately involved should be identified and understood. Any differences in views should be acknowledged and respected. Then the discussion should move to settling on the feasible choices or decisions. Of course, because doing nothing is a choice, it should be included in the list of options.

Next there should be *a thoughtful examination and recognition of all the ethical values or principles relevant to the situation*. These may be achieving fairness, respecting self-direction, promoting benefits, avoiding or limiting harms, telling the truth, keeping promises, and caring for one another. The available resources for action, any prior commitments, and constraints on decisions should be included in the deliberations. Then the discussion should look for how the relevant principles would be expressed in each of the possible solutions.

Weighing the relative importance of several ethical principles and their relevance to a specific situation can be complex and time-consuming. Divergent views should be heard respectfully and examined for their fairness in the situation. A question that may be useful when considering possible solutions is whether it would be fair in another, similar situation or whether some sort of special treatment is being offered. Likewise, would the basis for a decision be convincing to someone outside the situation? Could this solution be defended in public? Would I want it to be applied to me?

Many ethical dilemmas cannot readily solved, so imperfect choices will continue to be made. Before jumping to accept such a solution, those involved should take the time to work toward the best choice possible, with the best justification they can find together. It is important that the decision be agreed on and a commitment made to try to resolve the problem together, without leaving someone out on a limb of individual responsibility (or blame).

Once a solution has been decided on, it should be implemented and then its impact monitored. Subsequent events may shed more light on the original problem or may lead to others needing attention. Those involved in the decision should take the time to meet again to discuss what happened and also what they learned from their earlier analysis of the issue. Useful questions for learning are

- What were our assumptions going into the original analysis of the problem?
- Did our deliberations include full information about the situation? Complete recognition of the relevant ethical principles? Thoughtful examination of how they should be weighed and applied in reaching our conclusions?
- What did we miss, or to what should we have given more attention?
- What could we have done to come to a better decision?
- How would you feel if others decided on this solution when you were the subject of the decision?
- What lessons should we draw from those experiences and reflections that we could apply in the future?

Discussion Exercise

Jeff Arnold, the head of development at the Jacksonville Memorial Hospital, was stunned by the call from Howard Ritter, who said he wanted to make a gift of $600,000 to the hospital immediately, on the condition that the hospital publicly acknowledge receiving the gift from him. This would be a great, last-minute boost to the hospital's three-year fund-raising campaign. Ritter owned one of the two large drug companies in the area, and the hospital regularly bought drugs from him. His request for recognition seemed appropriate to Jeff, so he had no qualms about committing to it. But the day that Ritter's check arrived, Jeff spotted a short article in the newspaper that said Ritter's drug company was under investigation for possibly colluding on price rigging with the city's other drug company. He began to wonder whether Ritter was trying to influence public opinion by making the gift and whether the association with him might damage the hospital's public credibility. But no formal charges had been made, and the investigation might well find nothing. Ritter had made smaller gifts to the hospital in the past. His current large gift would enable the hospital to follow through on its plan to expand its services to a very underserved area of the city.

    1. What are the ethical values and principles relevant to Jeff's situation?

    2. What aspects of the situation would be emphasized by a consequentialist?

    3. How would you recommend that Jeff go about working out a solution? Why?

    4. What decision do you recommend? Why?

In conclusion, people in nonprofit organizations face many ethical challenges. Thoughtful attention to them is essential to a healthy organization. Building a culture of ethical awareness and responsibility is important for the well-being of the participants and the trust of the public. Avoiding problems or just continuing to treat them as has been done in the past will eventually damage the organization and its people. Leaders should take the time to address ethical issues as they arise and work toward for the best possible solutions. They should anticipate recurring issues and develop fair policies and practices that promote ethical behavior and prevent or minimize damage to people and to the organization. They should demonstrate courage in recognizing and examining problems, acknowledging limits, persisting in efforts to reach good conclusions, and learning from past experiences to improve practices in the future.

Discussion Exercise

The Bill and Melinda Gates Foundation recently awarded your nonprofit community center a $500,000 grant for programs related to HIV/AIDS. The board is currently debating three competing needs. Clearly, many patients and their families in the community need services and respite care. In addition, the schools have requested educational programs and materials to help educate and prevent others from transmitting or becoming infected with HIV. The dean of the City University's School of Medicine also has requested funds for further research that could kill the virus.

Have one class discussion group advocate for treating those currently in need of care. The second group should stress the importance of education as an intervention. The third group should take the position that research for a cure is the most important need.

How should the clients' short-term needs be balanced against the longer-term aspiration of a cure or a vaccine? If educational programs have not worked in the past twenty-five years, then should this midrange approach use the center's limited resources?

How can the board allocate the generous grant to help the most people? Is helping the many at the expense of the few the position you would adopt if you were a trustee?

Case for Discussion

Melinda Banks, executive director of the Norwood Youth Services Organization, was delighted to open a letter in the morning mail and find a check for $5,000 for the organization's new expansion plan. What a difference it would make! The cover letter was from Sam Lewis, a wealthy local manufacturer, who set as a condition of his gift that the organization issue a press release today that identified him as the donor. Melinda wondered about this condition, especially since the organization had always thanked its donors.

That afternoon, Melinda saw on the front page of the town's newspaper that Sam had been indicted for embezzling money from his company. Melinda wondered whether Sam was trying to use his gift to her organization to counteract the negative publicity from his legal situation. Then she wondered how others in the community might interpret her accepting and announcing the gift. She asked herself, Should I just accept this money and send out the required press release, or should I protect our esteem in the community by declining it and returning it to him?

4

Creating Effective
Nonprofit Organizations

This chapter shows how ideas can become realities. The founders of nonprofit organizations are visionary people who seek to address a need or problem in their communities. The organizations they create require several basic components and must comply with federal and state laws regulating nonprofits. The objectives of this chapter are to enable the reader to

1. Understand the basic steps in establishing a nonprofit organization.
2. Describe the federal and state regulations governing the required components of such an organization.
3. Explain and apply the basic legal duties of nonprofit leaders.

A nonprofit organization often is established when a few dedicated people see a need that they believe must be fulfilled. Although committed individuals can make a difference by starting a nonprofit organization, all the decisions they make, or do not make, before it begins operating will influence whether or not it is successful.

We should begin by defining what is new and different about this proposed organization. How will it meet a specific, documented need that has not been addressed by others? Why is this new organization needed in the first place? These are some of the basic questions asked in *The Nonprofit Kit for Dummies*.[1] We also recommend using appropriate professional advice to save time and resources that would be wasted in misdirected efforts and overlooked requirements.

This does not mean that good ideas require high-powered law firms with their accompanying high hourly rates. Instead, use local pro bono opportunities, law school clinics, and community service agencies. For example, in New York, connections might be made through the Web site http://www.probonopartnership.org, and in the cultural world, Volunteer Lawyers for the Arts (http://www.vlany.org) is a good resource. Searching for available resources is critical to starting (and building) a nonprofit organization. The Internet Nonprofit Center's Web site, http://www.nonprofits.org/npofaq/16/41.html, is a valuable resource, and try the Clearinghouse for Volunteer Accounting Services if you need guidance in these complex issues.[2] Another option is BoardSource, at www.boardsource.org.

This chapter explains how to start a nonprofit organization. You must have the required approval from the Internal Revenue Service and the appropriate departments in your state and local governments. When you have this, the organizers of the nonprofit will be ready to begin the extensive planning process.

Most nonprofit organizations are incorporated. Forming a corporation, either for-profit or nonprofit, has some advantages. Except under very unusual circumstances, the officers, administrators, and employees of a corporation are not personally liable for the organization's lawsuits and debts. In addition, their personal assets are shielded from legal judgments against the organization and from creditors of the organization if it goes out of business. The income of a corporation is taxed at a much lower rate than that for individual persons' income, and the income of nonprofit corporations is exempt from taxes. An organization that has legal documents ensuring its order, authority, continuity, and a system for paying its bills and accounting for its income and expenses has more public credibility than does an individual or unregulated group of people working on a project that interests them.

A disadvantage of incorporating is that decisions cannot be made by one person with no accountability to others. In a corporation, even though a charismatic leader may have a grand vision, that person's decisions must come under the scrutiny of others. Ideas and options are examined by the corporation's board of directors, and control is held by a group, not an individual. Another disadvantage is the extensive amount of paperwork, forms to be filed, reports to be submitted, expenses for operation, and penalties to be avoided for not complying with the laws and regulations applying to any kind of corporation, whether nonprofit or for-profit.

Those who establish a corporation agree to formal rules of operation to promote and sustain its purposes. The corporation's founders define those purposes, select a name for the organization, and decide on the procedures by which it will be run.

A For-Profit or a Nonprofit Organization?

An important early decision is whether to form a for-profit or a nonprofit organization. There are compelling reasons to choose one over the other. The organization's distinctive benefits, services, products, and purposes should drive the decision, and it is helpful to consider some of the benefits and drawbacks of nonprofit status.

The benefits of a nonprofit are, first, the exemption from most federal, state, and local income, real estate, and sales taxes. Donors can benefit from tax deductions for their contributions to the nonprofit, and the U.S. Postal Service has special rates for nonprofit mailings, which can result in significant savings. Another benefit of nonprofit status is the public's awareness of and respect for doing the public good. Public service has a higher civic image than does generating profits for a few people. Nonprofit organizations also may have an advantage when applying for grants from foundations and governmental programs, since their limited funds cannot be used to pay dividends to stockholders.

One of the main disadvantages of the nonprofit organization is the limitations on its programs, services, and possible ventures, as they must be directly related to its overall mission. Even if the nonprofit's board of trustees comes up with a great idea to generate revenues to support mission-related activities, the activity itself must be directly connected to the organization's mission, or other tax laws may apply. Nonprofits may not generate profits or financial advantages for its members or trustees, and they typically pay their employees and leaders somewhat less than do for-profit corporations. Although this is not a requirement, the salaries in human services, fine arts, religious organizations, performing and cultural systems, and charitable service often are lower than those in the business sector. Nonprofit organizations cannot engage in partisan political activities.

Federal Tax Regulation of Nonprofit Organizations

Both for-profit and nonprofit organizations are regulated by the U.S. Internal Revenue Service (IRS), as well as the laws of the state where they are located.

Whereas the same IRS rules govern all nonprofits in the nation, the state laws vary. We examine the basic components of both. More details are available at www.irs.gov and the Web sites of most states' offices of the secretary of state or attorney general (www.nasconet.org). The principal reasons that a nonprofit should be familiar with these rules are that the exemption from paying taxes on net income is a major benefit to the organization, and federal and state laws require it and its supporters to comply with these rules. The exceptions to these regulations are public organizations, religious organizations, and nonprofits with gross receipts of less than $25,000 per year.

The IRS recognizes and regulates a variety of nonprofit organizations, the most familiar of which are those providing charitable, educational, or scientific resources to the public. These organizations are recognized as having 501 (c) (3) status, the section of the IRS tax code that applies to them. They are distinguished by the IRS rule that allows donors to receive tax deductions for their contributions. Other types of nonprofits are foundations, civic leagues, labor unions, social and recreational clubs, fraternal societies, mutual insurance companies, and other voluntary beneficial associations. Although these types of organizations may be exempt from taxes, most of their donors may not take income tax deductions for their contributions. For more information about determining the category of an organization and the specific rules governing it, see IRS publication no. 557. Because understanding these rules and completing the required forms can be difficult, you may want to consult the Internal Revenue Service's Exempt Organizations Division and its publications to assist would-be filers.[3]

When starting a nonprofit, its leaders must obtain an employer identification number (EIN), which is the organizational counterpart of the Social Security number. Every nonprofit must have an EIN, whether or not it has any employees. Form SS-4 (available at www.irs.gov) is used to apply for an EIN. If an organization does not already have such a number when applying for exempt status, a completed copy of form SS-4 must be included with the application for recognition as a 501 (c) (3).

FOUNDING DOCUMENTS

The basic documents on which any nonprofit is established are its articles of incorporation and its bylaws. The articles of incorporation are the first official document by which the organization is created and governed. It must list the organization's official name, purposes, governance structure, uses of assets, registered office and agent, and a plan for distributing its assets if it is dissolved. The articles must explicitly limit the organization's activities and use of assets to the purposes identified in section 501 (c) (3) of the federal tax code, as in IRS publication no. 557. These limitations also address what is to be done if the organization fails and goes out of existence. At that point, the organization's remaining assets must be passed along to either another, similarly exempt nonprofit or otherwise to a federal, state, or local government to be used for public purposes.

Another required official document is the organization's bylaws, the rules by which the organization is governed. This document defines the structures and functional roles of its board; the procedures by which the members will be chosen and will make decisions; the board members' duties and rights; when and how new members will be selected; the schedule for and way in which meetings will be called; and the process by which the board will amend, adopt, or repeal specific rules.

Examples of an organization's articles of incorporation and its bylaws are offered in appendices A and B. Note that their provisions are for illustration only and that a particular nonprofit may have variations that accommodate its circumstances, although IRS limitations may not be omitted.

Exercise

Ask the executive director of a nonprofit organization to show you its articles of incorporation and bylaws. Ask that person to cite at least three important ways in which these documents guide the organization's work. Do some rules interest or surprise you? Can you find out why those provisions were included?

These founding documents should be included with the organization's application to the IRS for tax-exempt status. The application itself (IRS Form 1023) requires the organization to give a full description of its purpose and activities, financial reports for the current and recent years, names of board members and top staff, financial information, and other organizational details. Other than financial data, much of the information requested should already be available in the organization's founding documents. Attorneys in many cities are available to complete this form (for a fee), but anyone patient enough to work carefully through all the details can complete it by oneself.

The completed application form and attachments should be sent to the Internal Revenue Service, P.O. Box 192, Covington, KY 41012–0192. An application fee must be enclosed. For nonprofits averaging less than $10,000 in their first four years of operation, the application fee is $150, and the fee for those averaging more than that amount is $500. Incomplete applications are returned without being considered, but the part requiring further attention is noted.

LETTER OF DETERMINATION

When the IRS is satisfied that the applying organization has met all its requirements, it will send the organization a ruling or "letter of determination," the official notice of approval for the organization's tax-exempt status. This status is effective retroactively to the date on which the organization was founded. If the organization has paid taxes during the time between its founding and the IRS ruling, it may apply for a refund. Conversely, if the application process results in substantial changes in its founding documents or activities, the tax-exempt status will be effective on the date of the letter. After the organization obtains its exempt status, if it substantively changes its purposes or major activities later, it must report them to IRS and obtain approval. Depending on the extent of such changes, the IRS may require the nonprofit to prepare and submit a new application for exemption.

STATE REGULATIONS

The laws of the state where the nonprofit is located also regulate it. These regulating offices are often under the state's attorney general or secretary of state. Every nonprofit must obtain and complete the required forms and procedures for recognition by its state government. Usually the required forms include a Charitable Organization Registration, which again asks for defining information (much of which can be found in the nonprofit's founding documents). The state application also requires a copy of the IRS letter of determination. Often, the state registration must be renewed each year, along with a copy of the nonprofit's most recently completed Form 990 (discussed later).

In many states, nonprofits that raise funds also are required to file a separate solicitation registration at the beginning of each year in which such activities are undertaken. At the end of the year, they must file a financial report on the amount of money raised and the portions of the total spent on the organization's services, as distinct from the costs of the fund-raising activities themselves. Nonprofits that raise money in several states should use a Unified Registration Statement (URS) to obtain approval to solicit funds in each of those states (www.multistatefiling.org).

Web Assignment

Look for the office that regulates nonprofits in your home state by going to www.nasconet.org and clicking on "U.S. Charity Offices." Select the state where a nonprofit that interests you is located, and click on that state in the menu. Then click on the Web site of the state office, and look for the rules and forms to be used by a nonprofit for registration or recognition there. Ask a leader of a nonprofit in that state to let you look over copies of the forms it files with the state government.

ANNUAL FILING REQUIREMENTS AND DISCLOSURES

Every tax-exempt organization must submit annual reports on its finances, using IRS Form 990. A simplified version of this form (990-EZ) is available for nonprofits with an annual income below $100,000. Form 990 asks for income and expenses from contributions, gifts, grants, dues, sales, special events, and other sources as well as estimations of the market value of all in-kind gifts, operating costs and payments to others, and net assets or fund balances at both the beginning and the end of the year. Expenses must be itemized by categories of programs and services, management and general administration, fund-raising costs, payroll taxes, supplies, equipment, telephone, rent, travel, accounting and legal fees, and other such categories. Compensation to officers must be specified by individual and the amount paid.

In one section of Form 990, the organization must state its purposes and describe its related accomplishments during the year. Information from the organization's year-end balance sheet is required, as well as the amounts in the major expense categories (these financial documents are covered in chapter 15). If the organization has received income from a for-profit business it operates, that source and amount must be documented as well.

Each year the organization must also send copies of its completed IRS Form 990 to the state office regulating the nonprofit and also make them available to anyone in the public who asks to see it.

Even though nonprofits benefit from their exemption from taxes on their income, they still must pay other taxes. Federal and state withholding taxes on employees' incomes must be deducted and filed regularly along with Social Security payments. The state may also require workers' compensation payments.

Web Assignment

Go to www.guidestar.org and search for the recent financial reports from a non-profit that interests you. Look for its types and amounts of income and expenses, descriptions of its accomplishments, and other information that tells you about the work of this organization and what it does with its money.

DONORS' GIFTS TO NONPROFITS

People who make contributions to nonprofit organizations classified as 501 (c) (3) are entitled to include the amounts of such gifts in their itemized deductions when filing their personal income taxes. The nonprofits receiving such gifts are required to give each donor who gives $250 or more a written receipt of each gift and the amount. This documentation helps donors substantiate their gifts if the IRS audits them.

Nonprofits should send donors statements that list the name of the organization, the amount of the gift, and a sentence affirming that no goods or services were provided in exchange for the gift. If the gift is not cash but an in-kind contribution, it should be described and a good-faith estimate of its value provided. If the giver receives a benefit, only the amount of the gift exceeding the amount of the giver's benefit is deductible. For example, a nonprofit sells tickets to a benefit banquet, for which the value of each meal served is one-half the cost of the ticket. The donation thus is one-half of the ticket cost, and so the giver is entitled to only that amount as a deduction. IRS publication no. 1771 provides further details on how to substantiate charitable gifts.

UNRELATED BUSINESS INCOME

Nonprofits are not taxed on the contributions and income they generate from activities that are directly related to their missions. Some nonprofits sell items for a profit, such as scout manuals and uniforms, which are clearly linked with their missions. Other nonprofits, however, run businesses that are not directly related to their missions. For example, a college may organize foreign travel tour programs for alumni and friends which are run by a private travel agency. Because the tours do not include classes or instruction related to the countries visited, they are not an important component of the college's educational mission, even though they do generate income for it, so the income from them is taxable. Another example is a museum that owns property that it leases for private use. If the income from such operations exceeds $1,000 in any year, it is taxable, and the nonprofit must file IRS Form 990-T (in addition to the regular 990 form for its tax-exempt income) and pay taxes on the operation's net gains. Participants may not deduct payments to such businesses from their personal income taxes. IRS publication no. 598 contains extensive information about differentiating mission-related from unrelated activities. We turn now to the basic legal principles that guide nonprofit organizations.

Legal Duties of Organizational Leaders

Nonprofit organizations operate within the general legal framework for all organizations. State and federal laws require that the officers of all organizations exercise some basic responsibilities. Fiduciary responsibility is not a new idea. As section 102 of the ancient Hammurabi Codes ruled, "If a merchant entrusts money to a broker for some investment, and the broker suffers a loss in the place to which he goes, he shall make good the capital to the merchant." Today, this responsibility also is specified in both policy and legal terms. Most definitions of fiduciary include the phrases "held in trust," "have faith in," be responsible for," or "acts in the best interests of."

The U.S. Department of Labor's definition is a general guideline: Trustees have "an allegiance to the organization, an expectation of confidentiality, a responsibility not to use the position for personal gain, and an obligation to act in the best interest of the organization at all times."[4] Fiduciary roles implement the ethical principle of *nonmaleficence*, the duty and obligation to do no harm. This term is not limited to the medical context; people in nonprofits (and elsewhere) also can cause harm by their actions and inaction.

The "best interest" phrase contains the key to effective fiduciary relationships. Formal mechanisms are required to ensure no real or apparent conflicts of interest in all the actions and decisions of the board and its members. Simply stated, due diligence to the organization's mission in all matters is mandatory. Thus, some decisions may need to be reviewed or delayed until more information is available. Effective leaders must make sure that the board and staff have all the information they need to act in accordance with their fiduciary responsibilities and requirements.

Two important aspects of the fiduciary role are the duty of *loyalty* and the duty of *care*. Together, these duties and obligations help ensure that no personal interest or individual benefits accrue from voluntary service to the system or interfere with an impartial decision-making process. Both these duties ensure that decisions regarding programs and services keep in mind the best interests of the public. Indeed, entrusted responsibility is part of the fiduciary relationship.[5]

DUTY OF LOYALTY

Trustees and managers must rigorously adhere to their own bylaws, policies, rules, and procedures. Competent third parties must conduct an external audit of all financial transactions on a regular (if not annual) basis, to make sure minimum compliance and accountability processes are in place. Beyond this, effective managers should review decisions to see whether they have accomplished their program and service objectives. Regularly reviewing financial matters is necessary but not sufficient to meet this legal and public expectation. Complete disclosure is the best policy, since allegations of negligence can cripple a board, harm an organization, and create almost insurmountable problems for its staff and managers. Suspicions undermine the organization's reputation. Even though innocence is presumed until otherwise proven in court, for public relations and philanthropic purposes, just hearing about charges or investigations can send supporters elsewhere in a hurry.

DUTY OF CARE

The duty of care obligates the leaders of an institution to make sure that all decisions are the best ones to fulfill the organization's mission. Art museum trustees may have to balance expenditures for their educational mission against creating a new fund-raising position (short-term versus long-term impacts). Area Agencies on Aging face the dilemma of cutting programs such as Meals on Wheels or curtailing information programs on the new Medicare Part D program (individual service versus public education). These are difficult choices, and the board and staff must weigh the impact of each alternative on their mission and its ability to move the system forward. It is acceptable to consider not offering a service or program if the nonprofit organization cannot offer quality efforts efficiently.

The duty of care pertains to both the means and the ends of a program. If the decision process is problematic, perhaps there are problems with the duty of loyalty. When services are ineffective or too costly, not delivered in a timely manner, or provided by untrained staff members, the duty of care may have been compromised. Careful internal managerial reviews are a better strategy than responding to lawsuits, donor inquiries, or media interviews on the subject.

Malpractice is the term most often applied to the failure to meet the duty of care, with substandard services only one element of such failure. The failure to maintain confidentiality is another aspect of malpractice, since confidentiality between an individual and a professional forms the basis for many service programs. The duty of care may also apply to how an organization treats and protects its own employees, vendors, contractors, and visitors. If radiation exposure is a known hazard in the workplace, managers must address this problem adequately. Not acting to protect people violates the duty of care, as well as myriad laws, regulations, and accreditation standards. This duty also requires employers to take seriously any allegations of improper behavior against or by clients, volunteers, staff, visitors, and prospective employees.

Getting the Organization Under Way

Once the necessary documents have been filed and approved by IRS and the state agency that regulates nonprofit organizations, the founders are ready to proceed with implementation. The following are the next four steps:

1. Develop a strong business plan, beginning with a clearly defined mission statement, goals, and objectives and detailing the needed revenues and expenditures, anticipated donations, space, staffing, and community support. This plan should be well documented with relevant facts and current data-based information supporting the organization's needs and showing how it will address them. It should explain how this effort differs from others in the community, state, region, or country. The business plan should also show how the organization will continue operating after its start-up period ends. No one wants to support a new venture that will end in a year.

Sometimes failures are caused by the little things that are needed to be successful. Consider that offices require everything from telephones and fax machines to computers and duplicating equipment. Stationery and general supplies must be stored in desks and other furniture. The costs of permits, licenses, insurance premiums, leases, and utilities must be included in the start-up costs. Headd notes that "more resources tend to lead to better odds of survival."[6] While seemingly obvious, money is a necessary, but not sufficient, prerequisite for success. Consider the following two different approaches to obtaining the needed capital to start a new program or organization:

The first approach is *debt financing*, in which the new nonprofit asks for a loan from either individuals or commercial lending sources. These can be secured or unsecured, but the loan carries with it an obligation to repay both the principal and interest. Not fulfilling such obligations will cause numerous problems for the organization.

The second approach is *equity financing*, selling "stock" or a percentage of the business to others. In return for their money, the business investors receive equity in the venture and thus become part owners and share in its profits. But because nonprofits do not have shares to sell, equity financing becomes philanthropy, or gifts or grants that do not require repayment; otherwise they would be listed under debt obligations on the organization's financial statements. Although individual donors and foundations can be the major sources of these start-up funds, they may not own shares in or receive dividends from the nonprofit.

Having a nice balance in the checking account does not mean success. Rather, the source of the funds and the business acumen of the nonprofit's top managers must determine how those assets will be used and how they will help the organization carry out its mission.

The space to carry out the program's activities always is an issue and often a costly one. In some communities, the local chamber of commerce or a local college may have developed model public–private partnerships, which are called *business incubators*.[7] These buildings can provide space and logistical support for new entities, including nonprofits. In addition to important system maintenance functions such as housekeeping, telephone-answering services, security, and computer assistance, participants also have access to technical support to develop marketing plans, human resource policies, internal control procedures, payroll and financial transactions, and evaluation or assessment processes.

In summary, a strong business plan must define what services the nonprofit will offer to meet specific documented needs. The business plan answers questions regarding who the clients will be and how they will be served and describes the organization's financial needs and resources. The plan also should spell out the qualifications for the organization's leaders so that outsiders will have confidence in the organization's potential for success and donors will want to contribute.

The organization's founders should consult with the relevant professionals to make sure that its purposes and plans meet federal, state, and local laws and regulations. Lawyers, accountants, service consultants, grant writers, and management experts can help translate the mission and goals into operational realities. Although these do come at a cost, success is not likely without expert input and guidance. Many new ventures have found that they can benefit by offering their ideas as a real-life case study for students in a university's MBA course on strategic planning. Students gain firsthand experience, and the start-up agency learns from a guiding professor and supervised students.

2. Build an effective board of trustees. Members of the board must understand their role in the new venture; they are to be trustees, not managing supervisors, despite their desire to help. The board should be sure that a manager or managerial team and all the required rules, polices, procedures, and financial controls are in place. All decisions should be recorded, and the records must be maintained in accordance with professional and public requirements. (For more information about the board's role in determining an organization's success, see chapter 8.)

3. Build good relationships with community leaders. In some cases, the charismatic personality that is driving the development of the new organization may know some of the "movers and shakers" in the community. This leader must then reinforce these relationships in his or her new role as an advocate for recognizing and supporting the organization. Political leaders, other nonprofit directors and executives, foundation officers, media representatives, and members of financial institutions and businesses all are important to the organization's development.

Excessive debt, low-quality programs, or insufficient revenue can stop an organization very quickly; in fact, a significant percentage of new organizations fail within the first year. A study of the U.S. Department of Commerce study shows that almost 25 percent of all new firms fail within the first two years,[8] and according to Dunn & Bradstreet, "Businesses with fewer than 20 employees have only a 37% chance of surviving four years and only a 9% chance of surviving 10 years."[9]

4. Develop a strategic plan. An essential ingredient of success is a solid strategic plan. It should identify specific, challenging, and attainable goals that show how the organization will carry out its mission. Good intentions are not enough. An assessment of the needs of a community or target population should be followed by plans and priorities for addressing them. Whether starting a new nonprofit or managing one with a long history of service, clearly defined goals are the foundation. This issue is so important that this book devotes a full chapter to it (chapter 10).

Highly committed individuals can make a difference in the success of a strategic plan. Through personal efforts, many aspects of our society have changed for the better. Starting a new organization, whether it is for-profit or not-for-profit, requires more than just energy, commitment to a cause, and a dream.

Is your organization prepared to deliver the best work and best-quality services it possibly can? One view is that no system ever operates at its maximum effectiveness and efficiency. If it did, then how long could it maintain this posture? Consider "the paradox of pride: pride in being the best comes from knowing that we are not good enough."[10] This statement illustrates the seeming contradiction between the pride of success and the continuous improvement of quality. The paradox lies in ever increasing expectations and changing needs or goals. If organizations become dispirited, complacent, or overwhelmed by these challenges, they are doomed to eventual failure. Leaders should set the organization's goals high enough to be challenging yet reasonable enough to be attainable.

Linking with National Associations

Many prominent national nonprofit systems have local affiliates that form the national network. Examples are the American Red Cross, United Way, American Cancer Society, labor unions, political organizations, Habitat for Humanity, American Humanics, numerous religious organizations, symphony orchestras, and museums.

Perhaps the first and most important benefit of a national connection for the local unit is the ability to contribute to the *overall mission*. This works both ways; the national group can only be as strong as its local affiliate's effectiveness. The overall mission has been a magnet for public figures to get involved. Former Presidents Bill Clinton and George H. W. Bush became partners in the tsunami relief efforts in 2005, and former President Jimmy Carter volunteers for Habitat for Humanity.

Being part of a national system can produce important *cost savings* through economies of scale, legal representation, group purchasing, or insurance plans. The national umbrella organization also enables the local units to learn about the *best practices* being implemented across the country.

Studies of the relationships between local organizations and their national associations have identified some of the sources of tension between the two groups.[11] Sometimes these tensions result from different views on the proper means to achieve common goals. In other cases, the problems may arise from having divergent goals and questions about the power to achieve them if they interfere with the other party's aspirations. In summary, these problems are as follows:

1. Payments to headquarters: How much money should the national organization require the local units to pay? What is the impact of this on the local unit's ability to meet its goals? We all have heard the complaint that "too much of the money we raised goes outside and does not help people right here in our community."

2. Resource allocation: What voice should the local affiliate have in national fund-raising efforts? Conversely, how much control should a national movement have over local allocations?

3. Delivery of services: Local units often feel empowered to deliver services consistent with community and professional standards, but national headquarters may have different views and use other methods or reporting requirements.

4. Using "the" name: The name may cause perhaps the biggest tension. National associations own the name and logo and may authorize local units to use them, albeit with strict limits. These limits include conformity with national policy requirements about what can be done and how. Conversely, a local unit may see departures from the standard package as important to local conditions. Nonetheless, most national offices retain the right to accept or reject any such changes. Sometimes the central office's policies conflict with local concerns. Remember the national publicity that the Boy Scouts received for their conflicting policies on homosexual males in their programs?

5. Governance: Where does national governance end and local governance authority begin? Who serves on these boards, and what systems are in place to facilitate communication between them? One group's strategic plans may part from the other group's agendas, causing tension over allocations, payments to the national center, or staffing issues.

The main message from these principles is to think globally and act locally. The purpose for the national association must complement the local plans, which in turn must support the national group's overall mission. Whereas legislation, tax codes, national public relations, and information campaigns and financial controls are best dealt with by both the national and local associations, the programs and services to clients and stakeholders should be local.

In summary, nonprofit organizations are regulated by the IRS and the laws of the state where they are located. Those nonprofits that carry out charitable, educational, or scientific activities that benefit the public are eligible to apply for status as a 501 (c) (3) organization, which exempts them from having to pay taxes each year on their net income. Their donors also benefit by being allowed to deduct the value of their gifts to the nonprofit from their individual income tax. Nonprofits are founded in accordance with articles of incorporation and bylaws, which define their purpose, structure, operations, uses of money, and limitations on their activities. The IRS and state governments require annual reports of the nonprofit organization's income and expenses. Rigorous business plans guide the development of thoughtful strategic goals which in turn should guide every aspect of the nonprofit organization's work. Resources can come from a variety of donors, foundations, government agencies, and national associations, although many such resources are restricted in how they may be used.

Education or Politics?

Jane knew it was going to happen. As soon as she saw the telephone message from the television reporter, she called the executive director. Knowing that the election for county commissioners was only six weeks away, Jane did not want to get embroiled in a controversy that would bring negative publicity to the homeless shelter. Instead, as the director of community relations, she preferred to work quietly with other providers rather than call attention to the five other shelters in local neighborhoods.

But all this changed when one of the trustees publicly supported the incumbent commissioner. Lagging in the polls, the current commissioner was getting endorsements from across the community. The trustee's response to Jane's telephone call about the matter was that he was "only trying to inform the commissioner and the public about the homeless families' needs." But as a nonprofit organization, the shelter was not permitted to engage in partisan politics.

As you enter a meeting with the executive director, what approach will you use? How can the shelter respond to the reporter's queries? What are the advantages and disadvantages of issuing a prepared statement?

5

Understanding Nonprofit Organizations

Nonprofit organizations have many differences from, as well as many similarities to, their for-profit counterparts. All their workers have defined responsibilities, supervisors and managers that oversee them, lines of accountability, disputes to settle, budgets, and many other common traits. Understanding the components of any organization is a good starting point for discovering an organization's distinctions. This chapter traces the major developments in organization theory and management practice with applications for those who lead, manage, and supervise nonprofit systems. Its objectives are to enable the reader to

1. Describe the conceptual frameworks for understanding organizations.
2. Identify the major strengths and limitations of these frameworks.
3. Specify their applications to nonprofit organizations.

Conceptual Frameworks for Contemporary Views of Organizations

Since the Middle Ages, from government to private enterprises, scholars and practitioners have tried to understand human organizations: what works, what works best, what works well in distant lands, and what works with different class structures. We begin with the classical approach and move to how theories about structure and organization gave way in practice to models of employee motivation and managerial roles and functions.

THE CLASSICAL APPROACH

The *classical approach* began in industrialized Europe to define management principles for effective practice. By characterizing ideal organizations, classical thinkers hoped to remove experimentation and ad hoc solutions, which was the way that most managers solved most problems at that time. A French industrial engineer, Henri Fayol (1841–1925), is considered the father of this approach. His principles pertain to an organizational structure with power consolidated near the top and delegated down through immediate and remote subordinates. Fayol was the first to delineate the basic functions and actions of management: planning, organizing, directing, coordinating, and controlling. With great success, he used these ideas in his own mining and drilling company. Published under the title of *General and Industrial Management* in 1916 but not translated into English until after World War II, Fayol's following fourteen principles were adopted throughout the world with varying degrees of commitment and success:[1]

1. A division of labor requires that jobs be broken down into discrete tasks.
2. Authority must coincide with responsibility, as one without the other will yield poor results. Lower-level employees have less of both authority and responsibility, thus defining their position in the organization's hierarchy.
3. Discipline is required to keep employees working toward predetermined goals. Managers must ensure that rules are followed obediently and with little leeway. Ideally, disciplinary measures are clearly defined in advance and then applied impersonally and equally to all who violate the rules and regulations.
4. Unity of command means that each employee should report to only one supervisor, forming the typical pyramid structure of most organizations.
5. Unity of direction comes from the top of the organization to ensure that all units in the organization are working toward common goals. The idea of "keeping your eye on the ball" (or the prize) reinforces the system's overall mission.
6. Subordinating individual objectives to overall organizational goals is critical to success. A generation ago, the saying was that "what is good for General Motors is good for America." Similarly, when an individual's goals are aligned with those of the organization, motivation increases and positive results accrue to both the employee and the institution. But when their goals diverge, either the

individual benefits or the organization gains, one at the expense of the other, in a win/lose situation.

7. Remuneration should be fair, equitable, and just. These are sound human resource principles; when practiced, they help avoid discontent by preventing salary and compensation inequities. Even if the agency is able to pay someone a bit less, this does not mean that it should. All decisions about compensation have both short- and long-term consequences.

8. Centralization is the cornerstone of coordination. Decisions made by management are necessary because they are the organizational leaders. Most military structures operate in this way. "I was only following my boss's instructions . . . " indicates this in practice. Fayol believed that organizations could become so decentralized that individual units would or could not work together, which would hurt the organization, its leaders, managers, and employees.

9. The scalar principle dictates that effective organizations have a clear line of authority from the top to the bottom of the structure. Many religious and military structures exemplify this principle.

10. Order is a key component of the classical approach. Each piece of the system must fit into its proper place. Employees, service delivery procedures, production systems, support processes, and external linkages all must be designed in advance. Then, these plans should be executed within tight margins and monitored for compliance. There is a right place for everything and everyone in the organization. Management has the responsibility to find that place or job for each person.

11. Equity means that managers must supervise employees with fairness and understanding. It does not mean that everyone should be treated the same; rather, it allows managers discretion and individual supervision. Fayol believed that the desired ends of efficiency, quality, and productivity would be enhanced if organizations motivated employees by dealing with them properly, not just as hired hands.

12. Job tenure and security help retain employees. Without fear of losing a job, and thus their livelihood, staff are motivated to perform for the good of the system. Long-term employment provides organizational stability and security for the employees, who in turn will remain loyal and productive. It can be a symbiotic relationship.

13. Incentives stimulate work and productivity, especially if employees are believed to be motivated by extrinsic rewards, which can extend beyond just economic incentives. Managers must find out what individuals need and try to meet some of them. These incentives benefit both the employee and the system.

14. Esprit de corps is the backbone of teamwork and helps maintain morale. Fayol was concerned about both horizontal and vertical communication patterns, as teamwork is effective only when communication is timely and open.

Fayol's views of organizations were based on what later became known as *Theory X* assumptions; that is, workers are by nature lazy unless motivated and pushed by management. Wages are management's best leverage to motivate employees to work harder, and discipline is the best, if not the only, way to maintain order.

Although Fayol's principles may have defined the early theories of management, we have some concerns about applying these models today. First, the unstated assumption in this paradigm is that the external environment is relatively stable. Because the world in Fayol's time was not changing very rapidly, organizations could be designed to match almost every contingency, but this is not true today. For example, a food cooperative may serve people employed in low-paying jobs, the unemployed, and retired senior citizens living on modest savings (if lucky enough) or Social Security. Each of these people has different nutritional needs, mobility, access to transportation, and ability to contribute to the co-op's programs and needs.

Second, classical theory focuses on the organization's formal elements, its reporting structures, compensation plans, and management's spans of control, task definitions, job descriptions, and lines of authority. These are critical issues in all organizations, but classical management approaches understate the importance of the informal employee network, the role of a strong personality, organizational politics, group behavior, role conflicts, and interpersonal animosities. We know that these informal, and often covert, processes can determine an organization's success or failure. When employees choose not to share information, this will have consequences. We know that when employees want to give excellent customer service, the system thrives, clients benefit, and employees have the satisfaction of doing their best work. *USA Today* sponsors an annual Make a Difference Day showing how individuals can and do go far beyond what is minimally required for their jobs to help others.

Some of classical theory's principles also do not apply to professional nonprofit organizations and complex settings. For example, the unity of command and the scalar principles argue against an organizational matrix design in which a professional on a team may report to more than one supervisor. In community mental health settings, a counselor might report to both the head of social work and the team leader for a specific clinical site. Although this raises issues of coordination and communication, it can be an effective organizational design, despite its violation of Fayol's classical principles of organization and management.

A fourth concern about applying classical models to contemporary non-profit organizations is the belief that work and productivity can be rigidly structured. Perhaps the original impetus for this approach came from the idea that there was almost always a most efficient way to organize tasks and work flow. The goal was to maximize productivity, which may work better in manufacturing than in human services, educational settings, or the cultural, performing, and fine arts. Of course, a museum would be twice as efficient if it doubled its collection on view at any one time, but would the quality of the visual presentation remain as high—or would it just look cluttered?

Finally, Fayol and others may have believed that employees prefer to work alone rather than in teams or groups, but in many nonprofit organizations, this is not true. Many systems have built-in interdependencies. For example, the delivery of health care requires the input of current, reliable, and complex information from numerous staff members in order to complete a diagnosis and determine the proper treatment. Administrative control in professionalized settings may be limited to contextual concerns, such as which shift each employee works and when he or she is granted time off for professional development or vacation. It does not mean that one professional may order another to do something just because that person has the title of Chief. Instead, nonprofit systems replace positional authority ("Do it because I am the boss") with knowledge and information ("Let's do it because it is the best thing to do").

The Ideal Bureaucracy

Living at about the same time as Henri Fayol, Max Weber (1864–1920) had a similarly significant influence on the development of organizational theory. Born in Germany, Weber studied law, religion, economics, history, and military science in Heidelberg. At age twenty-two he passed the examinations required to practice law but continued his interest in history, and his dissertation was on the development of medieval business. Weber's academic and professional career, however, can best be described as checkered, as he abruptly left his position at several universities and spent time in an institution for a nervous breakdown. Nonetheless, his work is still the foundation for organizational theorists today.

A strong believer in capitalism, Weber's thesis rests on rationality. That is, studying a system is the best way to organize it; reviewing production processes is the best way to determine a more efficient method; and structuring work is the best way of making it effective.

The "ideal bureaucracy" is based on the assumption that most inputs can be predicted. Weber believed that it was possible to structure jobs and specific tasks to meet predetermined goals both efficiently and productively. Therefore, the following characteristics serve organizations well:

1. The division of labor and specialization allows employees to learn what exactly is required of them in (almost) all circumstances. Employees can become specialists, a concept that Weber endorsed as evidence of well-trained and educated staff.

2. A clear hierarchy of authority clarifies responsibilities throughout the organization.

3. Policies, rules, and requirements should be specifically defined, clearly written, and widely disseminated.

4. The impersonal administration of these rules and policies is necessary to maintain morale and productivity. Employees should not conduct their personal affairs on company time.

5. Employees are recruited, retained, rewarded, promoted, and disciplined in accordance with their technical skills and contributions. They are trained as needed as their jobs evolve over time. If this is done properly, employees and the organization will develop long-term commitments to each other, and both will benefit. Weber also believed that employees should be on salary to avoid potential conflicts of interest.

In this perspective, managers are the central feature of all organizations, whether they work in Weber's ideal bureaucracy or a small community nonprofit. Although many of his principles still are relevant, some of them now would only create problems like the following:

Problem 1: The ideal does not exist today, nor did it really exist in Weber's era. Nonetheless, the concept of efficient and effective organizing principles and approaches that vary from circumstance to circumstance does have merits.

Problem 2: Employees are not just hired hands who work completely by the rules.

Problem 3: The information age requires faster adaptation than ever was contemplated a century ago.

Problem 4: Technological changes can make jobs obsolete. Weber's notion of specialization must be altered from accomplishing tasks to understanding processes. If employees use only one computer program, they can quickly become out-of-date.

Problem 5: Authority always comes with one's position, but unfortunately for the ideal organization, compliance does not. Charismatic employees can undermine positional authority.

Problem 6: Following the proscribed rules and procedures can be the correct way of doing the work. But these same rules may also lead to inefficiencies and lack of services. For example, when the nation's air traffic controllers wanted to make a point about safety, they followed the rules to the letter, delaying departures until the proper time, altitude, and distance requirements were met, which slowed air travel for days.

Problem 7: Whereas Weber advocated an impersonal administration of rules, policies, and procedures, we know that managers have personal preferences, which do enter decision making and lead to charges of patronage, political influence, or personality conflicts.

Problem 8: In theory, the ideal bureaucracy is managed by people who do not own the business, but in reality, many successful companies are family-owned enterprises.

Problem 9: The ideal system relies on a stable cohort of employees, but the reality of today's nonprofit organizations is that "soft-money" funding often requires layoffs, transfers, and reassignments. Many nonprofits are so understaffed that many employees have a wide range of responsibilities, so replacing one person may be difficult because of the complex and ad hoc nature of his or her job.

Weber's actions and advice during World War I gave critics fuel to oppose his ideas. After serving as a hospital administrator during the war, Weber was a delegate to the Versailles peace talks, arguing against signing the treaty. He was, after all, a strong nationalist and believed that industrial success was critical to rebuilding Germany. Today, however, we remember the sociologist Max Weber not for his political views but for his understanding of organizations and his efforts to develop a framework for effective and efficient production.

The Managerial Acronym: Applying Science to the Work of Management

Luther Gulick's (1892–1993) career had numerous highlights, which may be best summed up by a set of initials and an acronym. During his career, Gulick served in numerous roles, one of which was as an adviser to President Franklin D. Roosevelt to reorganize the federal government in order to increase both the efficiency and service delivery of the government's programs. Gulick's writings, models, theories, and implementation strategies helped managers around the world. To encourage the research and emerging scholarship of administration, he cofounded the *ASQ*, the *Administrative Science Quarterly*, a journal that is now among the most respected publications in the field.

Gulick is perhaps best remembered today for coining the acronym POS-DCORB to define the principal elements of organizational administration: *P*lanning, *O*rganizing, *S*taffing, *D*irecting, *C*oordinating, *R*eporting, and *B*udgeting. His commitment to understanding and improving large systems led some people to refer to him as the dean or father of public administration.

Despite the difference in the size of governmental structures from that of businesses or nonprofit organizations, Gulick believed that the effective management of all such enterprises had to be specific, hence the acronym POSDCORB:

Planning focuses on the organization's mission, goals, plans, objectives, strategies, and tactics. Organizational missions become the "why" for any system. Strong planning defines the system by answering the questions of who, what, where, when, and how. Effective planning specifies the goals to be attained and the resources needed to do so.

Organizing requires the establishment of a formal structure of authority, through which work subdivisions are arranged, defined, and coordinated for the particular objective. In practice, this refers to the roles of top leadership, middle management, first-line supervisors, and employees. How these roles work together on all functions is partly connected to the ways in which the manager chooses to organize work and tasks, by process, service, program, location, profession, or another criterion.

Staffing focuses on the organization's human resources, including their recruitment, selection, training, evaluation, retraining, and even firing or termination. The goal is to have competent staff members who are capable of successfully doing their specific jobs and meeting their department's goals.

Directing is leading and managing employees, staff, volunteers, and others to achieve the organization's goals in the most effective and efficient manner by means of clearly enunciated directions. Effective directing means accomplishing the designated tasks with the available resources in as timely a manner as possible. It is noteworthy that Gulick did not think that anyone should supervise more than six employees. Instead, he believed that a small number of employees allowed maximum control and compliance with the predetermined work flow and production.

Coordinating is the all-important duty of connecting the various parts of the work, by creating the proper organizational structure, maintaining open lines of communication, and keeping the overall goals in mind. Shared concerns and aspirations form a bond among the employee, the manager, and the organization itself.

Reporting means sharing results with all those in the organization who rely on such information, including supervisors, peers, subordinates, external organizations, and stakeholders. This function relies on strong assessment practices and an effective performance appraisal system. Predetermined goals serve as targets for individual and unit performance, the benchmarks for assessing progress.

Budgeting refers to both formal financial planning and managerial decision making in regard to all resources. In its original use, managers were responsible for only the organization's finances, but now budgeting includes decisions about other resources, from space allocations to equipment assignments, from employees' work schedules to the use of consultants, and from training to professional development. Since most organizations have limited resources, budgeting is the process of deciding how to use them in the most effective and efficient manner.

After World War II, POSDCORB became the favorite term for many business school students, as a handy way to remember the major functions of management. In turn, POSDCORB formed the battery of skills, abilities, and tasks that effective managers needed to perform. These functions also provided the foundation for performance appraisals, university courses, training programs, and placement testing.

How do these apply to today's nonprofit environment? Gulick understood that because the external world changes, organizations must adapt as well, in contrast to Weber's ideal bureaucracy, which depends on developing rules, structures, tasks, and controls to ensure as much standardization as possible.

Second, the principles underlying the division of labor may not be as useful to the system if they become too efficient. Speed can cause problems, especially when quality services and programs define outcomes. For example, at the extreme, shorter counseling sessions may not improve clients' abilities to solve their problems or change their behaviors more quickly. Since quality is ultimate barometer for many nonprofit professionals and programs, job design must consider effectiveness, not just efficiency.

Professionals are not on assembly lines or paper-processing entities. Experts can be beneficial but not, as Gulick assumed, always narrowly focused. Rather, today's professional requires collegial input from other professionals. That is, the symphony conductor may guide an orchestra through its music, but the input of each member is needed to help improve the program.

Rigid hierarchies can cause problems as well. The top-down model implies that essential information travels down to the other employees from the top. But we know that often the system's most current, reliable, and useful operational data are not at the top of the organizational chart. Without proper and timely information, poor decisions, low-quality programs, poor morale, and reduced satisfaction can result. The problem is not the staff's competence or skills; rather, it is resistance to sharing needed information that will help others perform up to their fullest potential.

Divided loyalties are not uncommon in professionalized organizations. In addition to wanting to help move the organization forward, many employees also are members of a formal profession. As such, they must adhere to its codes of ethics, recertification processes, continuing education requirements, and state licensure laws. This situation contradicts Fayol's grand notion that employees should have undivided loyalties and total allegiance to the organization.

We have seen the development of Weber's concepts for structuring the ideal system and Fayol's principles for effective organization. Gulick's analysis of managerial functions extended their efforts. He understood that the individual manager and employee make a difference in every system's productivity and outcomes and that structure alone does not guarantee success. This leads to the work of Frederick Taylor, who advocated rigorous methods to define workers' productivity and management's responsibility for making sure that these goals are reached.

The Scientific Management Movement

Born in 1856 in Pennsylvania, Frederick W. Taylor became known as the father of scientific management, a giant step beyond his initial employment as a machinist. While earning his pay, the young Frederick Taylor began to understand the subtle collusion of managers and employees. Managers seemed to push their employees only halfheartedly to reach production goals until there was a major problem. Only then did they strive for more output. This problem intensified when one employee saw other, less productive peers making the same wage for less effort. These inequities cut into the employee's morale and hurt the company's bottom line.

Taylor earned a degree in mechanical engineering and, as a consultant for Bethlehem Steel, began to apply the lessons he had learned on the shop floor to redesign a common household tool, the shovel. Taylor believed, and ultimately proved, that each worker should be given a shovel that fit his body size and strength. Before this, each employee was given the same-size shovel and expected to produce equally. Did this make a difference? Yes. Total production costs went down, and (fortunately or unfortunately, depending on your perspective), more than half the employees lost their jobs while productivity remained at the same level.

From these experiences, Taylor believed that management's decision making was really a science, and he showed that information could be gathered and used to increase a firm's productivity and profits. In his view, over time, such practices would also increase wages for the workers, so that both sides would benefit.

Taylor's basic principles make the following four points:

1. Through a rigorous examination of each job, management can determine the one best way to accomplish every task.
2. Through good personnel practices, management can select the best person to perform each job.
3. Through continued training and development, each worker will receive the training enabling him or her to perform the needed tasks as well as possible.
4. Through proper financial incentives, employees will work at their highest levels to meet the demands of the job.

Managers, employees, and their unions, however, soon found reasons to question Taylor's competence, ideas, and practices. Supervisors saw these efforts as intruding into their prerogatives and discretion. Employees resisted being judged against the relentless ticking of the stopwatch. Unions believed that the speed of the production line and worker outputs should be negotiated through a collective bargaining process. Science was not an integral part of labor agreements.

On a personal level, opponents tried to discredit Taylor because he had essentially been fired from two jobs. But it was the political clout of the labor movement that energized the most successful attack on Taylor's beliefs, principles, and practices. He believed that workers would produce more when they adhered to scientifically developed standards, received ongoing training, and used the proper equipment. These beliefs lead to the development of time–motion studies. In 1911 Taylor was questioned by the U.S. Congress, and as a result of these hearings, new laws prohibited the use of stopwatches to time the work of federal civil servants. This law actually remained on the books until the late 1940s.

During his lifetime, Taylor's work[2] was both praised and criticized, but undeterred, he became one of the first professors at the now famous Tuck School of Business at Dartmouth College in Hanover, New Hampshire.[3] One of the sharpest critiques of "Taylorism," as it became known, centers on the underlying assumption that based on scientific results, human nature can be controlled by strong management. In reality, though, it is difficult for theorists, staff, and managers alike to overlook the political process in organizations, interpersonal conflicts, informal networks, and the impact of an organization's culture on both how the system operates and its bottom line, whether that is profits or the quality of services.

Like earlier approaches, the research base and resulting models were typically derived from and applied to production systems and manufacturing organizations, and their direct application to nonprofit systems was minimal. Thus, how these principles were translated into different practices were legitimate targets for the opponents of such approaches. How can productivity and efficiency be measured? These are no simple ways of measuring the productivity of an orchestra; in fact, speed works against most symphonies. A concert played to the beat of a marching band might be efficient, but it certainly would not be effective, accurate, or enjoyable.

One of the underlying principles of scientific management was the use of history and research to predict the future performance of employees, work speed, and system outputs. Science strives for objectivity to counter individual biases, and this is true in any organization. Managers are just as prone to see the results they want as any other profession is. In addition, scientific research strives for repetition; the results of one study must be able to be replicated again for reliability and validity. No single data point should serve as the sole basis for a decision. Furthermore, by using clear procedures, Taylor believed that past performance could help predict future behavior and determine appropriate goals, which would give an edge to one firm over its competitors. For example, if a particular intake process were known to result in shorter treatment times, clients and patients would go to the location that served them quickly and effectively.

Human Relations Movement

In typical Hollywood Westerns, the boss refers to the ranch workers as "hired hands," a term that symbolizes both the classical and scientific approaches to organizational design and managerial roles. But employees come with hearts as well as hands. Workers have information that they may or may not use to influence productivity. Studies of employee satisfaction demonstrate that feelings (the heart) do affect workers in a variety of ways. Absenteeism, sabotage, and turnover can be negative consequences, whereas going the extra mile, teaming with others, retention, and longevity are positive outcomes for which most organizations strive.

It is not a surprise, therefore, that another approach to management and organizational behavior emerged, one focusing on employees' attitudes, behaviors, motivations, ability to adapt to different work settings, and feelings. The core assumption was that satisfied employees are productive employees. Management's role thus was to help employees meet their own needs, so that they in turn could help the organization meet its needs. This is the human relations movement.

From 1927 to 1932, a major research project at Western Electric's plant in Hawthorne, Illinois, helped stimulate the growth of the human relations movement. Harvard University researcher Elton Mayo and his associates were planning to conduct a time–motion study as part of the scientific approach. What they found, however, was that productivity increased almost without regard to the changing variables. Whether or not the workers were given extended rest periods, their productivity remained the same or improved. When similar experiments were conducted, such as changing the available lighting in the work area, productivity generally improved whether the room was brightly lit or nearly dark.

The researchers concluded that something else besides objective science was operating at the Western Electric plant. Even though the scientific method documented that work variables could be manipulated, productivity nonetheless increased with little correlation to them. This finding became known as the *Hawthorne effect*. The Hawthorne effect means that the very act of studying someone can in fact change that person's behavior. Workers gave their all because they perceived that they were important enough that this Harvard group was studying them. Management's interest in their work and physical environment meant that they were valued employees. Or so they thought.

"They" became a critical variable, for it was the group, the employees themselves, who made these decisions. The scientific method of analyzing each individual job and task overlooked the reality that communication among employees can have a significant impact on results. Thus, it is not just individuals acting alone, but a larger entity. This realization gave rise to the concept of social rewards, group influence, informal leadership, organizational culture, and, ultimately, "groupthink."

Elton Mayo's conclusions were quite different from those of Taylor, who believed that economic motivators were sufficient to ensure production, motivation, and commitment. Mayo noted that, instead, the team was critical. Instead of assuming that workers were passive "hired hands" who would respond as expected to changing conditions, this research revealed that power and authority are not vested solely in management. At Western Electric, the employees as a group made assumptions about what was happening—that is, they were proud of the imagined recognition from management—and acted accordingly.

The Hawthorne results also gave rise to the broader concept of *systems theory*, that what happens in one part of a system has a direct or indirect impact elsewhere in the system. For example, if there is an accident in one part of an organization, others not only learn about it but also react in ways that influence their motivations and performance. Management's role expands from controlling information to sharing it in ways that do not undercut the organization's goals. Similarly, when a new employee is hired, his or her peers will look at the new employee's starting salary. Because the consequences of paying the new recruit more than longer-term employees can be predicted, the Hawthorne experiments demonstrated the interrelatedness of numerous parts of the organization.

The Hawthorne effect can have a significant impact on nonprofit organizations. First, many nonprofit organizations use team approaches to deliver their services. These teams can be both formal and informal, and their supervisors should understand the important role they play in helping a team form, operate effectively, manage disagreements, build consensus, and facilitate open decision making. In addition, the Hawthorne effect shows the folly of imposing rigid production requirements on each individual. Outcomes often are successful because several staff members bring their specific professional perspectives to collaborate in a work situation, something that cannot be codified and placed under the time–motion study microscope.

Finally, nonprofit organizations tend to be more decentralized and flatter structures in both their decision making and delegated authority. Power is vested less in the positional authority of the supervisor than it is in the expertise of the staff members.

Theory X/Y

Fayol, Weber, and Taylor made a series of assumptions about workers, which were later challenged by the work of Mayo and others. In turn, in his landmark book entitled *The Human Side of Enterprise*, Douglas McGregor (1960) developed a perspective that helps managers understand their assumptions about employees.[4] These assumptions represent the two poles of a paradigm, with theory X assumptions reflecting the view that most employees

1. Do not want to work or like to work.
2. Will only do what mangers direct them to do.
3. Prefer not to accept responsibility.
4. Want job security more than advancement.
5. Work only for their paycheck.

Theory Y assumes that most employees

1. Are internally motivated to do their best work and contribute to the organization's overall goals.
2. Will accept responsibility when earned.
3. Have more potential than the organization recognizes.
4. Are committed to the organization.
5. See work as a natural part of their lives and the social order.

The theory X manager rarely delegates, spending the majority of time overseeing the work process and outcomes. There is less time for planning because *control* dominates. Theory Y managers plan more effectively because they have the time to do so. They monitor work outcomes through a variety of methods and help solve problems when needed. Theory Y managers are not threatened by employees' successes, whereas theory X managers may see a promising employee as a challenge to their own safety and security. The X-type is parsimonious with praise and does not easily accept criticism or negative feedback without deflecting it onto others. One-way communication characterizes most of a theory X manager's conversations with peers and subordinates.

Theory Y makes quite different assumptions about people. From this perspective, staff members are assumed to be internally motivated to do quality work and contribute to overall goals. They have more potential than organizations often recognize, and they will accept responsibility when it is earned. They understand work to be a natural part of their lives and the social order and are committed to the organizations where they work. Most people prefer to work in environments where such assumptions are made about them. The best-prepared managers of nonprofit organizations proceed from the basis of theory Y, although theory X assumptions are occasionally encountered.

Discussion

Does the theory X/theory Y model describe anyone you have worked for? If so, what was your experience as an employee in that situation?

The Leadership Continuum

Devised to help managers select a style with which they can be most comfortable, the Leadership Continuum has provided useful ideas for the past fifty years. It is based on the interaction of three variables in any work situation: those factors that specify how a manager will approach a situation, other factors that compel subordinates to act in various ways, and those factors in the situation that both the supervisor and subordinate find themselves. This is the hallmark of the situational approach to managerial style and decision making. It adds a level of complexity and further refines the bimodal theory X/theory Y approach. Developed by Tannenbaum and Schmidt, the Leadership Continuum, shown in table 5.1, flows from autocratic to democratic and describes specific behaviors at various points along its path.[5]

Point 1: The manager decides and announces the decision. In this approach, the manager possesses all the information about the situation, weighs the alternatives, decides how to proceed, announces the plan of action, and expects compliance.

Point 2: The manager makes the decisions and then "sells" them to his or her subordinates. At this point, slight movement is found in the selling of the decision. Rather than expecting only one-way communication and implementation, the manager recognizes that the employees should accept the decision. Thus selling is added to the manager's style.

Point 3: The manager presents decisions and asks for comments or questions. Now the manager has moved into a dialogue with those who must implement the decision. They have the opportunity to ask questions, share reactions, and perhaps learn about the decision process. This is a long way from the first point. Here, involvement, interaction, and conversation can clarify vague aspects of the decision. But power, responsibility, and authority still remain with the manager.

Point 4: The manager makes a tentative decision and requests ideas. The power to define the problem, options, and approaches remains with the manager, but the decision can be changed if the employees and others providing feedback raise valid opposition. Ownership has shifted more toward becoming jointly shared.

Point 5: The manager shares a situation that needs to be resolved with staff and seeks their input into the decision. After receiving whatever others have to offer, the decision rests with the manager, but subordinates usually have a clear idea of the choices being considered. Greater involvement can expand ownership of the solution and hasten its implementation.

Point 6: This point differs in that the manager raises the issues, provides some guidance to and limitations on final actions, asks the department to explore the options, gets needed information, and decides on the course of action. Involvement increases. When subordinates are empowered to work in this model, the manager's style has moved from an autocratic to an enhanced democratic approach.

Point 7: Finally, the most democratic style is the manager giving subordinates the autonomy to raise issues, develop plans, implement their choice, and assess the results. This is not abdication, since the subordinates are still required to report to the manager. The manager at this point delegates more than in any of the previous styles. The greatest sense of staff motivation, autonomy, responsibility, and risk/reward is found in this style.

For this model to be applicable, the factors relevant to the manager, the subordinates, and the situation must be in alignment. Factors regarding the manager greatly influence what style will be considered. Most important, if the manager has little confidence in the subordinates' skills and abilities, priorities and values, then a more autocratic style might be appropriate. When managers view their role as action oriented and in charge, they are more likely to remain autocratic than if they assume that the workers are competent and motivated.

Part of the manager's choice of styles depends on the factors regarding the subordinates. When subordinates have been trained to achieve and perhaps have a history of achievement, managers will be encouraged to move toward a more democratic style. When employees have a direct stake in the issue, they can see how their choices will affect their work, and this increases the likelihood of a responsible development of options and the inputs or decisions needed to face the challenge. If the employees' goals are aligned with the department's and the organization's objectives, removing a conflicting interest can lead to effective action. Even under the most democratic approach, the manager still oversees the situation and bears final accountability for the results.

Of course, the situation itself can influence the choice of managerial style. If the culture supports one style, the manager will take a great risk in adopting a different approach. But if the situation is an emergency, there may not be enough time to involve others to the degree that one might prefer. If the promotion system encourages managers to help train their replacements from

Table 5.1
Leadership Continuum

Manager's Use of Authority				Subordinates' Area of Responsibility		
Manager makes decision and announces it	Manager "sells" the decision	Manager presents ideas and invites questions	Manager presents tentative decision for input	Manager presents problem, seeking ideas, but still decides	Manager defines limits, so group can make decision	Manager permits employees to define issues, options and actions within predetermined limits
1	2	3	4	5	6	7
(Most Autocratic)						(Most Democratic)

within, that will encourage a more democratic style than one whose traditions are based on seniority or test scores for promotional opportunities. It is also noteworthy that the employees' experiences with one another can influence a manager's approach. If there are underlying conflicts, political infighting, high turnover rates, and absenteeism, a more autocratic style might be in order, even if it reinforces some of these concerns.

As managers move toward more democratic styles, certain positive consequences can result. When given adequate training and resources, a more democratic style increases most people's motivation, which can help the manager change the system's culture from dependency to interdependent action. Thus, goal congruence will help align the employees' goals and objectives with those of the organization. This supports Fayol's and Weber's theories of design and organization.

Employees in nonprofit organizations have a stake in providing the needed services and programs, and their input will enhance the development of options for decision making. When programs rely on effective collaborative teams, the more democratic approach encourages decision making based on information and experience rather than on merely positional authority. These are valued outcomes for nonprofit managers and supervisory personnel.

Management by Objectives

In the 1950s, Peter Drucker coined the term *management by objectives* (MBO) which became a national movement in the 1970s.[6] MBO is an organization-wide process that starts by establishing the goals of the overall system. Then, each unit, department, division, and team decides on its own goals and objectives. Each one's goals must support the broader goals of the system's higher-level units, and the sum of all these objectives should be the attainment of the overall goals. The whole is at least equal to the sum of the parts. For MBO to work effectively, the agreement on the goals is only the first step. Managers must make sure that all the needed resources are available so the employees and the department can carry out their assigned tasks. Then, an effective performance appraisal system monitors their progress over time. The MBO model was used extensively in the corporate world and formed the basis for strategic planning.

Watkins, Holland, and Ritvo extended the MBO model to human service organizations by distinguishing two different types of objectives: service and impact.[7] *Service* objectives specify how much of a particular service will be offered in a defined period of time. These objectives generally can be measured by quantitative data. For example, how many clients will be served during the first half of a year? How many staff members will attend professional development programs?

Impact objectives are the difference that receiving these services will make. For example, what was the impact of serving 543 clients during a six-month period? Did the staff who attended a training program on intake procedures make fewer mistakes? Were they able to enroll new clients more efficiently? Were clients better off after completing the services?

Specifying objectives and their indicators has direct utility in preparing proposals for external funding, developing volunteer service programs, establishing partnerships with other organizations, training staff, and reporting each year to an organization's numerous stakeholders. Objective information is more persuasive than subjective opinions.

Peter Drucker's work extends to nonprofits and, in fact, exhorts corporations to learn from the experiences of successful large and small nonprofit organizations. For example, many companies can benefit from understanding how nonprofit organizations define their missions and use these ideals and parameters to focus their programs and services. Accountability to funding sources and the frugal use of resources are hallmarks of nonprofits; documenting results and ongoing assessments fit closely with the management by objectives process. Finally, Drucker knew the value, in both real and symbolic terms, of committed employees and a strong cohort of volunteers.

Web Assignment

Go to the Web site of a corporation or a national nonprofit organization, and find its "strategic goals and objectives." What do you find when you compare these against the criteria of specificity, challenge, resource availability, and evaluation methods?

In conclusion, as organizational theory has developed over the past one hundred fifty years, organizations have learned how to structure their managers' roles and tasks. Managers must learn how to adapt to changing conditions both inside and outside their systems. Effective organizations are those that can predict and respond to change by means of a culture that supports excellence, adaptation, efficiency, and effective service programs. Most nonprofit leaders aspire to these ideals.

6

Leading and Managing Nonprofit Organizations

This chapter examines the core skills, abilities, and perspectives that supervisors, middle managers, and leaders in nonprofit organizations need to be effective. The objectives of this chapter are to enable the reader to

1. Describe the components of an organization's culture.
2. Identify the skills of leadership.
3. Understand how to improve staff performance.
4. Describe the characteristics of effective staff teams.
5. List the steps to improve one's use of time.

As Peter Drucker pointed out many years ago, nonprofit organizations have long been ahead of businesses in understanding how to respond to the needs of staff and consumers, develop a commitment to mission, and carry out quality work with limited resources.[1] They differ dramatically from the "buyer-beware" attitudes that characterize commercial transactions. As Steve McCormick, president of the Nature Conservancy, noted in the Stanford University Graduate School of Business Newsletter, "Great management is really a matter of leading and capitalizing on the value of people in the organization."[2]

Leadership may be one of the most abused terms in organizations and politics today. It has become synonymous with positional power; that is, only those with a title can lead. This misses the fact that leadership comes from many sources. The nonprofit organization's board of trustees and a commercial organization's chief executive officer and its management team certainly have a leadership role. But any staff member can provide leadership as well as influence others in the organization. Leadership is as much a function of the person as it is vested in any one position. It depends on the issues at the moment and the leadership skills of those addressing them, as well as on the level of conversation and the decision making required.

Leaders create environments that influence people to identify and work toward shared goals. Good leaders know that people support a world they help create, while managers tend to focus on keeping the work organized to accomplish those goals. Both require skills to be cultivated by every person in the organization.

Understanding an Organization's Culture

The context for leadership is the organization's culture. Effective leaders know how to assess and shape an organization's culture to improve its performance. They understand how culture develops and how they can change those elements that do not support effective and efficient operations.

An *organization's culture* is the interaction of attitudes, values, norms, customs, history, traditions, and beliefs. It is "how we do our work here." Culture is composed of the *shop talk*, the *theories-in-practice* (not the espoused theories), the *what we do, not what we say*, the *unspoken rules around here*, the *tacit assumptions*, and *what they forgot to tell you during the job interview*.

People come to work each day with their own expectations, values, attitudes, fears, ideals. and aspirations which interact with the department or the work unit's norms. For example, in some settings it is acceptable to come to work five to ten minutes late. Of course, there is no rule allowing that; it just happens because the department's culture allows it by either inaction (no one is reported) or public acquiescence (cracking a joke by asking, "Did you bring me coffee, at least?").

Once at work, the job itself helps define a system's culture. Consider the stereotypical emergency room. It is often a culture of quick action, fast movement, and rapid decisions based on limited information. Contrast that with a professional association serving a national constituency. Of course, it occasionally has emergencies, but the normal work flows through various standardized, predictable communication systems. Thus the work itself helps define the culture.

Following are ten elements to think about when analyzing an organization's culture.

1. The organization's *mission* helps define its culture. Sometimes a mission becomes a slogan or organization motto that is widely recognized by the public, for example, the United Negro College Fund's "A mind is a terrible thing to waste" or the American Red Cross's blood drives, "Give Blood, Give Life." The point to remember is that people commit to a vision as well as to those who work toward it. Peter Drucker defined several dimensions of an organization's culture: (1) its mission; (2) its clients/customers' needs, desires, wants, values, and attitudes; (2) its plans to meet these; and (4) its progress toward meeting them.[3]

2. According to Fayol and Weber (discussed in chapter 5), an organization's *structure* and control systems play an important role in establishing its culture. If all decisions must be cleared by upper management, then the culture may not support planned risks or creative ideas.

3. *Power* is spread unevenly through most organizations. Even two supervisors at the same level on the organization chart may exercise different forms or extents of power. In some systems, position defines power. In others, knowledge, needed expertise, and information are more important. In still others, power accrues to those seen as rising stars or popular favorites.

4. Culture often is revealed in how *perquisites* are allocated. These may take the subtle form of the favored corner office, proudly displayed certificates of achievement on office walls, the close-in parking space, or the selection to attend the meeting in Hawaii. Perquisites may also be more obvious, such as having an administrative assistant, being invited to special meetings, or receiving a new job title. The distribution of rewards, inducements, punishments, and discipline thus contribute to a system's culture.

5. Every organization has its own *rituals.* Whether they are the celebration of the organization's birthday each year or an annual reward banquet, rituals provide stability and help reinforce the status quo. In turn, the status quo can help maintain the excellence that has built the organization's reputation, or it may be a major impediment to any proposed change. Whether the ritual focuses on the retiring employee or the new coworker welcome luncheon, employees learn through rituals what is valued and expected of them.

6. Organizational stories about the organization's *history* help define its culture. The legendary empty office shows what happens when a former employee challenged the boss. Stories help employees learn about the system's history, values, and ideals, whereas legends become food for gossip and distortion. It is important to distinguish the stories about the past from the myths that develop over time.

7. *Patterns* define both the individual worker's approach and the work unit's culture. Some people want to meet others over morning coffee before starting their jobs. This social time helps people reconnect. Chats by the water cooler sat-

isfy more than just thirst. Required staff meetings serve many purposes, some of which are so routine that they may lose their meaning.

8. Culture is transmitted through *language.* Every organization has its own codes, acronyms, and ways of communicating. Such shop talk might include MBO, Docs, Rule 10, the sixth floor, and EAP, which probably mean nothing to an outsider. But to those in certain organizations, these code words refer to, respectively, Management by Objectives, physicians, the policy that allows certain employees to carry weapons, the location of the top management offices, and an employee assistance program.

9. An organization's culture contains numerous *subcultures* created by different programs, divisions, teams, buildings, job classifications, and groups over time and embedded in the larger system. When cultures clash, the workers' energy and focus shift from effective work to protecting their subculture and their friends in it.

10. Individuals and groups develop their own culture in part by *observing* others. Rewards, punishments, promotions, access to resources, and other decisions become ingrained in the culture of each unit. McCaskey concentrated on "the hidden messages that managers send" as an important variable in developing and maintaining a unit's culture.[4]

Organizational cultures develop in many ways. Consider the particular type of consumer. A museum serves a different constituency than does a food co-op. If your work unit deals with affluent, independent clients, it will have a different impact than if it serves people in homeless shelters. This does not mean that the employees give less attention to each consumer, but it does mean that different assumptions may govern the interaction. So, for instance, instead of enjoying an elegantly decorated lounge, convicted felons on a work-release program may have to relax in more modest surroundings with more visible security.

Leaders must be concerned about whether the organization's culture supports the most effective and efficient work habits to attain its goals. Their reactions to events will almost always affect the culture, and the culture will affect the workers' reactions.

Leaders learn to identify important dimensions of organizational culture and find ways to strengthen the organization before it changes them and they begin making the same assumptions as everyone else. Culture therefore is shaped by what leaders want, support, and do, and effective leaders understand the organization's culture according to the following processes:

- Effective groups share an understanding of their goals and the tasks needed to achieve them. Consensus helps maintain commitment to the group and the organization, though it may constrain creativity.

- Effective cultures define who is on the team, who supports the members of the team, who is outside the group, and who may impede the work. The effective leader becomes a boundary spanner for these different roles.
- A common language builds cohesion and encourages the support of other team members.
- Shared power builds stronger member-centered groups. If this is the desired culture, then leaders must delegate as appropriate and build the needed skills for the group members to function in this environment.

A common understanding of the organization's rules and procedures must complement a consistent application of these guidelines. If the culture accepts unequal treatment, low productivity, or conformity, then work teams will not maintain high levels of excellence. Individual employees still may perform well, but the culture might stress survival or access to rewards at the expense of the unit's goals. Effective leaders take steps to cultivate the norms and expectations that guide the organization's work and reinforce them in their relationships with everyone in the organization.

Exercise

1. Describe the characteristics of organizational culture in a nonprofit with which you are familiar.
2. How does such analysis help those working in a nonprofit organization become more effective?

Building High-Performing Systems

John Gardner's exceptional essay on renewal explains why leaders should support a culture of success and how they can maintain a high level of performance once they have begun to reach their goals.[5] These guidelines apply to every kind of nonprofit organization. His first principle is that *every system needs effective steps to develop and recruit new talent*. An organization's developmental role focuses on how their leaders train and support all the current staff. The options may include in-house training programs, support for college courses, professional conferences, a change in shifts, and use of the Internet for access to current information.

Recruiting new talent means more than just filling personnel vacancies. It requires an analysis of the organization's strengths and weaknesses before the personnel department begins to seek candidates with the requisite values, skills, and information. Recruitment means getting out of the office, going to programs that educate new professionals, and using the professional networks to find out who the best available people are.

Gardner's second principle is that *the organization must have a "hospitable" environment for all employees at all levels.* Since each person's job contributes in some way to the overall success of the organization's services and programs, the workplace must be conducive to productivity. A fear of criticism, job loss, or political agendas undermines effective work and positive outcomes. Clues to these problems can be found in high turnover rates, continued absenteeism, anonymous messages on bulletin boards, or a dirty work environment in which employees have no pride.

Third, *organizations need built-in mechanisms for self-criticism, evaluation, and assessment.* Leaders must know how they can maintain and improve the organization's programs, services, tasks, and processes. The public demands accountability and transparency, and taxpayers, companies, regulators, creditors, and other must be continually reassured that their funds are being spent in the most effective and efficient manner. Successful organizations thus regularly monitor their work. This is Gardner's idea of "continuous quality improvement."

Fourth, *adaptable structures and policies support successful planned change.* Many of the rules, policies, and procedures that we have today were put in place because something happened in the past that was not covered by another rule. As time passes, however, rules become outdated. For example, the notion that every employee must sign in by 8 a.m. in the morning seems archaic when some jobs can be done at home or while flying on an airplane. Text messaging allows distant connections, a process unheard of just two decades ago.

Related to the previous concept is the fifth principle, that *the organization must find a way to prevent people from becoming prisoners of their own procedures.* When the phrase "That is the rule" becomes a normative reply, then problems likely exist. Leaders help others find new solutions to issues, not announce more rules.

Finally, *successful organizations foster a culture that supports planned risk taking.* This does not mean that every employee can do as he or she wishes. Rather, it recognizes that new solutions may be more effective than previous approaches. With proper review and clearance, attempting something new may enhance outcomes, save resources, open new partnerships, or lead to other ideas. If an organization is standing still in today's environment, it may indeed be falling behind.

Leadership Skills

Successful nonprofit leaders cultivate several sets of skills, which differ depending on an individual's position in the organization. The three sets of skills are conceptual, interpersonal, and technical. *Conceptual* skills refer to the broad understanding of the organization's purposes. Examples are the ability to develop and articulate strategic goals, to define and resolve major problems, and to help connect the organization to the external environment. *Interpersonal* skills refer to why someone may be referred to as "a people person." They include adapting a leader's approach to each worker by recognizing differences in backgrounds, contributions, abilities, education, and role. *Technical* skills refer to understanding the numerous aspects of the organization's work. The following box shows how people in top management and midlevel and first-line supervisors can balance these skills. Every manager should have some of all three; the relative balance is what distinguishes the work of top managers from that of first-line supervisors.

Skills of Effective Leaders

1. *Advocating* for the organization's vision.
   Building interdependencies and partnerships to strengthen the vision.
   Stating the vision to others.
2. *Explaining* the vision to others.
   Clarifying the required steps.
   Showing how actions help realize the vision.
3. *Applying* the vision.
   Acting in a manner consistent with the vision.
   Applying activities across the system to illustrate the vision as practiced.
4. *Adapting* the vision.
   Ensuring that the organization's goals and programs fit the vision.
   Being willing to revise and adapt to changing conditions.

Leadership is characterized by certain qualities that can be harnessed at appropriate moments to change a system, to resolve a problem, and to move the organization forward. Leadership is often connected to the organization's mission and vision, which helps answer the question "leadership for what?" Effective leaders have strong skills in those areas shown in the preceding box.

These actions do not happen by chance but are learned and practiced every day and improve when using feedback to find out what can be better. Tom Peters and Robert Waterman's landmark book *In Search of Excellence* stresses that effective leaders have a bias toward action, not inaction and standing still.[6] Effective leaders accept information from outside the agency and do not challenge or dismiss data that may reveal problems or concerns. They establish goals that are challenging yet attainable. Effective leaders know how to develop other persons' skills and remain committed to doing so. Although others' success threatens some people, effective leaders recognize and applaud them, since they help the organization reach its goals. Effective leaders know how to allocate resources toward the vision, not just toward the political power of the moment. They use their usually high energy level to inspire others, not to shame them by making them feel ignorant or lazy. They believe that others can and will contribute their best if given information, resources, recognition, and feedback. They maintain high levels of ethical behavior and integrity, treat others fairly, and model the attitudes and behaviors they want others to follow.

Managers as Leaders

People in nonprofit managerial and supervisory roles can develop and exercise effective leadership, and they also are responsible for seeing that the day-to-day work is done. Managers that cultivate leadership skills become even better at moving the organization forward. There is no single best managerial style; high-performing organizations result from many factors. Becoming a quality organization also means learning how to assess performance and grow in excellence. Not surprisingly, the search for the perfect manager has resulted in thousands of books and models. At one point, the tall man theory, that effective managers were mostly tall men, was popular. Surely Margaret Thatcher and Napoleon disproved that notion. The desire to understand effective management styles also concentrated on the assumptions managers make about their employees, which led to theory X and theory Y.

Kenneth H. Blanchard advocates a functional approach that pulls together elements of other approaches into one framework.[7] Management uses influence because people tend to comply with the vision and goals of good leaders. But managing is more than just persuading some hired hands to follow orders. Blanchard described four complementary roles that managers can use when dealing with different people.

Directing is a skill that works well with employees who need precise directions spelling out specific tasks. Whether they do not have all the requisite information or just require close supervision, directing is based mostly on positional power; that is, the supervisor or manager occasionally needs to say, "I am the boss." That already is understood, and compliance usually follows. In this style, the employee often brings problems to the supervisor and expects him or her to offer solutions, and the supervisor complies by announcing the solution, decision, or new approach.

Directive supervision is continually appraising subordinates' performance. Performance feedback, evaluation, or appraisals require planning and prompt execution. It is not fair to employees to reserve feedback until their annual performance review. Waiting too long will not reinforce work that has been at or above expectations, and delay will not change problematic behaviors.

Even the best work assignments do not always achieve the intended results. Part of the problem may be that the plan itself overreached, promised too much for available resources, or was not realistic. In such situations, the plan must be revised. Sometimes an employee does not perform up to expectation, which is a managerial problem and requires prompt attention. These actions are part of directing employees toward desired individual and unit goals.

Coaching works best when employees already have the needed skills and information but need confidence or help identifying the steps to take once they understand the goal. Effective managers-as-coaches combine information, support, shared goals, with clear direction and feedback. Appropriate recognition should follow successful implementation, since the person being coached is part of the solution.

Supporting helps employees reach the same conclusions as the managers. The manager discusses the problem with the employee, who understands that the manager might have information that can help the employee redefine the problem, develop joint options, and decide with him or her how to proceed. Listening and exchanging ideas and ideals, or two-way communication, are characteristic of this style.

Delegating works best when the employee is familiar with the job, has the needed information, can access resources within predetermined limits, understands how the work will be evaluated, and knows how to communicate the results to the supervisor on a predictable basis. Delegating is not the same as supervisory abdication. Rather, effective delegation is a planned process appropriately using responsibility and authority along with checks and reviews.

The bully pulpit is often used to refer to the power of the president of the United States to announce the country's agenda (the pulpit) and to encourage compliance (the bully). This same power applies to managers as well. Even though they can make decisions unilaterally, "do it because I said so" does not foster commitment to an organization's ideals. Rather, when difficult choices must be made, effective leadership requires that a manager use the bully pulpit and carefully lay out the goals to be achieved in carrying out the organization's mission.

One style or approach will not work for all employees, as they have different needs, information, skills, abilities, pressures, problems, and aspirations. Instead, the manager should spell out his or her expectations, allow employees to do their best job, evaluate their performance, and then offer specific and timely feedback.

Exercise

1. Describe the skills demonstrated by a leader or manager in a nonprofit organization with which you are familiar.
2. What other skills may that person need?
3. Assess your own level of skill in each of the forms of leadership.

Building Teamwork

Almost everyone in a nonprofit organization works with others as part of a team. Whether referred to as departments, units, sections, or divisions, effectiveness means that the unit's goals are communicated and met. These structures reflect different aspects of the organization's work and often are based on professional skills. For example, most rehabilitation centers have occupational therapy and accounting departments. Whatever the rationale and organizing principles, most departments function best when the staff members work well together. Their supervisors' annual performance appraisals include attention to how well the team functions. For example, assume that all staff positions are filled with qualified individuals. The single most important characteristic of effective teams is having clear, specific, challenging, and achievable goals. Each team should understand how its work fits into the organization's mission, culture, values, and strategic plan. What difference does doing the job well make to the lives of others? Has management clearly articulated its performance expectations? Do team members accept them fully? Does the team understand its goals, resources, and boundaries?

The team has the best chance of success when these conditions are met. But highly productive teams have other defining characteristics. First, effective teams are small enough to get the job done without redundancy. If the team does not have enough members, some of the goals and objectives may need to be altered or eliminated as unrealistic and unachievable. But teams that are too large may have communication or morale problems, based on their members' differing contributions. Some members may be regarded as slackers by those who are strongly committed and harder working.

The team must be composed of people with the skills needed to achieve its goals, and these skills must be augmented by the delegation of appropriate responsibility and authority for doing the job. In order to create teamwork, the team members must also have access to all the information, resources, and supports they need to use their skills effectively. Although not all members need to be able to do every job, the composition of the team should be reviewed to be sure that its members have all the skills needed. A good time to conduct such reviews is when there is a staff vacancy but before writing the position description.

As the team's work continues, managers should make sure that their performance evaluations cover both individual contributions and the success of the unit. It is useless to reward individual successes if the team fails to reach its overall goals and objectives. Sometimes the team's needs should take precedence over an individual's preferences, with such interdependence characteristic of a highly productive team. In this era of growing accountability, an organization's top managers expect individuals, departments, the organization, and the public to be interdependent. When they are, managers should recognize and celebrate success. Money is one way to reward productive work. Public recognition and other symbolic rewards provide gratification and can also be powerful motivators for a team effort. The reward system should encourage innovation and accomplishment.

Effective teams know how to manage both their tasks and processes to meet specific goals. Although the team will always have a leader, members of effective teams "own" their own work processes, and a number of behaviors can help move teams forward. Although a dysfunctional team may have all the needed skills, resources, and information, its work process may discourage teamwork. The following behaviors are important to a team's process:

- Initiating new ideas.
- Seeking or sharing information.
- Providing information and opinions.
- Clarifying positions.
- Elaborating on ideas and building toward new ones.
- Comparing where the team is with where it needs to be.
- Harmonizing.
- Compromising to find win-win strategies.
- Ensuring that all members remain connected.
- Encouraging others when needed and appropriate.

No single team member should try to take on all these roles and responsibilities. Strong teams review their work, decide what went well, and make plans to modify when needed. The team's decision-making process and its methods for handling conflict, acquiring new members, filling in when someone is absent, taking risks, giving and receiving job-related feedback nondefensively all are areas for review and discussion.

Effective teams result from the leader's commitment to the concept and work processes need to develop and maintain high-performing teams. All this requires staff time, monetary support, and inclusion in the organization's culture. Planned professional development programs, periodic working retreats with professional facilitators, annual recognition occasions, regular staff meetings with time to discuss how the team is working, and social events such as holiday parties, staff recognition luncheons, and even family dinners are part of building and supporting the team.

Because many organizations use the concepts and structure of teams in their annual reports, recruiting materials, and professional training programs, team members should model their idea of effective teamwork for others throughout the organization. Teams should explain and demonstrate the practices they want others to follow.

Exercise

Evaluate the performance of a staff team in an organization with which you are familiar. How well did the team work? What areas need strengthening?

Managing Professionals

Nonprofit organizations often employ large numbers of skilled professionals. Even though members of many occupations consider themselves "professionals," the traditional (albeit changing) definition applies to people who

1. Have advanced knowledge, often from graduate education.
2. Are certified or licensed by authorized outside organizations or governmental departments.
3. Conform to an ethical code of practice.
4. Are committed to meeting emerging practice standards.

These characteristics apply to accountants, lawyers, physicians, occupational therapists, and engineers, as well as law enforcement officers, private investigators, beauticians, and financial planners. Although many professionals have their own practices and offices, the growing trend is for them to be salaried or compensated by an employing organization.

The administrative approach to professionals is different from that for less-skilled staff. Patricia Williams offers the following approaches to successfully managing and working with professionals in an organization, according to which management's and the organization's responses should be designed to maximize both loyalty to the organization and productivity.[8]

Professionals generally believe that they can and should *practice autonomously.* For example, physicians in a hospital typically believe that the administration has no right to interfere with the delivery of medical services. Professors expect autonomy in their teaching. But this does not mean that professionals can do anything they please but instead must follow rules, policies, and procedures. One of these is to make sure that their clients have access to all relevant information needed for a decision. If the professional does not provide this, then the administration must protect both the client's rights and the organization from possible liabilities.

Professionals generally expect ready *access to the latest information.* This means that managers must supply both the time and at least some of the resources needed to maintain professional currency, such as through training programs, books, seminars, continuing education courses, conferences, professional development efforts, and in-house training programs. Most professions have professional development requirements for a predetermined number of continuing educational units (CEUs). This should be a mutually beneficial and symbiotic partnership, as professional development serves the individual, the organization, and the recipient of the services.

Professionals have their *own language*, including acronyms. Although acronyms help people in the same discipline to communicate quickly with one another, they may be unintelligible to outsiders. Managers need to learn some of their staff's common terms and phrases. Effective supervisors are not afraid to interrupt and ask what something means, and they make sure that staff members communicate clearly with the organization's clients.

Professionals now face a growing demand for greater *documentation of services*. They must show what services were provided in response to the client's presenting issue, symptom, or diagnosis, with clear evidence of the actual results or outcomes. Managers need to provide technological and staff assistance for these requirements for both the provider and the organization.

Professionals expect *equitable rewards*. Their advanced education should be considered in their compensation package. However, deciding what is "equitable" may be difficult. For some it means internal equity: "How does my salary compare with of others in this organization?" To others, it may mean external equity: "What does my colleague in another similar organization make?" Managers must constantly monitor the internal and external environment to maintain the organization's competitive position. Absenteeism, low morale, ineffective services, or increased turnover may be signs that the organization's compensation and reward systems are falling behind in real or perceived terms.

Promotions may have different meanings to many professionals. In the typical chain of command and organization hierarchy, promotion up the corporate ladder brings intrinsic and extrinsic rewards ranging from recognition to salary, more or private office space, to more extensive secretarial support. Professionals, however, often prefer promotion within the profession to what they might regard as into a new profession, that is, management. In these cases, mentoring and teaching the next generation of professionals may offer a greater reward than becoming the supervisor of the weekend shifts.

Managing Demands on Time

How can people in nonprofit organizations gain greater control of the time that they are working? Time management is the process of reviewing and making decisions about how to spend one's time.

Flexible working hours have become common practice in many nonprofit organizations. An advantage for nonprofit organizations is that not all their consumers are available between 8 a.m. and 5 p.m., and so they can have both flexible hours and required hours. For example, employees could be allowed to come to work anytime between the hours of 7 a.m. and 10 a.m., with everyone expected to be on the job between 10 a.m. and 3 p.m. Outside that period, each employee can choose his or her own departure time as long it makes up an eight-hour day. Or perhaps employees could be permitted to work at home. Employees benefit by such arrangements because they allow time to meet personal and family obligations, and organizations benefit by having more productive and satisfied staff.

Even with flex-time arrangements, there often does not seem to be enough time to deal with all the work demands. Many people struggle to keep track of a multitude of tasks and deadlines. The accompanying box lists signs that time should be managed better.

Signs of Poor Time Management

1. Staff meetings last too long and accomplish too little.
2. I spend too much time on the telephone.
3. Too much of my time is spent on unimportant activities.
4. My staff does not work as productively when I am not in the office.
5. I tend to be involved in too many projects at once.
6. There are too many interruptions.
7. I cannot keep up with all telephone calls, mail, and emails.
8. I need to make too many urgent decisions.
9. I like being a hands-on manager.
10. If there are problems, I can always finish the job myself.

If these sound familiar, it is likely that you have succumbed to one or more of the following common myths of time management and are not using your time well:

Myth 1: Lots of activity gets the job done.
Myth 2: The higher the decision-making level is, the better the decision will be.
Myth 3: An open-door policy improves my relationships with subordinates.
Myth 4: Shortcuts save time.
Myth 5: I get faster and better results when I do the job myself.
Myth 6: Delegation saves time and worry.

The basic issue is using time effectively, and we next describe some of the principles of time management as they relate to the major organizational functions.

Planning

- An hour of planning can save three hours in implementation.
- Daily planning can save time each day.
- Time should be used to meet the more important priorities first.
- Avoid treating each problem as a crisis.
- Responding to someone's urgent problem takes time away from other, more important priorities.

Organizing

- Responsibility must be congruent with authority: Report to only one project or department supervisor at a time.

Staffing

- Results are directly attributable to personal motivation and skills.
- Orientation programs are effective uses of time.
- Training programs are effective when reinforced on the job.
- Encouraging employees to reach their potential provides a strong incentive for retention.

Leading

- If it cannot be changed, don't fight for it. That just wastes time.
- People tend to adopt the organization's culture and avoid taking risks.
- Implement strong plans, and revise weak ones.
- Do nothing that should be delegated to others.
- Delegate responsibility for the whole task, not just a part of it.
- Coordinate a process or service at the start, not at the end.
- Communicate clearly.

Decision Making

- Distinguish issues from causes.
- Build on what works.
- Indecision is in fact a decision, and it wastes time.
- Decisions should be made at the lowest possible level.
- Decisions should be made where the most information resides.

Managing time effectively requires planning and decisions about priorities for today, this week, this month, and this year. Some steps to consider are the following:

Drawing up a list of priorities may help some people think through their work and attend to those issues most important to the organization's goals. Some employees benefit from keeping a time log so they can see how they use their time.

Learning what your "prime time" is can help. For each person, some parts of the workday are more productive than others, so those are the time to do the most important tasks.

Preventing fires is better than putting them out. Effective time managers find ways to anticipate issues and help deflect them before they become serious problems or crises that require time away from other tasks. A to-do list can tell managers and staff what the boss is doing and when an interruption would not be welcome. People who always seem to be raising problems may be invited to take greater responsibility for finding solutions to them.

Assignment

Based on your own work calendar, conduct your own audit of your activities during a typical week. Are you planning, assessing, coordinating, or accomplishing assigned tasks? Are these the most important aspects of your job? Is this where you (or the other person) want to be spending time? Do nonessential tasks interfere with the more important functions?

Remember that part of time management means being able to keep up with the daily flow of information, requests, correspondence, spam, junk mail, e-mails, telephone messages, voice-mails, technological buzzers, and even family matters that intrude into your "normal" workday.

Exercise

Evaluate your own use of time. How well are you using it for your main goals? Does some of the time need more attention? How can you manage your time better?

Moving Into a Managerial or Supervisory Role

Once you sit at a desk with the word *supervisor* or *manager* on the nameplate, you have a new job, and your satisfying peer relationships of the past may become somewhat more hierarchical. Free time now is a luxury between scheduled meetings.

Nonetheless, other traditions must be honored, even if they require changing with the time. Nothing irritates subordinates more than the new manager who starts off every meeting referring to something "in my previous job." Learn the culture and incorporate your ideals and ideas into the new system. In many organizations, new leaders find that the first year is already put in place by the budget for the current year, which was drawn up nine months ago and approved three months before they even arrived. Remember that the organization's culture is transmitted from one generation to another through today's staff members.

Select your battles carefully. Nonprofit managers should concentrate on only a few goals at a time. Trying to work on too many initiatives at the same time will spread your resources so thin that only mediocrity can result. Moreover, merely satisfactory programs and services, however numerous, will never lead to organizational excellence.

Learn where the power resides. Sometimes—often, in fact—positional power is the least effective approach to wide-reaching decisions. Every organization, though, contains informal power centers. Is the power in your organization based on seniority? Is it based on access to a particular vice president? Do people use end runs to members of the executive committee or the board of trustees to get things done their own way? Examining why such maneuvers are used can help you deal more constructively with those in power.

Keep the big picture in mind. External events do have an impact on the staff and services of all organizations. When managers attend professional meetings, they should let others know something useful they learned. Whether this is shared in a notebook, in an e-mail, or at a staff meeting, such information will remind others that they work in a larger context.

In conclusion, becoming an effective manager in any organization involves cultivating a variety of skills. They include inspiring others through strong leadership, analyzing the culture and finding opportunties for change, nurturing teamwork, taking risks, using assessments to learn and grow, attracting and retaining the best employees, and making the best use of time. These are skills that can be learned and strengthened by practice. People who cultivate them help move the organization into high levels of performance and effectiveness.

Time Management Exercise

The following "in-basket" exercise is designed to show how seemingly simple matters can consume valuable time from other more pressing issues. Read the following three incoming items in your "snail mail" tray:

In-Basket Item 1

Memorandum

To: Dave Davis, Executive Director
From: Stan Karner, Director, Department of Community Services
Date: June 3, 2009
Re: Merit Pay Guidelines

I am writing to express the department's concern and my own reservations about the new merit pay guidelines. The recent Executive Committee minutes reflect the tentative decision to proceed with the new system. I want to be sure you are aware of the following issues:

1. The HR staff developed this proposal without any input from the professional services departments. Even though there was a committee, it never actively solicited input from either the Department of Community Services (DCS) or the Emergency Response Teams (ERT).

2. While I will not speak for the ERT staff, the DCS staff members feel that the proposed system penalizes them for three years of continuously exceeding written goals and objectives.

3. This raises a related question about the feasibility of having different targets for each unit. Shouldn't each department be expected to achieve at least 95 percent of their goals or, better still for the Center, shouldn't each unit be expected to meet at least 100 percent of its goals?

4. The proposed merit pay guidelines stress efficiency and quantity over effectiveness and quality services and program delivery. DCS proposes that more credit be given to the completion of cases through effective services and referral than to the number of new clients enrolled for care.

5. Finally, the proposal calls for a July 1, 2009, implementation date. That is exactly halfway through a performance period and the annual budget. We think the system should be structured to coincide with the budget cycles that provides the resources for the raises and the staff positions to meet our goals.

We appreciate your willingness to accept this comments in the positive manner in which they are intended. The idea of merit pay is valuable and valued. We want the new system to succeed and having a smooth transition is integral to that goal.

In-Basket Item 2

Memorandum

To: Dave Davis, Executive Director
From: Deborah Lieberman
Date: June 3, 2009
Re: Grievance

Two weeks ago, the committee concluded its review of the matter you referred to us. Operating under the procedures defined in the Staff Handbook, the committee met individually with Ms. Cotton and Mr. Roth. In addition, as the information unfolded, the committee requested meetings with three other individuals who were involved in the matter.

We find that Mr. Roth did not report to work for mandatory overtime as instructed by his supervisor, Ms. Cotton. Although the request was not put in writing, it is clear that Mr. Roth did know about the need for additional staff for the day in question.

Since this is a first offense, we reject the harshest penalty, terminating Mr. Roth. But we do recommend that

1. A letter of reprimand be put into Mr. Roth's personnel file. This will document the matter if something like this arises in the future.

2. Ms. Cotton develop clearer procedures to notify staff when such emergencies arise. The telephone tree is only as effective as its weakest link. In this matter, Mr. Roth's apparent unwillingness to answer his home phone on the morning in question became the link that broke the system.

3. The Executive Committee develop a process to recruit willing employees to work these mandatory overtime shifts. Additional funds may be worth using to prevent the situations like this from happening again.

4. Ms. Cotton should be reminded that weekend family obligations are important to many of our staff and that their reluctance to work weekend and midnight shifts does not indicate "a lack of support" for the agency, its programs, or its clients. We hope that you, as her supervisor, can make her understand this.

We thank you for the opportunity to serve in this role and will be available at your convenience to discuss these recommendations with you.

In-Basket Item 3

Association of Southern Executives
12 Peachtree Street, Atlanta, GA

May 31, 2009

Mr. David Davis
Executive Director
Center for Needed Services
34 Broadway
New Orleans, LA

Dear Mr. Davis:

Your presentation at the 2006 Annual Program Meeting of the Association was indeed the highlight of the meeting. Indeed, many of your colleagues and friends have commented to me personally that they learned a great deal from your experience integrating administration and policy issues into a coherent strategic approach for the Center.

Therefore, it is my pleasure to invite you to chair a panel to continue this theme at the 2009 meeting in Tampa, FL. I hope you will accept this honor. Your major tasks will be (1) to ask three or four colleagues to present complementary material with differing perspectives (15 minutes maximum for each panelist), (2) to introduce each speaker, (3) to moderate the Q&A session at the end of the 45 minutes allocated for remarks, and (4) give the Association your assessment of the session so that we can use it in conjunction with the participants' evaluations.

I shall call you in about two weeks to discuss this with you in greater detail and answer any questions you may have. Since you are aware that our financial situation is tight at the present time, we instead will waive your conference registration fee and instead give you a complementary banquet reservation.

In advance, on behalf of the Board and the Planning Committee, I thank you for your 15 years of active membership and friendship.

Very truly yours,
Steve
Steven Osborne

1. How long did it take you to read through the items?
2. Did you review all three letters before taking any action?
3. Which item was the most important? The least important? Why?
4. Was the most important item given the most time?
5. How many messages of all types do you receive in a typical day or week?
6. How much time can you spend on each one?

7

Key Issues in Human Resources

Executives often say that their people are their most important resource, and it is true. Skills in relating to others inside and outside the organization are crucial to its effectiveness. Developing and sustaining work environments with which staff, consumers, volunteers, and others are satisfied and motivated toward the organization's mission are key ingredients of success and effectiveness. This chapter helps readers

1. Identify the main purposes and components of personnel policies.
2. Understand the ingredients of a successful volunteer program.
3. Know how to diversify the staff.
4. Describe the components of accommodating the needs of people with disabilities.
5. Help an organization develop a more family-friendly work environment.
6. Prevent and deal with sexual harassment.

For a nonprofit organization to be successful, its staff and volunteers must be motivated, their jobs satisfying and challenging, the policies and practices guiding their work clear, and their work environment conducive to productivity. Finding the right person for a job means being able to describe the job clearly, including its purposes and tasks, required skills,

expectations and performance criteria, horizontal and vertical relationships, and benefits and limitations. The work of the organization is divided up into pieces or roles, which should be linked to a structure that
guides and coordinates everyone's efforts toward carrying out the organization's mission.

Before bringing in anyone for a staff or volunteer job, each position should
be described fully, specifying the work expected and explaining how the position relates to others in the organization, including what the person in this
position can expect from others as well as what they can expect from him or
her. The job description should list the criteria for assessing the performance
of the position, the salary or salary range for the position, and the benefits,
such as holidays, leave time, and insurance. The clearer the description is, the
less likely there will be any conflicts when reviewing applications or assessing
work performance.

Job descriptions are essential to comprehensive personnel policies, which
are the guidelines for how people will work in the organization. They define
and link the work of every position and set forth basic rules about how people are to be treated throughout the organization. For example, salaries and
benefits should be the same for everyone in similar positions, and the standards for promotion should be clear and open to everyone. The criteria for
performance reviews should be specific, along with the (fair) procedures for
conducting them. Steps for handling grievances should specify what people
should do in the case of disputes or conflicts. Rules about such matters as
discrimination, equal opportunity, sexual harassment, diversity, and use of
the organization's resources should be spelled out.

Sound personnel policies are the foundation of productivity and effectiveness for everyone in the organization and for dealing with the issues that
every organization faces, such as establishing volunteer programs, using diversity for organizational success, addressing issues relating to persons with
disabilities, creating a family-friendly work environment, and preventing
and dealing with incidents of sexual harassment. The organization's personnel policies should be readily available to everyone in the organization;
they must be followed consistently; and they should be reviewed periodically to ensure that they adequately address all issues relating to people in
the organization.

Case 7.1: Helping Out When Needed

As the head of Professional Services, many personnel issues have come across your desk in the past fifteen years. But recently things have become a bit more serious since the cutbacks, layoffs, and mergers during the past eighteen months have settled in. As part of this process, everyone has been asked to "do more with less." Many staff members have seen their workload increase, and the center's work environment has lost its happiness and sense of contribution. Those were the good old days.

Mary James has come to explain to you why she feels her performance is dropping. She was formally assigned work that is not part of her job description. Even though she has the credentials and skills to perform these tasks, she asserts that it "is not my job." Yet if she balks, Mary fears being seen as uncooperative, which will be reflected on her annual review and affect a possible salary increase.

What advice can you give her? What might happen if she files a formal complaint against her supervisor? What other issues are involved in this situation?

Developing a Successful Volunteer Program

To supplement the efforts of paid staff, many nonprofits use volunteers to do a large portion of their work. Volunteerism is an American tradition, with currently more than half of U.S. citizens involved in some sort of volunteer activity. This amounts to more than 100 million people donating more than 19 billion hours each year, with an estimated annual value of more than $150 billion. In recent years, however, there has been a shift toward shorter-term commitments, for a variety of factors, including a greater proportion of people working and for longer hours. A successful volunteer program thus must take into account the volunteers' needs and interests, minimize barriers, and offer tasks that require short commitments of time and more flexible scheduling.[1]

Among the many motivations for and reasons why people volunteer are the following:

- Devotion to the organization's cause.
- Interest in helping others.
- Interest in a specific activity offered by the organization.

- Friendship with someone else who is involved.
- Desire to gain experience.
- Social interaction.
- Available free time.
- Religious concerns.

The volunteers in a nonprofit organization bring many benefits. They extend the organization's reach of activities and serve many more people than the paid staff alone could do. They enable the organization to deliver programs at less cost, expand its services to clients, bring additional expertise to the organization, and extend its contacts across the community. Volunteers are well worth the investment of resources required to make a volunteer program succeed. Thinking of volunteers only as free labor does not work, and rushing through the planning process only guarantees problems later on.

Nonetheless, developing and sustaining volunteer programs do have costs, among which are the following:

- The lack of control over and reliability of volunteers.
- Supervision requiring staff time.
- Potentially negative effects on some staff.
- Difficulties of recruiting and retaining qualified volunteers.

Sometimes staff members fear that volunteers may overlap or interfere with their positions, and without the trust and support of the organization's staff, a volunteer program will not work. Staff must help build the volunteer program and feel a sense of ownership of it, even to the point of deciding not to use a volunteer. Staff should help define the volunteers' tasks and duties, help train and supervise them, and provide feedback to management about the results of their using volunteers. There must be trust and appreciation on both sides.

A good volunteer program has the following basic components, similar to those for paid staff positions:

- Job development and design.
- Recruitment.
- Screening.
- Orientation and training.
- Supervision.
- Recognition.

Volunteers need clearly defined roles and tasks, described in as much detail as the paid staff positions are. These job descriptions specify the volunteer's duties and the objectives or results to be achieved. They list the volunteer's responsibilities, the position's objectives, the activities to be carried out to achieve those objectives, and the criteria for assessing performance. Lines of accountability and authority should set the limits of the position and the volunteer's appropriate reporting responsibilities.

Recruitment is identifying qualified volunteers and inviting them to consider the opportunities in the organization. Some volunteer positions require few qualifications other than a willingness to do the tasks. People for such positions can be recruited through brochures, posters, presentations, notices, and word of mouth. Positions that require specific skills must be filled through more targeted recruitment steps, beginning with finding those places where people with such skills can be found. For example, looking for a person to fill a volunteer position that requires skills in event planning or public relations may start with exploratory telephone calls to businesses that employ or contract having people having those skills.

The recruitment message should be compelling and persuasive. It should explain why this organization is worthy of contributed time, the need that exists, and the good that can be done by volunteering. It should emphasize the needs of the community, not merely the needs of the organization. One danger is overrecruitment, drawing in more applicants than the organization can use constructively. Overrecruitment can result in either accepting more volunteers than the organization can actually use or rejecting applicants and running the risk of resentment.

Applicants are usually screened in individual interviews that ask questions about the applicant's interests, skills, and motivations for the position. At the same time, an interview gives the applicant more detailed information about the position and the organization.

Once suitable volunteers have been brought in, the next phase is introducing them to the organization and training them in the specific tasks to be performed. The volunteer should be told the organizational context of his or her position in order to understand the goals and structure that guide the job and the policies and procedures that regulate it. Training emphasizes the expectations of the tasks to be carried out, the skills required and how they are to be applied, the resources for and constraints on them, and the reporting requirements.

Supervising volunteers is much like supervising paid staff. Clearly enunciated assignments and expectations are crucial. One difference pertains to the flexibility needed for volunteers. Supervisors must accommodate volunteers' different styles, motivations, and time availability. Indeed, the volunteer position may not have the same priority as a paid position does.

Good volunteers are retained by recognizing their good work. This may be tokens of performance such as certificates, lapel pins, T-shirts, or other small rewards. Or performance may be rewarded by lunches or picnics, trips, parties, or other celebrations. More intangible rewards are saying "thank you" frequently, showing respect and esteem, involving volunteers in organizational events, and even enriching or upgrading their work. Volunteers should be recognized publicly, and others should be invited to acknowledge them. Such recognition should be timed close to the achievement for which the person is being thanked and should be tailored to the individual's preferences about how to be recognized. Keeping good volunteers is essential to most nonprofit organizations' long-term success.

The following is an example of a volunteer recruitment announcement:

Museum Volunteers: You Can Help

Volunteers play an integral role at the Montgomery Museum of Fine Arts. You will find all types of opportunities to help the Museum, all tailored to the interest of the individual. Volunteer opportunities have very flexible time commitments, so choose a position that fits your schedule.

Special Events: The Museum sponsors numerous projects for which volunteer help is needed, including the Flimp Festival in May and the Holiday Open House in December.

Visitor Services: First Impression volunteers work at the Information Desk as information specialists and hosts to Museum visitors.

Museum Gift Shop: Shop volunteers enjoy greeting and assisting in sales to customers of the Museum Shop.

Administrative Assistants: Administrative assistants help with general office duties on a schedule that fits their individual requirements.

A.N.T.S. (Assistance Needed Today): These volunteers enjoy the congeniality of working together regularly to help with Museum mailings.

Hospitality: The duties of hospitality volunteers include planning and carrying out an event, such as making decorations, arranging flowers, and baking.

Membership: Membership volunteers help recruit and retain Museum members through campaigns, phonathons and exhibition openings, and recruiting and retaining members.

Education: Education volunteers are trained to interpret the Museum's collections and exhibitions and offer unique learning experiences in ARTWORKS, the Museum's interactive gallery and studio.

Docents: The word *docent* means "teaching tour guide." Docents lead tours in the galleries, and they may also teach art in the studio. The Docent Program is a comprehensive program for volunteers who have an interest in the visual arts and would like to learn more about them. No art or teaching background is necessary. You will learn all you need to know and learn how to lead tours for visitors of all ages.

Pick up a list of volunteer opportunities at the Museum Information Desk, or call the Volunteer Coordinator at (334) 240-4333.[2]

Web Assignment

Search the web for volunteer opportunities to see how different organizations recruit volunteers (www.volunteermatch.org and www.worldvolunteer-web.org provide links to many sites).

Case 7.1: The Retired Volunteer

For several weeks, the head of Volunteer Services has wanted to have lunch with you to get your informal advice on how to handle a tough situation at work. Ralph Turk is the retired executive vice president of a local manufacturing firm and has received several recognitions from your agency for his philanthropy and his volunteer service hours. But recently things seem to be getting a bit out of hand. He has complained somewhat loudly about recent decisions, saying that they are not what he would have done or that the actions did not reflect the agency's priorities as he sees them. Ralph even was quoted by others as having said he might even chat with his colleagues at his former job about "how they could help get the agency" back on track.

What advice would give the head of your agency's volunteer services? What is the proper role for volunteers? What leverage does the nonprofit organization have to make sure that Mr. Turk does no harm by criticizing the current director and trustees' decisions?

Diversifying the Staff

The term *diversity* usually refers to race and ethnicity, but in its broadest meaning, it includes job levels, education, language, religion, gender, skills, political beliefs, sexual identity, social standing, age, marital status, personal values, and physical abilities. Accordingly, organizations must find appropriate ways of recognizing people's differences in order for them to do their work most effectively.

Hispanics are now the second largest ethnic group in the United States, preceded by whites, and followed by African-Americans. One out of every six U.S. residents does not speak English as a first language. In addition, the demographics of the United States have shifted, with the baby boomers nearing retirement age.

Managing diversity focuses on what *actions the organization takes to build and reinforce a work culture that enables all members to contribute their best efforts to meet predetermined goals.*

How does managing diversity build on and differ from affirmative action programs? Diversity programs are not supposed to make up for past discrimination. In most cases, such efforts have not been ordered by the judicial system and would be broader than race or gender alone. In contrast, affirmative action often is directed to the number of employees in a certain category, such as those over the age of forty in midlevel positions or the number of women in supervisory roles. Diversity extends far beyond this.

A brief review of diversity and affirmative action helps put contemporary issues in perspective. Before the 1960s, the United States was assumed by many to be a great melting pot with little exposure to different cultures. Racial segregation prevented many organizations from hiring minorities, especially African American employees, for positions above the entry level. Then in the 1960s, the civil rights and women's movements began to change this. The Voting Rights Act was a small part of the larger mosaic of public interest and rising expectations for the inclusion of all members of society, with the emphasis on fairness, numbers, access, and regulation. These movements continued through the 1970s until Ronald Reagan became president in 1981, at which time the emphasis shifted from enforcement to the celebration of differences and the development of marketing strategies targeted to emerging minorities.

The current efforts are to include a variety of employee perspectives in the main work of the organization. A commitment to diversity extends beyond mere compliance; it now is a business necessity, and an organization's success depends on its managing diversity well.

Alcatel–Lucent Statement of Corporate Principles

To us, valuing diversity means not only recognizing the legitimacy of differences in the cross-cultural sense but relying on these differences to establish a global competitive advantage. In order to be successful as a business and build high-performing teams, we will respect each other, acknowledge others' ideas and appreciate what makes us distinct as individuals while we unite for a common cause. Respecting differences is an integral part of our culture and a key element for our success. We know that to achieve business excellence, decisions must be based on a wide range of contributions from people with diversity in ideas, backgrounds and perspectives.

Workplace Diversity

[The] Alcatel–Lucent workforce comprises people across a range of ages, backgrounds, nationalities, and cultures. We know that to achieve business excellence around the world, our decisions must be based on the widest range of perspectives and contributions. Alcatel–Lucent has taken steps to support diversity by formalizing the strong principles that govern its operations through the Statement on Business Principles.[3]

Before Lucent's merger with Alcatel, Lucent's Diversity Plan had six goals:

1. Innovation created by diversity in its workforce.
2. Increased international market share.
3. Documented cost savings from fewer lawsuits and higher retention of all employees.
4. Greater productivity through better decisions and lower absenteeism.
5. Improved quality.
6. Intangible benefits such as community and governmental recognition.

It now is common for many larger organizations to have a diversity plan. Similar to a strategic plan, the plan for diversity defines future goals, commits resources to achieving these ends, holds managers across the organization responsible for progress in their units, and contains an assessment process. Effective diversity plans encompass all elements of the organization; they are not just for the human resources department.

A successful diversity plan should include the following:

1. Statement of purpose
2. Organizational assessment
   a. Strengths of current practice
   b. Specific concerns
   c. Unique opportunities for the system
   d. Impediments to success
3. Goals and objectives for the next five years
4. Responsibility charts
5. Timetable for actions
6. Communication plan
7. Committed resources
8. Assessment criteria and plan

When successfully implemented, a diversity plan helps the organization's workplace match the realities of its marketplace. The organization's workforce can attract the best people available to meet its goals, mission, and values. The quality and creativity of the organization's decisions are enriched by having multiple viewpoints and life experiences around the table. This diversity should apply to clients, contributors, staff members, funding sources, trustees, community advocates, suppliers, interns, and others with a stake in the organization's services. Diversity plans and programs have extrinsic values as well. Organizations must always recruit and retain high-quality employees. Because their customers and clients are now more diverse than they were several decades ago, organizations may need bilingual employees just to conduct intake interviews.

Most colleges and universities in the United States now have well-developed diversity plans (many are posted on Web sites). The following example, from a noneducational organization, gives an idea of how the topic may be approached: Representing more than fifteen hundred member organizations, the American Public Transportation Association established the following goals.[4] Each section goes on to specify objectives and action plans, such as new training programs, budget items, implementation dates, needed publications, and membership aspirations.

Public Transportation Association (PTA): Goals of Diversity Plan

Goal 1: To promote diversity as a strength of the industry and implement diversity policies and programs at all levels of the organization.

Goal 2.: To communicate diversity as a transit industry value in PTA publications and communications.

Goal 3: To enhance opportunities for substantive contributions to the transit industry and participation in APTA leadership roles and activities by members with diverse backgrounds and capabilities.

Goal 4: To promote the development of transit leaders with a commitment to diversity.

Goal 5: To promote and recommend diversity policies for PTA staff and programs.

Goal 6: To increase business opportunities in the transit industry for minority/women-owned businesses.

Such goals can help any organization to manage diversity. First, the organization will be able to respond to changes in the environment actively, creatively, and in a timely manner. Second, attention to diversity can prevent problems from arising, thus saving time, money, forced change, and damaged reputations. Third, better customer service to a broader range of clients can be expected, which will have a domino effect and help extend the organization's image and reputation. In sum, a commitment to diversity is a sound business practice.

Web Assignment

Compare and contrast diversity plans for large and small nonprofit organizations from public data online. For demographic information on today's workforce, look at the Bureau of Labor Statistics at the U.S. Department of Labor's Web site (www.bls.gov).

Table 7.1

Diversity Program: The American Red Cross

Goals	To ensure that the American Red Cross "is viewed as the service provider, employer and charity of choice for all people in America."
Program Structures	1. Formed a top-level Diversity Management Council.
	2. Started the National Diversity Advisory Council.
	3. Selected national experts to serve on the Diversity Cabinet.
	4. Use senior ARC staff to form the Diversity Executive Council.
	5. Developed a network of trained Diversity Consultants.
Process Results	1. The board of governors and its committees annually monitor diversity across the organization.
	2. Top leaders include diversity in their regular presentations to the general public, its national affiliates, and partners.
	3. The president chairs the Corporate Diversity Management Council.
	4. Diversity is a designated goal in the organization's strategic plan and implementation programs.
	5. Formed partnerships with the National Association for Equal Opportunity in Higher Education (NAFEO) and the nation's Historically Black Colleges and Universities. (HBCUs).
Additional Information	In 1998, "the diversity effort was removed from the Human Resources Department and a separate Diversity Department was established. A (new) executive position of chief diversity officer (CDO) was created and report(s) directly to the president and CEO. The Corporate Diversity Department's mission of providing leadership and consultation to the total organization is helping to institutionalize diversity in the products and services provided and the governance, volunteers and employees. The CDO is responsible for tracking progress on the organization's diversity efforts for the president and CEO. The American Red Cross considers this leadership commitment a best practice among organizations."

Source: http://www.redcross.org/news/other/diversity/010316polk.html (accessed June 8, 2006).

Table 7.2
Diversity Program: The United Way of America

Goals	To reflect the diversity of the communities we serve
Program Structures	1. Reorganized board of trustees in 2002 to broaden diversity and accountability in other aspects of its operations.
	2. Charged Nominating Committee with task of ensuring board diversity.
Standards of Excellence	The Standards of Excellence contain a section specifically devoted to inclusiveness: "Standard 4.7: Inclusiveness—United Way recognizes that in order to effectively engage communities to achieve community impact goals, staff, volunteers, donors/investors, and community partners should include the communities United Way serves. The organization's culture, recruitment, partnerships, and other business practices demonstrate inclusiveness. Formal policies and practices promote and measure inclusiveness in all aspects of internal and external functions.
	Practices—4.7(a) Awareness. Develop and disseminate your United Way's inclusiveness principles and values. Include clear language affirming your commitment to and respect for diversity and inclusiveness in your vision statement, by-laws and strategic plan.
	4.7(b) Inclusive Culture. Demonstrate commitment to and accountability for an inclusive environment in which differences are recognized, respected, valued, and even celebrated."

Source: http://national.unitedway.org (accessed June 8, 2006).

Case 7.2: With Supporters Like This . . .

You are the Executive Director of a mental health center and receive the following memo. What are your options, and how will you respond?

Memorandum

To: Executive Director
From: C. D. Jones *CDJones*
Re: Diversity Program
Date: August 12, 2009

Let me begin by saying how pleased I was that you were receptive to the idea of a diversity training program for all the staff in our agency. Since we serve clients from a wide range of backgrounds, all staff members should make efforts to improve intercultural communication. That is why Smith, Duncan, O'Neal, and I proposed this idea. Your initial support encouraged us to develop the idea, and you shall receive our recommendations soon.

Thus, you can imagine my surprise when you mentioned that David Duncan had reservations about the plan. Not wanting to violate his confidence, you kept your thoughts private, but this left us in an awkward position. Your request that we continue to develop the proposal put us between the proverbial rock and a hard place. Diversity programs are hard enough to implement and to get people excited about even when the senior staff supports them. But this appears to no longer be the case, and this should be dealt with immediately.

We will help you in any way you deem appropriate and look forward to resolving this issue before designing the program.

People with Disabilities

Accommodating people's limitations in physical abilities is an important component of organizations. When the Americans with Disabilities Act was signed in 1990, it required significant changes in how organizations handled everything from job applications, salary structures, and recruitment to training, promotions, and discharge procedures. The requirement to provide reasonable accommodations made many supervisors anxious, mostly because they had little idea of what was required. In reality, most workplace accommodations cost less than $1,000, many of which are one-time expenditures. Of note, the Job Accommodation Network's data reveal that about half of all accommodations can be made for less than $500, more than 80 percent require less than $1,000, and 19 percent require no direct funding.[5]

The Americans with Disabilities Act (ADA) requires any employer with fifteen or more employees to provide reasonable accommodation for individuals with disabilities, unless it would cause undue hardship. A *reasonable accommodation* is any change in the work environment or in the way a job is performed that enables a person with a disability to enjoy equal employment opportunities. According to the Federal Equal Employment Opportunity Commission's Web site, "reasonable accommodations" and change can be found in three areas: (1) job application process, (2) the work environment and how the job is done, and (3) access to the "benefits and privileges of employment such as access to training."[6]

The growing national list of accommodations offers managers options to tailor each to the specific circumstances of the organization and the individual client or employee. It is important as well for managers to obtain the latest information about what they legally do not have to do. This does not mean they do not need to offer accommodations but no laws preclude exceeding the minimum. Rather, what organizations should not do is lower quality standards, overlook violations of personnel policies, hire someone just because he or she is disabled, or meet every request solely because it is requested. The following eight actions illustrate how some organizations have responded to these challenges;

1. Restructuring jobs can benefit the employee and the program. For example, responsibilities for maintaining secure client records can be assigned to someone else if an employee's disability makes it impossible to do that task effectively.

2. Adjusting work schedules is a common practice in many organizations. Working hours can be changed to accommodate individuals who need a different schedule. People requiring some types of medications or treatments may require different work schedules.

3. Many organizations use technology more extensively. Bulletins, work schedules, and performance appraisals all can be completed and delivered online. Some equipment can be inexpensively altered as a reasonable accommodation. For example, larger computer screens can help people with vision problems. Special equipment can solve other problems; now hundreds of office supplies are designed for people with muscle weaknesses and those who are paraplegic.

4. Dividing work spaces for privacy can help certain employees perform up to their potential. Cubicles are modestly priced and can increase employees' ability to concentrate on the tasks at hand.

5. Problems with commuting can be resolved by assigning parking spaces nearest to an elevator or a handicapped-accessible entrance.

6. Employees who have developed a disability after being on the job may need aides or assistants. A disease called *macular degeneration* may require special computer programs to magnify and/or read text, and people who lose their hearing may need interpreters and transcribing help.

7. Coaching is one of the best interventions a supervisor can make. Helping employees and applicants prepare fully builds confidence and allows people to use all their skills.

8. Training programs have a positive impact. The organization should make sure that all employees, and especially people with disabilities, receive up-to-date information and training in all areas of their work. These employees are often overlooked in regard to professional development and therefore promotional opportunities.

As these interventions illustrate, reasonable accommodations can take many forms. While some carry a financial cost, others do not. All reinforce a sound human resource practice: to enable all employees to perform at their highest level in order to meet organizational goals and objectives.[7]

Case 7.3: Now You Tell Me!

After extensive interviews, you decide to hire a fully qualified and interested applicant named Mr. Samuels as a new member of your community's outreach counseling team. At this point, he mentions that he is under the care of a professional counselor and needs to start work "a little later in the morning" so that he can keep his regular counseling appointments. Can you require this applicant to work the standard eight-to-five shift?

In-Class Activity

Role-play this case for a fifteen-minute postinterview meeting. Select participants to be the applicant Samuels, the supervisor who must make the decision, and the head of the organization's human resources department. What are your options? How can you reach a decision that meets all three parties' needs?

Dealing with Sexual Harassment

In its simplest form, sexual harassment is unwanted and repeated sexual contact or communication. When it occurs, or is perceived to have occurred, it harms employees' morale, productivity, and efficiency and increases absenteeism and turnover. If not handled properly, sexual harassment can place an organization in harm's way for both liability and public relations disasters.

What constitutes sexual harassment? This issue has become one of the greatest difficulties of defining the problem and causes more confusion than need be. Employees should be aware that certain words and actions must be avoided. Examples are calling a staff member sweetheart, honey, babe, doll, cookie, dyke, stud, chick, buns, sex slave, homo, bitch, broad, hooters, boy, girl, dear, or playmate. Beyond single words, consider your reactions to the following: "That is damn good work for a woman"; "The weaker sex cannot do that job"; and the old-fashioned "It's women's work" or "That's a man's job."

Office Depot's corporate Web site provides a detailed discrimination and sexual harassment policy:

> Unlawful harassment is a form of associate misconduct that interferes with work productivity or creates an intimidating, hostile or offensive work environment. Harassment may take many forms, including, but not limited to uninvited verbal sexual innuendoes, propositions, suggestive or offensive comments, or ethnic, racial, sexual or other offensive jokes, ethnic or racial slurs or name calling, uninvited and unwanted physical contact, including kissing, hugging, grabbing, repeated brushing against another associate's body, touching, pinching or pushing, displaying sexual or other offensive objects, posters, graffiti, cartoons or calendars.[8]

Physical touching, sexual innuendos, jokes, and facial expressions may be misinterpreted, so employees need to know that these, too, can cause problems. Think about the voice tones, facial expressions, body movements, arm gestures, and pats on the back or backside, even if good natured and in the context of fun. Referring to public events also can cause problems. For instance, the plot lines of television shows such as *Sex & the City* probably should not be discussed in the office.

Effective sexual harassment policies meet six criteria. First, they clearly define the harassing conduct that must be avoided. Second, they must maintain confidentiality throughout the process to protect both the person who is making the complaint and the individual(s) who are accused. Third, the policies should spell out the complaint process, which should be conducted by an impartial individual with the authority to gather the relevant information. Fourth, the policies must protect the complainant against any form of retaliation for using the organization's complaint process, even if the allegations cannot be substantiated. Fifth, the organization must be able to take needed remedial or punitive action to correct the situation at hand and perhaps revise its training, policies, or workplace culture if necessary. The sixth requirement is for the organization to keep detailed records of the entire matter for a period specified by law.

Most organizations now publish their sexual harassment policies for both their employees and the general public. The following is another example:

It is the policy of the Community Mental Health Center to maintain and ensure a service and working environment free of any form of sexual harassment or intimidation toward staff, clients and the public.

Sexual harassment is generally defined as any repeated or unwelcome sexual advances, requests for sexual favors, and other verbal or physical conduct of a sexual nature when (1) submission to such conduct is made either explicitly or implicitly a term or condition of an individual's employment or receiving services, (2) submission to or rejection of such conduct by an individual is used as the basis for employment or service decisions affecting such individual, or (3) such conduct has the purpose or effect of unreasonably interfering with an individual's work performance or treatment plan, or creating an intimidating, hostile, or offensive environment.

Harassment on the basis of sex is a violation of Federal regulations under Title IX, state laws and the Center's board-approved policies.

Any individual who feels that she/he has been subjected to sexual harassment or intimidation is encouraged to contact her/his immediate supervisor and/or the Equal Opportunity Officer. The Community Mental Health Center recognizes the sensitive nature of a sexual harassment incident and the need for confidentiality. Every effort will be made to consider the sensitivities of the parties involved and protect them from retaliation.

The Center does not tolerate sexual harassment in any form and will take all necessary and appropriate action to eliminate it, up to and including, discipline of offenders. It shall be a violation of this policy for any employee to harass another staff member, client, vendor or member of the public through conduct or communication of a sexual nature as defined by this policy.

Having an up-to-date and well-disseminated policy is the first step. The policy also should specify how the organization will handle allegations of sexual harassment. The procedures should be clearly defined and easily ac-

Exercise

Review, in appendix C, Tufts University's guidelines for dealing with complaints of sexual harassment. Do you have any questions about it?

cessible, as ambiguity creates confusion and frustration for both the person making the allegation and those who must respond to it.

Effective practices include an educational approach to prevention. Sometimes staff and clients need to be told what actions and words are permissible in this organization and which ones may be deemed offensive. What is common sense to one person may not be to another, and regional phrases can take on new meaning elsewhere. "Honey" in the deep South means something different from what it might elsewhere, even though it can be pejorative.

Prevention is the best way of eliminating sexual harassment. Effective prevention activities include training programs that explain the basics of federal and local laws; clear, updated, and enforced policies that are posted in public places and distributed to all employees; a nonretaliation policy to protect those who report or witness sexual harassment; and support programs for victims. But prevention is not the only tool, and it does not work in all instances.

Victims and individuals who think they are or have been subject to sexual harassment should be supported, often by a supervisor or manager, although the Human Resources staff may become actively involved. Victims have the right and the responsibility to refuse; to document events; to report as appropriate to a manager, personnel department, union, professional association,

Web Assignment

Find three sexual harassment policies. Review their goal statements and process for filing complaints. Based on each of these policies, would you know what to do if it were necessary to deal with a sexual harassment concern?

trustee or director; and/or to go to outside agencies such as a federal, state, or local civil rights office.

Part of the process for understanding the impact of diversity, sexual harassment, differing styles, and workplace culture on our personal and professional lives begins with self-awareness. What values, beliefs, and biases do we bring to work with us? Stereotypes are perpetuated on the slimmest of evidence. How many of the following have you heard before?

- Blacks are not as smart as whites.
- Asians excel in science and math.
- All Hispanics share the same cultural heritage.
- All Jews are rich.

- Black women are hired because they fill two affirmative action categories.
- Republicans want to end social welfare programs.
- Whites will never vote for a black mayor.
- Asians work harder than do other employees.
- Muslims support terrorists.
- Most hairdressers are gay.
- Women succeed because they sleep their way to the top.

Unless challenged, many of these notions can enter our daily lives, including our decisions and behaviors in the workplace. Changing stereotypes is always a challenge, especially when they are embedded in an organization. But there is hope for change. Organizational training programs can initiate and support new behaviors. Ultimately, it is behavior change that remains the organization's most important objective. Even if an individual's attitudes or values do not conform to appropriate and legal standards, his or her actions must.

The Family-Friendly Workplace

In the past, the term *family friendly* probably referred to theme parks and sporting events. Now, no organization wants to be accused of not being family friendly. How did this new social responsibility come into existence, and what does it mean for nonprofit organizations and their managers?

In some ways, the issues of family are connected directly to the changes in the role of women in our society. Historically, Norman Rockwell's famous painting of Rosy the Riveter highlighted the important industrial jobs that women took during World War II. While the men were away fighting, many women helped keep the manufacturing sector of the United States' national defense running smoothly. Things never returned to their former state. Over the next several decades, more changes shaped the social roles of women. No longer Harriett Nelson and June Cleaver stereotypes, women found positions and excelled in all sectors of U.S. society. Medicine, law, politics, corporate roles, traditionally male positions, and hundreds of other jobs and occupations became more than mere possibilities. Federal laws barred gender bias in theory if not always in practice.

These changes had important consequences for families. Now, because both partners have careers, many families delay having children, and how organizations respond to the changing demographics of the workforce becomes crucial if they want to hire and retain top-quality workers. The U.S. Bureau of the Census notes that the year 2000 marked the first time that working married parents with children outnumbered nonworking parents with children. Thus, the traditional family picture has moved from TV's Ozzie and Harriet (she stayed home and was perfectly charming and elegantly groomed while waiting for Ozzie, David, and Ricky to return for dinner) to the working family model.[9]

Congress recognized these changes when it passed the 1993 Family and Medical Leave Act (Public Law 103-03, referred to as FMLA). As designed and implemented, the law and its accompanying regulations allow employees to meet family demands (such as caring for a sick spouse, child, or senior parent) without fear of being fired or other negative work consequences. The law also requires organizations to provide up to twelve weeks of unpaid leave to qualifying individuals to care for family members.

Organizational policies, practices, and individual supervisors have learned to respond to these social and legislative changes. Some adaptations are easier than others, and not implementing effective programs can cost an agency more than $800 per employee per year.[10] Collectively, when actions accomplish desired goals, organizations are seen as family friendly. The following are some actions that organizations have successfully implemented and used to change their culture, though few can be put into practice easily:

1. Making available flexible work schedules across the five-day week or four days of ten hours per day.
2. Supporting work at home (also known as telecommuting).
3. Offering child care at work or child care vouchers so employees can choose where to send their children. Some employees prefer that their children remain in the local neighborhood rather than at the workplace.
4. Extending maternity and paternity leaves.
5. Analyzing the unit's needs, not just the employee's job, to find possible solutions.
6. Asking the employee for suggestions about how he or she would like to handle the situation.
7. Supporting the employee with periodic assessments of how the policy is being used.
8. Reviewing benefit programs to determine their impact on families.
9. Developing flex-time policies and encouraging managers to support their implementation.
10. Arranging for job sharing in which two people share one job.
11. Allowing conversion to part-time status, with a right to return to full-time at a later date.
12. If available, encouraging the use of employee assistance programs.
13. Allowing employees to take professional improvement leaves with specific tasks and requirements, including the duty to return.

Collaborating with other agencies may help organizations to develop, implement, and evaluate information, programs, services, and ideas that will benefit employees and be cost-effective. Family-friendly policies are good for both the employee and the organization. The following are some of the likely benefits reported for institutions that develop and implement programs that employees actually use:

- Employees with flexibility work much harder.[11]
- Productivity increases.[12]
- Morale and employee satisfaction increase.[13]
- Employees have fewer distractions and spend less time worrying about home and family.[14]
- Employees have less non-job-related stress.[15]
- Retention rates are higher.[16]
- Recruiting efforts improve.[17]
- Absenteeism is reduced.
- Greater teamwork and cross-job understanding result.
- The community's reputation is enhanced.[18]

Thus there are valid reasons for organizations to consider the impact on the employees and their families when developing, implementing, and reviewing policies, rules, and regulations. Both organizationally and personally, supporting the proper workplace culture has short- and long-term benefits. As a gentle reminder of the importance of such programs, *Working Mother* each year releases a list of the most family-friendly firms.

In conclusion, finding ways to improve the morale and job satisfaction for people who work or volunteer in a nonprofit organization is important to its success. Clearly worded personnel policies that describe job expectations and criteria are the foundation. Volunteers can greatly extend the reach of an organization and enable it to serve many more people than paid staff alone can do. Diversity is a great resource for enriching an organization's creativity and effectiveness. Accommodating the needs of people with disabilities can contribute to that diversity and may be carried out in a variety of inexpensive ways. Clearly worded and detailed policies regarding sexual harassment are important to preventing it and to dealing with it when it occurs. Family-friendly work environments are another good way to improve staff morale and job satisfaction.

8

Governing Effectively

Every nonprofit organization has a board to ensure that the organization is using all its resources appropriately to pursue its mission and sustain public confidence. A board is required by law for the establishment of the organization, and it can be of enormous practical use in guiding the organization's work. Yet, despite being in this position of power, authority, responsibility, and visibility, many boards are not as effective as they should be. The material in this chapter is designed to help the reader

1. Understand the most important responsibilities of nonprofit boards and their members.
2. Learn the competencies that research and practice demonstrate are the keys to the board's decision making and functioning.
3. Explore how various boards use these competencies.

In this chapter, we begin by looking at the board's basic responsibilities and then at several specific aspects of its functioning. Then we examine the characteristics of exemplary boards and discuss ways of improving their performance.

A Board's Basic Responsibilities

Boards have a number of important duties. How they carry out those duties may change over time as the organization grows and matures, but the duties themselves never go away.

The board's first responsibility is to decide on the organization's mission and then make sure that it is using all its resources to carry out that mission. When the organization is established, the founders issue a statement of mission which is incorporated into the organization's bylaws and articles of incorporation (discussed in chapter 4).

A *mission statement* is a brief summary of the purpose for which the organization exists, its reason for being. A good mission statement identifies the ends sought but does not explain the means used to get there. It states what the organization aspires to be and to attain. The statement describes the distinctions of this organization and its limitations, thereby enabling people to understand what the organization stands for and why it is important. A good mission statement is

- Brief and succinct, no more than a sentence or two.
- Focused on the main purpose of the organization.
- Inspiring, motivated toward a visionary cause.
- Memorable and easy to explain.
- The foundation for setting organizational goals and priorities.

The following are examples of such mission statements:

The mission of the Hearing Center is to restore connections with the world for people whose hearing is diminishing.

The mission of the Forest Hills Retirement Community is to sustain the dignity, health, and well-being of retired people.

The mission of The Tree House is to prepare children for success in school.

The mission of Safe Haven is to provide a secure and healing resource for women who have been the victims of domestic violence.

The Open Hand Agency restores people to satisfying, productive, and self-sufficient lives.

All the activities of an organization and its board should directly support the mission, but translating the mission statement into programs may mean carrying out that mission in circumstances that the founders may not have anticipated. The community's changing demographics, new laws and policies, and different needs of the organization's consumers may prompt the board to reconsider how the organization has been carrying out its programs and look for better ways to serve its basic purpose. For example, in one city a nonprofit that provided day care for children of homeless parents found that more than enough day care programs had become available that would accept those children but that the problem now was that the parents of those children could not afford to pay for the care. So the board of that organization decided it would switch from providing day care to raising funds to pay for that care.

Exercise

Obtain a copy of the mission statement for a nonprofit that interests you. Look for both ways that it demonstrates some of the characteristics of a good mission statement and ways that it could be improved. Ask a leader of that organization to describe how well the mission statement helped establish or change a program of the organization.

A board's second basic responsibility is to select and oversee the top staff person, who may hold the title of executive director or chief executive officer. In the organization's first years, it may have only one staff person and, as it grows, hire more people. In any case, the board selects the top person, who then hires and oversees all the other staff. The board should state its expectations of the director and specify the goals it wants that person to achieve, a budget for attaining those goals, and the criteria for planned, formal, performance appraisals.

The roles of board and staff evolve over time and should be revisited periodically to make sure that the expectations for each are clear. During the first years of any organization, the small group of volunteers who started it are responsible for everything. Then, as the activities expand and money begins coming in, that group usually decides to hire someone to carry out the operation's routine tasks. This transition period may be difficult for the board, since most founders see themselves as the true carriers of the organization's vision and the best-informed experts on all its aspects, a tendency called "founders' syndrome." If the duties of the staff are not clearly distinguished from those of the board, conflicts and turnover may result. At first, boards usually blame the staff for not understanding the organization and their duties, but eventually the board must look at itself. Indeed, the board is responsible for differentiating its roles from those of the staff and changing its own approaches to work, with mutually acceptable expectations of each.

An operating board differs from a governing one. An *operating board* usually is a collection of volunteers who do everything in the organization. After they delegate operational tasks to the staff, the founders may be unsure of their roles, at which time they must learn about governance. *Governance* is setting goals for the staff, monitoring their activities and expenditures to make sure they are used to achieve those goals, raising funds for the organization, and formulating the policies guiding the staff's activities. Sometimes the board finds it difficult to keep its attention on planning for the future and monitoring priorities and evaluative criteria, though others make the transition more easily. Differences in interests and talents should be respected, and those who prefer more operational tasks should be encouraged to resign from the board, an awkward, but necessary, step.

A complicating factor in this transition is that many board members continue to wear the two hats of board member and program volunteer. Indeed, serving as a board member is a kind of volunteer position. But governing is different from carrying out programs. Wearing the hat of board member means learning and mastering the distinctive tasks of governance. In that role, the board as a group has the authority to set goals and policies. Only the board has this prerogative, not its individual members. In the role of program volunteer, however, the individual has no more authority than any other volunteer and must carry out tasks as instructed by the staff and within the parameters set by the governing board. Keeping these two roles separate can be a challenge for anyone, but doing so is essential for harmonious work. Writing job descriptions for the positions of staff, volunteer, and board member is one way that many organizations underscore the differences among these roles.

Exercise

Ask the leader of your nonprofit organization whether it has a statement of the board's duties or a job description for its members. Examine these materials to see whether the expectations are clear. Ask how the board differentiates its own roles and responsibilities from those of staff and volunteers. Have ambiguities in expectations led to problems or changes in the ways in which the three groups work?

A board's third responsibility is to ensure that the organization has adequate resources to carry out its programs. Nonprofits can be effective only if they have enough income to fund their activities and services. While staff may write grant proposals to support specific projects, the board must direct the fund-raising activities. These may include special events, such as golf tournaments or banquets. But nonprofits compete to draw people into such events, and seldom do they generate substantial income. There is no substitute for board members' personal conversations with potential donors, seeking their support for the organization. Chapter 12 explores fund-raising for nonprofits more extensively.

The board's fourth responsibility is providing proper oversight of the organization's income and expenses. The board works with the executive to develop budgets for each year, trying to break even between anticipated income and expenditures. Generating some surplus of income over expenses is desirable, since the difference can then be used to expand programs or upgrade staff skills and expertise. The board should receive regular financial reports from the executive and compare them with the budget and the goals for the year. Larger nonprofits usually hire an external accountant to review the financial records annually (audits). The financial reports are the basis for completing IRS Form 990 every year. Financial summaries should be included with the organization's annual reports that go to donors and others, showing that the organization is accountable for the resources it receives and is trustworthy for further support. Finances are discussed more fully in chapter 15.

Related to accountability is the board's duty to ensure the organization's legal and ethical integrity.[1] This fifth responsibility of the board has several dimensions:

- Conducting all work according to the organization's bylaws.
- Keeping careful records (minutes) of all the board's decisions.
- Honoring the limits required by federal and state laws.
- Establishing and following clearly worded and fair policies for the work of the board and the organization (such as personnel policies).
- Avoiding conflicts of interest.
- Providing accurate annual reports of the organization's finances and programs.

Chapter 5 examines matters of ethical integrity in more detail.

Every board must keep official, approved minutes of its meetings, which serve as a record of its actions, decisions, votes, and discussions and document how the board is fulfilling its fiduciary responsibilities. Over time, minutes can help resolve conflicts, especially those arising from differing memories of events. When needed, minutes can demonstrate compliance with legal, regulatory, fiscal, policy, and procedural demands and requirements. The record of past actions also is an educational and recruitment tool for a committee considering prospective board members. Each board can decide whether it wants the minutes to document every point made during a meeting by each member, note the point made without attribution, or just summarize the outcome. Minutes are an organization's formal memory.

A board's sixth responsibility is setting the organization's strategic goals and then following them in all its work. The board must continually monitor the organization's external and internal environments for any trends or changes that are relevant to its future. Internal strengths and weaknesses as well as external opportunities and threats are important considerations for planning, and changes in these areas should prompt the board to examine the organization's goals and directions. Indeed, the board should periodically revisit its goals and formulate new ones or revise old ones for the future. Board members should review the past year's goals, the progress toward achieving them, any obstacles and challenges, and lessons to take into the next round of goals.

The board and the executive must agree on the goals and priorities for the year ahead and should seek input on trends and possible goals from a wide range of people, not just themselves. Goals may have to be limited by anticipated income, and scarce resources may mean that not everyone's preferences can be honored. The board then must divide up its work. Although the staff should concentrate on goals pertaining to programs or services, the board must decide on the criteria or standards by which progress will be monitored and the format of and timing for reports on progress it wants from the executive. Strategic planning is discussed more fully in chapter 10.

Strong boards take this a step further and also set goals for their own performance, what they want to accomplish to enable the board to add greater value to the rest of the organization. These goals should be distinct from, but lead toward, the goals that the board sets for the whole organization. Examples are completing a board manual that specifies duties and responsibilities, carrying out a series of board education programs that extend members' understanding of the industry, learning about policies of other organizations like this one, using meeting evaluations to improve productivity, and better understanding the concerns of the organization's staff, consumers, and sponsors (see figure 8.1).[2]

The board is the link between the organization and all those who have a stake in its work, and accordingly, its seventh responsibility is enhancing the organization's reputation and esteem in the community. Examples of those with a stake in the organization's work are the staff, the consumers or members, donors, community and government leaders, the media, and the organi-

Figure 8.1
Responsibilities of Nonprofit Boards

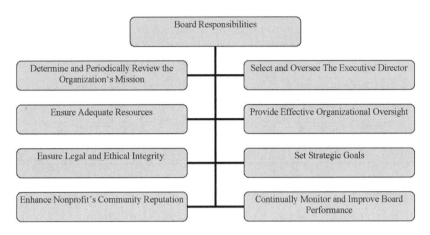

zation's neighbors. In order for the board to make good decisions, it must understand the interests and concerns of these groups and use this information in its deliberations on matters of policy and strategy for the organization.

As well as listening, board members should also tell others about the organization's work, its accomplishments, and the reasons why others should continue to trust the organization and support it. The board should pick up those items of "good news" it wants its members to disseminate and stress these in conversations outside the organization. The board should always speak with one voice on the organization's goals, commitments, accomplishments, uses of funds, and contributions to the public good. No member should discuss his or her own interests when they may diverge from those of the rest of the board, as doing so reveals weakness in the board and undermines public confidence. As one board chair put it, "If you can't be enthusiastic about a board decision, at least have the grace to remain neutral or even silent when it comes up outside."

Exercise

Ask leaders of your nonprofit whom they regard as their key constituencies or stakeholders. How do they keep abreast of those groups' concerns? Have these conversations produced any changes or surprises? If so, what did the organization do with the new information?

The eighth responsibility of the board is to recruit and orient new members and to continually improve its own performance.[3] Term limits are necessary for new ideas and perspectives. The board should identify the skills, experience, influence, and representation needed to achieve the goals it has set for itself and the organization. Rather than accepting anyone onto the board who wants to join, the group should look for the gaps in its expertise and seek those who have it. Prospective members should know exactly what is expected of them, so there are no surprises for them once aboard.

When new members come in, the board should help them become familiar with the organization and the board as quickly as possible. Any questions about why something is handled in the way that it is are great opportunities for the board to ask itself whether there may be a better method of dealing with such matters.

Board members must be closely involved in the organization. Attending the quarterly meeting for three hours is not enough if they do nothing between meetings. Accordingly, they might consider visiting the organization between meetings to observe its daily activities. Some organizations organize a "shadow" experience in which trustees and key community leaders spend extended periods (perhaps an entire day) observing the programs, interviewing clients, attending meetings, and engaging in informal discussions. Trustees should try to attend annual employee recognition and holiday programs.

The board should periodically evaluate its own work and examine ideas or practices that could be improved. Inviting brief oral or written comments at the end of meetings are useful for identifying aspects of the board's work that may need attention. More extensive annual assessments can lead to reflective discussions about basic changes the board could make and goals it could set for itself.

Serving as a trustee is like having another job, albeit an unpaid one. Every board should have a job description of its members' obligations and responsibilities. These can often be found in a trustees' handbook or the organization's bylaws. Best practices indicate that each committee and perhaps each trustee should decide on and approve the organization's annual goals and tasks. Then trustees know what is expected of them, and the entire board's work for the coming year or so is laid out.

Sometimes a longtime board member has difficulty saying that the time has come for a change, and the other trustees may have difficulty encouraging that person to leave the board. One solution is to have the trustees fill out a form each year noting what committees they would like to serve on, what areas of activity they prefer, and whether they want to be reappointed. In this way, the process remains private and the chair of the board or the governance committee can discuss transition issues without public pressure.

The Executive Search

As chair of the board of trustees, you have been asked to speak at John Ray's funeral. Affectionately known as Johnny, he served as the CEO of the museum for the past seventeen years. You also know that it is time to move forward and begin selecting a new leader for the organization. The board wants your suggestions about how it should conduct the search. List at least five issues you need to cover with the board.

Are some elements of the strategic plan more salient than others? If so, do these help define the qualifications for the next CEO?

What should you say about inside candidates, including Mary Franklin, who has been appointed as the interim director?

Practices of Highly Effective Boards

Boards have been cynically described as "high-powered people doing low-powered things,"[4] based on the common observation that many board meetings tend to be characterized by passive listening to numerous committee reports, followed by a few halfhearted questions to clarify insignificant matters, often bracketed by interruptions from latecomers and early departers. Attendance is a problem for many boards, and sometimes they are prevented from making any decisions because they fail to meet the bylaws' definition of a quorum. Finding ways to strengthen the board's performance is a challenge faced by many members. An excellent resource for a range of materials for this purpose is www.boardsource.org.

Some boards become proficient in their work and add great value to their organizations. Research into the characteristics of highly effective nonprofit boards has found several distinguishing features that set them apart from ordinary boards, as well as practices that others might want to adopt.[5] The six dimensions of highly effective boards are (1) contextual, (2) strategic, (3) analytical, (4) political, (5) interpersonal, and (6) educational.

The *contextual dimension* focuses on the board's understanding and use of the organization's culture, norms, and values. Boards that are strong in this area use the distinctive characteristics and culture of the organization and its environment; rely on the organization's mission, values, and traditions as guides for their decisions; and exemplify and reinforce the organization's core values.

The *strategic dimension* focuses on the board's envisioning and shaping the organization's directions and devising a strategic approach to its future. Boards that are strong in this area cultivate and concentrate on procedures that sharpen the organization's priorities; direct their attention to decisions of strategic or symbolic magnitude for the organization; anticipate and resolve potential problems; and set their priorities and then stick to them.

The *analytical dimension* refers to the board's recognition of complexities and subtleties in the issues it faces (see figure 8.2). The board draws on multiple perspectives to analyze complex problems and to decide on appropriate responses. Boards that are strong in this area approach problems from a broad organizational outlook, search widely for information and seek different viewpoints from multiple constituencies, tolerate ambiguity, and recognize that complex matters rarely have perfect solutions.

Figure 8.2
Board Competencies for Effective Governance

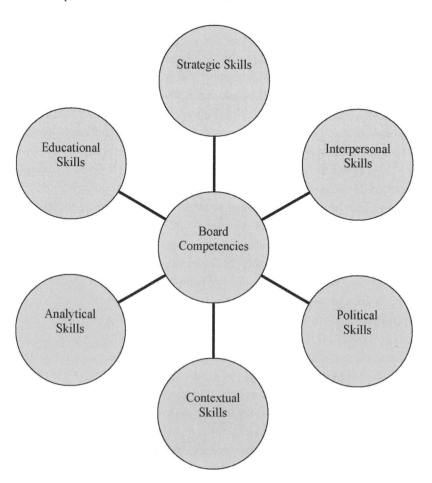

The *political dimension* focuses on the board's responsibilities for developing and maintaining open, two-way relationships with the organization's key constituencies. Boards strong in this area consult often and communicate directly with constituencies, listen to them, and understand their concerns. They minimize conflicts and win/lose situations and respect the integrity of the governance process and the legitimate roles and responsibilities of the organization's other stakeholders.

The *interpersonal dimension* pertains to the board's development of its members as a group and attending to its collective well-being and sense of cohesiveness. Boards strong in this area create and sustain a sense of inclusiveness among their members, settle on goals for the group, recognize their achievements, and encourage leadership and teamwork within the group.

Finally, the *educational dimension* refers to the board's ensuring that all its members are well informed about the organization, the professions represented in it, and the board's own roles, responsibilities, and performance. Boards strong in this area create opportunities for their own education and development, regularly seek information and feedback about their performance, and pause periodically for self-reflection to diagnose strengths and limitations and to learn from their mistakes.

Three Models of Governance

Because boards carry out their work in many ways, no single style is best. Most boards use a different mix of elements of the preceding strategic, contextual, analytical, political, educational, and interpersonal dimensions, as well as different ways of practicing these competencies as dictated by local circumstances and responsibilities. Board members should examine their work style for ways to maximize their own particular strengths and the group's overall effectiveness.[6] One way of doing this is to observe other boards and then adapt their best practices to local needs.

For example, certain boards focus on maintaining harmony in interpersonal relationships (with executives and among members), whereas others emphasize efficient planning, task completion, and goal accomplishment, even if that emphasis sparks conflicts among players. Some boards give top priority to the external environment and focus on raising funds and generating resources for the organization to carry out its mission. Others are more concerned with keeping track of internal expenditures and leave the fundraising to the executives. Another board style is careful compliance with past commitments, policies, and organizational traditions, and its more forward-looking counterpart challenges longtime practices in the interest of innovation and experimentation with the organization's mission. Accordingly, board X may be concerned primarily with satisfying consumers, constituencies, and the community as the ultimate measure of success, and board Y is more protective of its organization's survival and growth.

All boards probably go through periods of emphasizing first one style and then another, often because of individual members' own personalities, skills, and interests. Boards tend to emphasize certain values and downplay or ignore others. The result can be a one-dimensional, stagnant, underperforming board.

High-performance boards feature a diversity of skills and flexibility, that is, an ability to change their approach as the situation demands. Like an orchestra or sports team, these boards offer a variety of skills represented by their members, who were selected for their talents to be used for the group's performance.

Comparing Boards Along Three Dimensions

Our observations of differences in boards' assumptions, work styles, and values found the following three dimensions, or profiles:

- How boards perceive structure and authority.
- How they perceive and carry out their work (duties and roles).
- How their attention is primarily focused or oriented.

These dimensions provide a comparative framework for examining boards' various approaches to governing.

STRUCTURE AND AUTHORITY

First we consider some ways in which boards understand and deal with structure and authority. Many boards (and individual trustees) see themselves as carrying out the interests or decisions of others—whether founders, sponsors, parent organizations, or legislatures—and operating within the constraints of that outside authority. The organization's mission and traditions, as well as past decisions made by others in formal leadership positions, guide all current board-related actions and prevent trustees from doing anything that might depart from the limits circumscribed by the higher authority. In this scenario, the founders' or donors' intentions are the most important guides for decision making, and the board's past legacy and commitments are the organization's major driving force.

A variation of this orientation shows up in boards that view the CEO, board chair, or executive committee as the formal authority, with the board relegated to a subordinate role. Faithful compliance with the rules or expectations of those in authority is essential to how these boards perceive their work style. This kind of board culture does not question the legitimacy of the hierarchy.

Contrast this perspective with that of boards and trustees whose operating guideline is creative adaptation to ensure future effectiveness. They regard their function as preparing strategically for the future and their most important value as finding innovative alternatives to position the organization for greater success in the years ahead. Because critical analysis, creativity, and experimentation are valued as springboards to bigger success, these groups tend to be willing to take risks and implement changes in the interest of carrying out their organization's mission more effectively. They view past legacies or others' decisions only as departure points, not constraints. Few of the members of such boards accept past traditions or hierarchical structures as being useful to their work.

These boards generally fall somewhere between two extremes: dedication to past legacy and authority and dedication to innovative changes geared toward the future. For a board whose trustees do not share this strong team mind-set, this dichotomy may cause conflict.

DUTIES AND ROLES

A second dimension along which boards and trustees may be examined is how they perceive their duties and exercise their roles and functions. Some groups assume that their principal responsibility is to sustain efficient and orderly movement toward explicit targets and results, identify tasks to complete, expect regular progress reports, and work to remove barriers to success. They prize instrumental competency and timely movement. For example, in reference to meetings, they want to "just get it done and stop talking about it,"

Trustees operating along this "what-to-do-and when-to-do-it" spectrum grow impatient with anything that interferes with their brisk and orderly progress toward established goals. They have a low tolerance of efforts to revisit decisions or discuss other perspectives because these trustees want to concentrate their time and energy on completing their tasks, even if their colleagues disagree with the underlying assumptions or the conclusions.

Contrast this outlook with a board culture that values relationship harmony and group cohesion over orderly and disciplined goal attainment. These boards embrace members' collegiality and friendship and try to avoid conflict and confrontations. Although they respect rules, laws, and policies, they see "keeping the peace" and group adaptability as bigger priorities. Their quest for harmony overrides their desire to complete tasks efficiently, so their lengthy discussions, digressions, and tangential issues can overburden the deliberation process. Frequently, the result is delay in reaching conclusions on important issues.

Again, most boards operate between two extremes: nurturing relationships (accompanied by inefficiency in completing tasks) and completing tasks efficiently (accompanied by interpersonal conflict). If the trustees cannot balance their instrumental and relational competencies, the board can become ineffective.

ATTENTION FOCUS OR ORIENTATION

The third dimension of a board's work style has to do with the members' primary orientation and focus of attention. Some boards concentrate on the internal maintenance of their organization, conserving and protecting its resources and improving the quality of its programs. These groups place high priority on building strong internal operations within the bounds of available resources. They seldom consider changes in the environment or criticisms from the external community as useful information, because board's focus is locked on internal maintenance.

Contrast this mind-set with the boards whose chief concern is external advancement, for example, positive community relations and increased market share. With their focus locked on strengthening the organization's competitive edge in the marketplace, they are willing to make whatever internal changes are deemed necessary to secure a greater share of external resources. They monitor feedback from outside sources and emerging regional trends, for example, to look for opportunities to advance the organization's cause and its competitive strength. Resources, whether measured in finances or community trust, are to be used as necessary to ensure the organization's growth.

The two extremes along this spectrum are boards that protect the organization and its resources (to varying extents) and those that take calculated risks in responding to opportunities in the external environment. The trustees' differing levels of attention may cause conflicts in the board's approach to its work.

Because board members in all three dimensions have different inclinations, those at one pole may find the style of the other two dimensions difficult to understand or tolerate. Finding a workable balance of skills and competencies and of mission and strategy is necessary for successful governance.

In fact, the importance of balance in all these styles is highlighted by considering the extreme forms that any one of them might take. For instance, the rational pursuit of competitive advantage and maximum output can lead to an oppressive sweatshop atmosphere, characterized by an obsession with gain, dogmatic control, and human exhaustion. Conversely, overindulgence in comfort can lead to a complacent country-club climate in which unproductive processes breed apathy and confusion. An aggressive response to every external change can generate random experimentation, opportunism, and anarchy within the organization. But a lack of attention to internal processes can produce sterile procedures and inertia. Although each approach contains some valid and valuable ingredient for success, avoiding extreme tendencies requires balancing each component of the board and using each value in tandem with the others.[7]

Three examples illustrate the ways in which boards deal with these aspects of performance. Concerned about the quality of their performance, all three boards tried to improve in accordance with their assumptions about how they wanted their board to work. Each of them evaluated its own performance and used the findings to design plans to make them stronger.

Comparisons and contrasts among these three examples—of a team of co-owners, an assembly of instrumentalists, and a booster club for the president—are instructive for understanding divergent approaches to governance as well as the potential strengths and limitations of boards.

BOARD A: A TEAM OF CO-OWNERS

Board A functioned as a team with a sense of shared responsibility and ownership of the organization. Its practice style closely approximated strength and balance among all three dimensions discussed earlier in the chapter, and its performance scores were high in the six competencies described earlier.

The members understood the importance of its goals, which anchored the group's attention. At the same time, they tried to nurture positive and cohesive relationships among themselves. The members shared a deep commitment to their institution and its core values and pursued ways to adapt and reformulate them as guides for strategic planning.

The group shared power, keeping each trustee closely involved in deliberations and decisions and with everyone regarded as equal partners with one another and with their organization's leadership. They held regular educational sessions to address a range of board issues and key organizational issues, and sought performance feedback from one another, the senior staff, and community leaders. Each year the board members attended a retreat dedicated to examining the past year's experiences so as to set the next year's improvement goals. They also spent retreat time reviewing assessment findings. Their interpersonal skills and analytical and strategic competencies were strong.

In addition to its strong appreciation of its organization's mission, board A respected its authority, as well as that of donors and sponsors, and also acknowledged the legacy of founders and past policies. But the members used past traditions only as guidelines for making changes in the interest of achieving its objectives to secure the organization's future. The group balanced its work emphasis between mission and strategy.

Board A tried to strengthen the quality of internal programs and board processes while at the same time paying careful attention to changes in the external environment that might pose opportunities or threats to the organization's advancement. The trustees pursued the organization's mission through judicious strategic planning while also enhancing their leadership skills and interpersonal relationships with one another.

Through its shared power as a team, this group emphasized the partnership of board and executive rather than a hierarchy steered by organization leaders or a board chairperson. The members valued the rigorous and critical analysis of all recommendations as a means of reaching the best conclusions. At the same time, the members paid close attention to their collegial relationships with one another and with senior staff. They followed trends in the environment and monitored regional and legislative developments for opportunities to advance the organization's mission.

The members debated proposed changes and innovation before drawing conclusions, and they paid close attention to potential disruptions to staff if policy or program changes were installed. The board identified its goals through extensive group discussion and consensus rather than voting. Although they valued diverse viewpoints in seeking creative solutions, members worked toward consensus rather than moving hastily toward "win/lose" conclusions by voting on motions.

Despite being close to balancing all dimensions, this board seemed to place slightly greater emphasis on the organization's legacies and traditions than on risk taking, experimentation, or innovation. It tended not only to value internal relationships among members over the efficient completion of tasks but also seemed more inclined to protect the organization than to satisfy the interests of those in the external environment. The group saw its role as providing strong, stable governance for the organization. The organization showed every indication of successful performance, and the executive attributed much of that success to the board's effectiveness. This organization's shortcoming might be its slow response to a fast-changing marketplace.

BOARD B: AN ASSEMBLY OF INSTRUMENTALISTS

Board B functioned as an assembly of "young turks": task-oriented instrumentalists focused on maximizing market share. The group's scores were high in the strategic and analytic dimensions but low in contextual, educational, interpersonal, and political skills. Compared with board A, board B had a much more aggressive, even opportunistic, approach to its work. Its leaders were chiefly concerned with advancing the organization's competitive position by rapidly taking advantage of new opportunities in the regional market for change or expansion. They valued strategic planning and efficient adaptation to external opportunities but remembered little of the organization's past legacy or traditions.

The health care organization governed by this board had grown rapidly in recent years and was emerging as a major and esteemed player in its region. Past ties to a founding religious denomination had been severed in this board's reorganization five years earlier, at which time the board made extensive changes in its administration and composition. By the time we came on the scene, almost all the newcomers, in both administrative and board positions, had corporate backgrounds.

These individuals believed strongly that the board's internal operational stability could be sacrificed for changes required by new funding opportunities or innovative programs for new clusters of consumers. The current members of the executive committee were especially proud of the new organization and believed that the board's more aggressive approach to governance had been a crucial reason for its success. Staff other than the CEO were unavailable for comment.

The current trustees appeared to fall into two groups: a few "insiders," who were members of the Executive Committee and made most of the key decisions by (and for) the board, and the "outsiders," who functioned chiefly to ratify the first group's recommendations. The board emphasized amassing power and status by exerting its influence over resources from other organizations and by solving problems adroitly and efficiently. The leaders compared the board with a meritocracy or oligarchy, in which those with the greatest economic power rose to positions of control. They felt that many trustees were disdainful of any talk about inclusive group processes or cohesiveness. Changes in the board's internal procedures or the organization's services were made quickly, based on the executive committee's conclusions regarding opportunities for organizational advancement. Outsiders and staff heard of these changes only later and were expected either to approve or remain silent.

The board had a centralized structure for decision making, with power resting in the executive committee. That committee focused on advancing the organization in the marketplace and was willing to make extensive and abrupt internal changes in operations, procedures, or past practices in order to take advantage of new opportunities. The executive was seen as an employee of the board: even though he might propose directions, the board clearly was the final authority in all decisions. Dissatisfaction among staff was considered a negligible and inevitable cost of doing business and ensuring success in a demanding marketplace.

Board B made slow progress in developing strengths in neglected aspects of its performance, specifically in its contextual, educational, and interpersonal dimensions. These changes may not yet be sufficient for it to deal with additional problems that we predict it will encounter with internal operations. Largely due to staff dissatisfaction and turnover, these problems may lead to difficulties with recruitment (although some professionals might be willing to make the accommodations required by this organization). Likewise, shifts in programs and services are likely to increase the community's dissatisfaction and distrust unless the board makes even greater gains in neglected competencies. We anticipate that this organization will either begin acquiring nearby hospitals to form a regional network or be bought by another network attracted to its strong financial position.

BOARD C: A PRESIDENT'S BOOSTER CLUB

The third governing body, board C, functioned mainly as a booster club, or auxiliary, for the executive. Its scores were very high in the interpersonal, contextual, and political dimensions but low in educational, analytical, and strategic skills. Board C's trustees seemed to have been selected for their professional skill or their personal contacts, which provided a resource important to the executive and social compatibility with other members of the group. Interpersonal relationships were strong and positive; much of the time the group functioned as a congenial social club.

Seldom were crucial issues first raised in board meetings; instead, the meetings served to ratify executive decisions that emerged from prior private consultation with certain trustees whose expertise or linkage was deemed relevant to the issue. The group's structure was similar to wheel spokes radiating from a central axis, the executive. Board meetings were confined to ceremonial functions (conferring awards, honoring traditions, and preserving procedure traditions). Business sessions tended to be short, with social time before and afterward.

The executive initiated issues, recommended directions, obtained advice whenever needed, and followed through on conclusions. Although the trustees were called on individually to consult on issues relevant to their areas of professional expertise, the final authority clearly resided at the executive level. In short, the president told trustees how and when they were to contribute (but privately complained about the board's passivity).

Board C's organization was very successful as well and was considered a leader among nonprofits in its region. Everyone attributed this success to an executive who had held the office for nearly two decades. His leadership skills, business acumen, and assertiveness were praised for having pulled the organization from near extinction upon his arrival to a position of high esteem in the community.

The board's members were proud to be associated with the organization, chiefly because of its strong and successful leader. While they appeared to conduct little work as a group, individual trustees were confident that their support had contributed to the organization's success and saw no reason to change any aspect of the board's operations. Only one member voiced concern about what the board would do if this executive were to leave. Meanwhile, the organization and board alike showed every evidence of success and satisfaction.

This example illustrates the weakness (covered temporarily by a dominant executive) that results from inattention to most duties of governance. Although its interpersonal practices are strong, the board is markedly weak in its attention to mission, problem analysis, learning, and strategic planning. Unless the board itself grows stronger in those areas, the organization may survive only as long as this particular executive remains. Most trustees will be unprepared to act when this person no longer runs the show, at which point the group may seek another savior to protect its past practices. But if the board's competencies grow stronger, the organization may not depend as much on a single individual.

All three case studies illustrate the diverse ways in which boards deal with the dimensions of governance and how board members emphasize one or another dimension. Each board has achieved a satisfactory and productive balance (even if only temporarily) in serving its organization. Board B continues to place financial growth and increased market share well above loyalty to its mission, staff, and community, although it has begun to pay closer attention to the interpersonal dimensions of governance. Such an imbalance may well lead to staffing problems and future changes attached to merger or acquisition.

Board C continues to depend heavily on a strong executive and will face considerable difficulty whenever that person leaves unless it improves its instrumental skills. It still has much to accomplish in developing sufficient leadership or teamwork strength for dealing effectively with succession issues, a basic responsibility of any board.

Board A was the strongest in most dimensions of competence and exhibited even more effective teamwork, drawing upon a variety of members' skills and interests. It continues to provide effective leadership but may respond slowly to changes in its environment (an area to which it has begun to direct attention). Experiencing steady growth, the organization continues to enjoy loyal commitment among staff as well as high regard in the community. In the long run, this example is the healthiest of the three and serves as a useful example of effective governance.

Exercise

Ask the director of a nonprofit that interests you to allow you to sit in at a meeting of the board. To prepare, ask to see a copy of the agenda and any materials or reports sent to members in advance of the meeting. After the meeting, see how well you can answer the following questions:

1. What are the principal issues this board faces?

2. How clearly were agenda items linked to the board's plans and goals?

3. How well were the participants prepared to analyze the issues?

4. What proportion of the meeting was spent on the past (such as descriptions of recent activities or listening to committee reports) versus on the future (where the board wants to go in coming years, information relevant to preparing for that future)?

5. What did you notice regarding relationships and interpersonal interactions among members of this group? How much was each member included in discussions and offering suggestions (versus passive listening)?

6. What evaluative conclusions did they (or you) draw about the meeting?

7. What suggestions would you offer for improving future meetings of this group?

At a panel discussion composed of observers at different board meetings, pick up common themes and differences. What questions do such comparisons stimulate, and what aspects of boards would you like to learn more about?

In conclusion, the boards of nonprofit organizations have a number of responsibilities to the organization. These include deciding on and following the organization's mission, selecting and overseeing the executive, ensuring adequate financial resources for the organization, providing proper financial oversight, maintaining accountability, setting and following strategic goals, enhancing the organization's public standing and reputation, recruiting and orienting new members, and using assessments to grow stronger. Building on those responsibilities, some boards have shown how to become very proficient in them and add great value to their organizations.

9

Organizational Growth and Renewal

This chapter explores the typical stages of organizational growth and development, examines the common challenges to success, and discusses intervention strategies for changing problematic situations, dealing with conflicts and resistances to change, and restoring a healthy work environment. The objectives for the chapter are to enable the reader to

1. Identify the phases of organizational life cycles and their typical features.
2. Describe "founder's syndrome" and its challenges to organizations.
3. Recognize and deal with mission drift.
4. Understand and apply some of the methods of organizational development and renewal.
5. Understand the basic principles and procedures for dealing with conflicts in organizations.
6. Plan for and respond appropriately when planned changes are resisted.

Organizational Life Cycles

Organizations are living systems that go through stages of development, much as people do. People begin life as infants and grow into children, teenagers, young adults, middle-aged adults, and old adults. The earlier years are times of rapid growth and change, while the later years are marked by more reflection, balanced decisions, reviews of the past, plans for the future, and discipline to carry through with the plans. Similarly, young organizations take in and use a lot of resources just to stay alive, and their leaders make quick, reactive decisions to keep operations going and growing. They do not spend a lot of time on long-range planning, formulating policies, or refining their methods of communication and decision making. As the organization matures, however, participants come to see the importance of establishing patterns of work, dividing up tasks into related work assignments, preparing for the future, and developing sustainable resources to support improvements in the quantity and quality of programs and services.

These developmental stages for organizations have been identified as *birth*, *youth*, *midlife*, and *maturity*.[1] The size of an organization is usually closely related to its stage of development. Start-ups typically are made up of just a few people and little structure, while mature organizations often have many employees and multiple layers of management. The birth stage for most non-profits starts when a small group of individuals see a need for addressing an issue in the community (for example, domestic violence or a lack of cultural resources) and decide to work together to address that issue. The group often is led by one charismatic individual who inspires others to join in the work. The work itself, though, is not yet well organized or defined into specific components and roles. Rather, everyone does a little of everything. There are few rules, no staff, and mostly informal communication. The main objective is to get the activities going that will address the need, and it drives everything the participants do. Those involved want to make sure that the dream is realized.

Soon this little group begins to notice that its members are stepping on one another's toes, duplicating efforts, missing important details, and using limited resources inefficiently. Misunderstandings and even arguments break out over who should have done what and when. Some begin to wonder whether the group can do what they had hoped to do at the outset.

To get things on track, an effective leader invites the participants to settle on some procedures and sets of tasks that can be allocated to each person. The members want to work on tasks that interest them and for which they have some natural talents. They look for gaps in skills and recruit others to join the group. They also work out the means of keeping one another informed of their progress. These steps of differentiating assignments and establishing expectations for members are the initial steps in forming an organizational structure, which then becomes more elaborate as the group enlarges and the organization grows.

As newcomers are recruited to join in the work, they want to know what is expected of them and what they can expect from others in the group. These questions help clarify roles and identify predictable patterns of work. Multiple demands and limited resources prompt the group to begin deciding what tasks should be given priority within the constraints of the available resources (such as money, space, equipment, and time). This leads to further role differentiation, with some people focusing on service activities, others on monitoring resources and documenting activities, and still others on searching for more resources to support and expand services. In these ways the organization's viability is strengthened.

FOUNDER'S SYNDROME

This early growth phase often includes struggles by founders who resent having "their baby" taken over by others who were not part of the initial concept. They see their informal patterns of work being replaced with more systematic procedures, carried out by newcomers with specific skills who approach work in more formal ways. These new employees and volunteers bring professional knowledge and skill, reliability, and quality standards, not just reactions to today's opportunities or threats. Many founders, however, cannot make this transition and distrust the emphasis on orderly procedures, accurate records, and new plans, and they may resist many of the changes they see taking place.[2]

Founders tend to be strong-willed risk takers driven by a passion. They are confident they understand the customers' needs best and are often highly skeptical about analyzing problems or planning for future possibilities. They make quick, reactive decisions and want other people (usually the board) to obtain the money needed to implement these decisions. They may handpick board members to ensure that loyal support is the dominant characteristic, rather than independent thought or objective assessment. In effect, the board works for the founder, who is (or was) the original champion of the organization's mission. The strategies that succeeded in getting the organization going in the first place become unquestioned assumptions, making the consideration of alternatives evidence of unsuitability for serving on the board. The founders seldom address the need for new approaches to help the organization deal with growth and change, thereby leaving the organization dependent on the owners' styles and interests (and blind spots). Nonetheless, responding to growth requires skills and approaches different from those that helped create the nonprofit in its early days and months.

Often serious conflicts arise between one or more of the founders and some of the newcomers, with the founders usually winning the first several rounds and the disaffected newcomers departing in frustration. In such organizations, the person hired as the first paid staff member is subjected to all the different expectations of those in the founding group. This person has as many bosses as there are founders, which quickly leads to problems over priorities. The founders blame the newcomer, and soon he or she leaves. Work continues to proceed disjointedly, and resources run out before tasks are completed.

This pattern of conflict and turnover may be repeated over and over until someone questions whether the problem may be an organizational one and not the individual failures of the staff members. An important stakeholder, often a board member or major donor, confronts the founder about the recurring problems, which typically causes him or her to become anxious and defensive. Without some sort of intervention, the stakeholder and the founder become polarized until one of them leaves. At such times, the organization risks going out of business.

Rosabeth Moss Kanter pointed out that "leaders are more powerful role models when they learn than when they teach."[3] Effective leaders understand the importance of change to strengthen the organization and enable it to accommodate to changes in internal and external circumstances. They value the expertise of staff and ask them to point out areas for improvement. They adapt their approaches to problems, seeking to strengthen the whole organization through the best ideas that they are given. Successful leaders value learning, solicit feedback, and engage others in reflecting on experiences and finding lessons that can improve everyone's performance. Although some founders can make such transitions, many cannot. Navigating this difficult crossroad is one of the biggest challenges in the early years of many nonprofits. Often these problems require the expertise of a community leader or an expert consultant to get the organization back on track.

Once this crucial transition has been resolved, the organization can return to healthy growth and maturation. As it enlarges, coping with and sustaining upward momentum becomes the main concern. More staff members are added, and their salaries must be paid regularly. Activities become further defined, differentiated, and linked, leading to formal job descriptions, reporting requirements, and performance assessments. More resources are needed to enlarge and improve many components of the organization, and budgets and records are needed to plan and document activities. Fund-raising becomes a more systematic concern.

Organizations may sustain this phase of growth and expansion for varying lengths of time. Some stay on a growth curve for many years, whereas others level off and remain at about the same size for long periods. Regardless of the trend, leaders in the organization continue to look for ways to improve both efficiency and effectiveness, which may mean changing or refining some activities or shifting resources to respond to new opportunities.

MISSION DRIFT

Some organizations become so concerned with keeping things on track and remaining stable that the mission becomes overshadowed by the needs of the organization itself. This is called *mission drift*. Organizations are tempted to begin following the money and adapting their operations to accommodate whatever the funders want. Sustaining the organization itself becomes the priority, instead of using the organization as a means to the ends set forth in the mission statement. Its mission drifts when the organization's leaders begin to forget why they are there and what the organization's real purposes are.

Signals that an organization may be declining into mission drift are having money drive decisions about program activities more than the mission does. There is a strong pull to go after grants just because they are available rather than because they would clearly support an important advancement of the mission. Sometimes such efforts are rationalized as having some of the grant money left over to support current services, but often the funded activities replace the original ones.

Frequent turnover among staff and board members and repeated crises also may signal drift, especially if there are questions about why the organization exists in the first place. Forming partnerships with other organizations or starting projects because they may be moneymakers, as well as repeated efforts to "make our organization look good" when the reality is otherwise also are danger signs. Trying to do everything that everyone wants is a sure route to frustration, and setting priorities clearly based on the mission is sometimes difficult. But as the old saying goes, "If you aren't sure where you are going, then any route will work."

Dealing with mission drift requires courageous calls from the organization's leaders to reexamine why the organization exists in the first place. Finding ways to reconnect with the founders' vision and passion is important even if the circumstances have changed so that the original methods no longer work. Effective leaders do not hesitate to invite others to reflect on the original purposes for the organization and to help find new ways to carry them out. This may include looking at how circumstances have changed for the organization and prompting it to move in new directions. But possible new directions are numerous, and only some of them can extend the organization's original purposes.

One leader may suggest, for example, an extended retreat to discuss questions like "What would happen to our mission if the organization's present form disappeared?" Or "Let's imagine that we are working from a clean slate, with nothing we currently are doing is required. We are creating a totally new organization that will be dedicated to this mission. What might that new organization look like?" Imagining scenarios of a changed organization can be powerful motivators to get out of drift and make the changes necessary to renew the excitement of pursuing a clear, shared vision for the organization.

Organizational Renewal and Development

While some people resist change and want to keep the status quo, others welcome it and welcome thinking about change and working to bring it about. It is easy to become bogged down by the resisters and miss the opportunities offered by the more imaginative people in an organization. Many members of the staff can point out aspects of the organization that could be improved. The challenge is to bring them together to identify the underlying issues linking their concerns. Layers of rules and regulations, requirements for approvals, and restrictions on discretionary choices frustrate many people who wish for less bureaucracy and more freedom to respond to challenges creatively. Channeling those concerns into systematic efforts to change an organization is a productive approach to renewal.[4]

Organizational development (OD) is a set of methods based on behavioral science research that deal with organizational change. It was developed by expanding models of practice and strong educational programs in many of the world's top educational institutions. OD uses "social science techniques to plan change in organizational work settings for the purposes of enhancing the personal development of individuals and improving the effectiveness of organizational functioning."[5] Common interventions falling under the OD model are Management by Objectives, Survey Feedback, Appreciative Inquiry, Team-Building Programs, Continuous Quality Improvement, Job Redesign, Job Enlargement, and Socio-technical Systems analysis.[6]

Deming's early work in Japan led to discovering ways that organizations could be structured to create and sustain a culture of quality.[7] This meant that managers had to turn from their usual role of being the top decision makers. In fact, critical information residing in an organization does not always reach the decision maker's desk in a clear, usable, or timely manner. Accordingly, management should create a culture that empowers employees to question their work process and results in order to find ways to improve both.

What would an organization look like if it had a culture of continuous quality improvement? First, it would focus on results: service outcomes, the number of clients successfully served, the appropriate time length of contacts, funded proposals, or other measures of success. Management would be committed to encouraging suggestions and feedback which would be reviewed and shared with those who made them. Managers would be held accountable for meeting their employees' professional development needs, and employees would have a stake in the organization's success. Clients would respond to the reputation of excellence through contributions, attendance, referrals, and other forms of support. Lou Gerstner, a former CEO of IBM, best summed up this underlying theme: "Never confuse activity with results."

Change strategies that focus on improving quality exemplify critical organization values: stakeholder satisfaction, ongoing assessment to maintain and improve the quality of outcomes and work processes, and effective teamwork. These programs can succeed only when top management's support is consistent, visible, and communicated as a priority. They are not designed to be a quick fix for systemic problems; rather, they focus on long-term changes that can be evaluated and institutionalized. As such, when proper training, resources, realistic time lines, and rewards are part of the process, the results can be positive.

Organizational change is an ongoing process and can be managed effectively. It is preferable to responding to events without information or guiding principles. Change occurs at three levels in any organization: the system, group, and individual. In order for any change to be successful, leaders need to account for how changes at one level affect the other two. Success over time depends on the connections across the levels. Middle mangers and supervisors often become the central point for translating the plan's requirements to departmental staff.

Mahatma Gandhi (1869–1948) preached and practiced nonviolence in India's long struggle to gain independence from British rule. He is quoted as saying, "If I believe I cannot do something, it makes me incapable of doing it. But when I believe I can, I acquire the ability to do it." Such positive attitudes toward the future form the foundation for success. In this case, Gandhi was discussing his personal beliefs. If this is translated this into an organizational setting, and advocates for change believe in their hearts, minds, and souls that they have a legitimate cause, it will empower them and their allies. But if they have doubts, even the best rhetoric will not cover them. Doubt disempowers the team. Leaders must believe and convey these positive goal-oriented messages to the rest of the organization, and supervisors and managers must make sure that subordinates are working together toward these goals.

In the United States, organizational development builds on a common assumption. We know how to solve problems, and as a culture our "can do" attitude is energizing. The typical process begins with a clearly worded problem statement. Too often, however, this statement carries an explicit or implicit solution, even though that is not what is called for at this point. For example, "We just do not have enough money for that program, even though it may be worthy." The unstated assumption is that we need more income. An alternative may lead to a different decision, such as reallocating funds from one program or service to another.

Clearly, one of the premises of organizational development efforts is looking beyond the presenting problem or issue. Since organizations are designed to be interconnecting parts, the impact of one issue (for example, pay scales) can have an impact on many employees' morale, turnover, office climate, and productivity. The following case is an example:

High Turnover?

You head the Human Resources Department in a large nonprofit that serves a multistate region. The last two annual reports contained graphs reflecting the rising turnover in the system's multiple sites. Information about turnover rates over the past four years is displayed in the following figure. Without a doubt, something is going on, but you are not sure what to make of these increases (see figure 9.1).

The director has asked you to prepare an action memo presenting your analysis of the situation and possible remedial steps to change this trend. Specifically, he has asked for regional employment comparison data on turnover rates, comparative salaries for the local communities the nonprofit serves, any data on employees' attitudes, and, most important, your short- and long-term recommendations for change.

How will you approach this issue? What kinds of information will you need? What approaches can you think of to meet this need? Which staff members might have relevant information that can help you understand this situation? What other issues besides pay rates affect these concerns and your recommendations for the director?

Figure 9.1
Turnover Rates

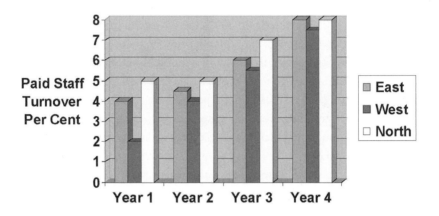

Appreciative Inquiry

Appreciative inquiry is an innovative alternative to the traditional, seven-step problem-solving process.

Step 1: State the problem.
Step 2: Describe the impact.
Step 3: Develop alternatives.
Step 4: Assess the pros and cons and costs and benefits of each alternative.
Step 5: Decide on an alternative.
Step 6: Implement it.
Step 7: Evaluate the results, which may then lead to a new problem statement.

This traditional model is generally taught in professional courses and forms the basis for how most organizations respond to most issues. And it generally works. But step 3 has a major flaw: developing alternatives. Alternatives are created as hypothetical solutions and often have no reality in the organization's day-to-day operations, services, or programs.

A new approach has emerged in the past decade called *appreciative inquiry* (AI). AI is "a practical philosophy . . . engaging people in building the kind of organization they want . . . with a formal and informal structure . . . [to accomplish desired outcomes] through a new approach to OD interventions."[8]

AI builds on a premise different from that of the traditional problem-solving model. Rather than constructing *possible* solutions, it helps organizations understand when and where they perform best. Then, through an analysis of what works well, or the strengths of the organization, decision makers can better understand the structures, process, information flow, task scheduling, and use of resources and other dimensions of high-performing individuals, teams, and departments. When a problem arises, the participants can look at their own *known* approaches and resources to see whether they can adapt what works well to the new realities and concerns.

Thus, instead of starting with a problem, AI begins with an inquiry into the system's excellence. Rather than citing the constraints and costs of various options, AI tries to replicate those processes and approaches that are known to work well in that organization.

How should leaders use appreciative inquiry? They should start by having open conversations with the members of their unit or team. Asking each staff member three basic questions can help change the frame of reference for the problem.

1. When were you most proud of your work, a project, or a service here?
2. Describe why (including the role of staffing, organization, resources, outcomes, recognitions, etc.).
3. In what ways did others contribute to these accomplishments? (Find out who and what they did).

By reviewing the answers to these questions, an alert manager should be able to find trends and points of congruence to use as the basis for addressing future problems. This process may be new and unfamiliar to many people. Employees are likely to want to share problems first and then talk about what they did to solve them, which is what most managers expect and what employees have been conditioned to offer. A good subordinate brings the boss solutions, not problems. AI changes that approach to emphasize building on the organization's strengths.

Quality Improvement

Another approach to organizational renewal is the process called *continuous quality improvement* (CQI), which sounds like a goal that can be valued and implemented easily and without much resistance. To implement CQI, an organization's leaders and its culture usually must make some major changes. Supervisors must give up their traditional emphasis on inspection, compliance, oversight of the work process, and the use of productivity as the most important measures. This can mean reviewing the organization's reward systems as well. If the system rewards the number of completed cases, for example, then it is rewarding quantity. The obvious next question is to ask is how well these clients were treated or served, thereby adding the dimension of quality to the review. The CQI model and approach require a focus on the ongoing quality of all products, programs, and services (see figure 9.2).

The goal of any quality improvement effort starts with describing the current situation, which requires current, reliable, and valid data as well as an effort to listen to stakeholders. As a program for the entire organization, the different departments must be aware of the organization's common goals and their individual contributions to them. Then, with effort and planning, the nonprofit can design the right programs at the right time for the right client with the right information at the right place. They should be augmented by appropriate follow-up and complete record maintenance. These are the goals of continuous quality improvement.

The following are characteristic of successful efforts to implement this approach across an organization:[9]

1. There must be good reasons for undertaking quality improvement efforts. Just because a nonprofit uses this approach does not mean that it will be successful. It also does not mean that the current programs and services are deficient.

2. Organizations should start by eliminating waste and obvious inefficiencies. Even the little things can help, like reducing the amount of supplies and materials in storage closets. These little changes become a tangible sign of commitment and can encourage people to see the result of their work: freed-up space and money available for other uses.

3. Review quality in real time rather than waiting until after the fact. An annual quality review does not ensure quality all the time; it means only that some lessons may be learned, but not until the end of the year.

4. Many organizations have too many suppliers which causes coordination problems, since each external contract has its own requirements and demands. Each supplier requires the nonprofit to develop a system to test, audit, and inspect each delivery or referral, which carries monetary and other costs. By focusing on particular suppliers, a nonprofit can develop stronger relationships that can also save some money and receive priority service. Clearly, there are political and community reasons for not becoming too isolated; the point is to reach a balance.

5. After a system of CQI conversations, training sessions, and professional development programs for staff and board members is implemented, everyone should be held accountable for quality. This should lead to improvement throughout the organization.

Figure 9.2
Characteristics of Effective CQI Efforts

6. In order for continuous quality review and improvement to work over the long term, leaders must try to eliminate fear and insecurity. If staff members feel that their job is at risk, they can undermine the effectiveness of the program and of their work team.

7. Quality is not just one person's responsibility and not one department's job. Rather, for a nonprofit to develop and maintain a reputation for offering high-quality programs and services, the entire system must be committed. Accordingly, interdepartmental competition and rivalries must be managed effectively, which means that information should be shared as needed and that collaborative decision making should complement internal reviews.

8. CQI is based on data from a variety of internal and external sources. This information should be continuously gathered and reviewed several times a year. All

staff can benefit from feedback throughout the year rather than waiting for the annual performance review just before salary raises are announced.

9. Instilling pride in the organization's work helps establish a culture of quality. Pride can follow from individual and team recognition programs, managerial support, sharing of information, and the knowledge of how one unit's work fits the nonprofit's overall goals and mission.

Although the team's role can be critical continuous quality improvement, not all functions are best handled by a team. The goal in a CQI model is to find the complex tasks and the information needed from numerous sources and then to combine them in making decisions. For instance, just to admit a patient, health care delivery teams need input from physicians, nurses, social workers, therapists, family members, home nurses, and the finance office.

If the roles of several staff are interdependent, that is a good place to start assessing quality. Is the information timely, accurate, and delivered in a form easily understood by others? Was all the needed information available? Was it used? How were errors noted and resolved? What steps could we take to improve these processes?

Staff members are the experts in their own jobs, professions, and roles, and they also must learn how to be effective team members. This means that they must attend team meetings, prepare for the sessions, ask appropriate questions, be willing to listen to other's differing points of view, and keep in mind the overall goal of the program or service.

A "best practices" approach can help any organization. By finding out how others in the field achieve their success, an organization can select issues for review and improvement. Though not a nonprofit organization, the Disney Corporation learned that its maintenance staff and groundskeepers were often the first points of contact when visitors had questions. Because Disney has a long-standing commitment to maintain a clean environment at its theme parks, the grounds crews are everywhere, and so it was understandable that visitors would question them. The initial problem was that these employees did not know as much as they needed to about the visitors' concerns. Training changed that, and Disney became a model for how organizations should respond to individuals in a large crowd.

Dealing with Resistance to Change

Given all the excellent thoughts, ideals, models, and reasons for effective planning, leadership, and renewal, we might expect the members of an organization to welcome needed changes and work diligently toward common goals. Too often, however, that is only the ideal. As former New York Senator Robert F. Kennedy announced in a speech, "Progress is a nice word. But change is its motivator. And change has its enemies." An essential ingredient of successful nonprofit leadership is the ability to diagnose and respond appropriately to resistance.

Next we examine some of the reasons for resisting change and how nonprofit leaders can respond effectively. The purpose is not just to overcome or drown the resistance; instead, effective managers and leaders confront it and channel it into productive work. The following quotations represent many of the common phrases used to show resistance:

1. *"Why do I need to change?"* Some people embrace change as opportunity, but others find change difficult. An often-used slogan notes that "change is debilitating when done *to* us, but exhilarating when done *by* us."[10] Sometimes employees do not understand the reasons for a change and wonder whether management is just following a whim. How many organizations jumped on the bandwagon for quality circles without understanding their purpose and the process needed for them to succeed?

When explaining or selling a change, threats and coercion rarely work in either the short or long term. Positional power ("Do this because I have decided it will be done this way") works only in emergency situations or very hierarchical systems. Instead, effective leaders personalize the proposals to show individuals how their work contributes to the whole. Avoid buzzwords. Shun techniques if you do not understand the conceptual framework behind them, and do not seek a quick fix. None of these lasts long.

2. *"What's wrong with what we currently doing?"* U.S. Navy Rear Admiral Grace Hopper (1906–1992) became an international leader in computer software engineering. On a somewhat humorous note, in 1969 she received the professional association's Computer Science Man-of-the-Year Award. She believed that the most change-resistant approach lay in the following six words: "It's always been done that way."

Resistance to change can be seen as fear of the unknown or the result of little feedback about current activities. When the focus is on the future, there often is a fear of the unknown. The known is safer, because we already know what works, what does not, and have developed coping mechanisms to deal with it . . . and most likely have dealt with it successfully. If the concern lies in a paucity of information about programs, then leaders' silence has been a contributory factor.

When some staff members have this fear, it will spread to others, especially in the absence of detailed responses. Just saying that "things will be fine" does not alleviate this problem, but information and clearly worded statements about the future, the purposes of the changes, and how each person fits into the larger picture all are helpful. Many people think first about what they have to lose now before considering how they may benefit in the future. Effective leaders want to be sure that staff can state in their own words the reasons for the change. Just repeating verbatim the text of the written goals is not the same as translating them into operational terms.

3. *"I do not trust top management to take our views seriously."* As noted in an earlier chapter, organizations create their own culture over time. If the culture supports shared information, open communication channels, and the mutual achievement of goals, the resulting trust will support the planned changes. Distrust usually grows as the consequence of past experience with the organization or its managers. When those affected by change do not trust their managers or board, their resistance will grow.

Trust takes time to build, and rebuilding it when it has been lost is indeed a long-term process. Isolation begets greater distance and fosters more mistrust. Leaders should confront trust issues by initiating clear explanations and information and listening to each person's concerns. In the long term, providing feedback on ideas, demonstrating a willingness to hear unwelcome comments, and adapting as required will rebuild trust.

4. *"Could I lose my job?"* At some level, change means a loss of security. In recent years, many organizational change programs have led to a reduction in staff positions. The language of publicity has adapted to these changes, so what used to be called *termination* or *reductions in force* is now called *downsizing* or (even worse) *right-sizing*. The organization's bottom line may be balanced, but the bottom line for employees is strong resistance and self-protection.

Some nonprofits have a culture of poverty; seemingly, there is never enough revenue to meet all needs. Thus if the economy is weak, some organizations' programs may be needed more than ever, but staff may see themselves personally as victims. This situation may spawn rumors and stoke employees' fears. When employees feel like they have lost control or even input, resistance should be expected.

If layoffs are in the offing, management must be clear about both the reality of the situation, the criteria to be used, and the details of the entire process, including appeals. Knowing that employees will feel that their hard work and dedication over the past years now have little impact, managers must find appropriate ways to share information about the process. Fairness is mandatory.

5. *"What happens if I fail or if my department does not meet these ridiculous requirements?"* This question shows two points of resistance. First, it portrays the new directions and expectations as being unrealistic. Second, it reveals a fear of failure. If the organization has a history of punishing those who do not succeed, no matter what the reason, then people will resist change. When the fear of failure equals the benefits of success, they will not support the new approaches, programs, or plans.

Leaders should define success as both the goals and the processes needed to reach them, including several opportunities for an open assessment of progress against predetermined objectives. If management demonstrates a willingness to adapt projected plans based on performance data, this will help reduce such fears.

6. *"This could not come at a worse time."* Planned change needs to fit into the organization's rhythms and cycles, whether they are based on calendar or program years, budget cycles, or civil service requirements. Trying to force the change against the work flow will undermine success.

People need to see the plan and know that there is a transition period while it is being carried out. Staff may have to develop new skills, work with different people, alter work schedules, change technologies, or fill out new forms. These all take time. Connecting one change to unrelated processes can hurt needed programs. For example, just because the budget is due on a certain date should not mean that all training must be final and complete before that schedule. To the staff, training is a longer-term undertaking, and its content may not be related to the budget preparation cycle.

7. *"We do not like this plan."* Sometimes group and collegial pressure swells to resist change. Even if an individual does not have much or anything at stake, each voice in a unit can be powerful. The Hawthorne experiments showed how powerful peer pressure, group standards, and subtle influence can be.

This kind of resistance comes from a lack of information directly from managers about a change, a new plan, or the process for implementing it. Sharing more information in a timely manner is important, and it is valuable to celebrate milestones along the path to permanent change. As positive results occur, give public commendation and support to those who made them happen.

8. *"It is not that simple."* Many staff members correctly understand the details and implications of proposed plans that top management and the board may not see. The views of those on the front lines are important to developing plans that will affect them. Even if training is included, it must be reinforced and supported. Systems theory notes that changes in one part of an organization have direct and indirect consequences throughout the entire enterprise. Failure to anticipate these complexities before they become reality can cause resistance.

Managers and supervisors should ask staff members to share feedback on proposed plans and then acknowledge their input. If the head of the change effort were to set up a "reality panel," this group would learn a great deal. Actively seeking ideas and reactions from everyone is crucial. The purpose is to prevent problems later by addressing them now. *Foresight* helps leaders define the organization's future goals and directions. As the great baseball player Yogi Berra noted, "If you don't know where you're going, you'll wind up somewhere else." *Hindsight* can show where you've been. Lessons of the past can provide guidance for today and tomorrow. *Insight* reminds everyone why this organization offers programs and services and how these implement the mission's core values.

9. *"But that is not how we do things around here."* When changes challenge relationships, go against the group's norms, change tradition, or affect the organization's culture, even the best plans will run into resistance. In such instances, leaders must show flexibility and a willingness to adjust. Getting input from others may reveal holes in the original ideas, so negotiation and compromise will serve the process well if the results enhance acceptance, movement, and change.

10. *"We just do not like that guy and the others who are behind these plans."* Such personality conflicts exist in all human organizations. This is not the problem; rather, the concern is that these personal issues have not been resolved and are draining productive energy away from planned change efforts. Sweeping interpersonal conflicts under the rug rarely works, as it forces people to take sides, creating a "we/they" mentality.

Leaders should show that the needed changes are not dependent on those who advocate for them. Rather, their purpose is to improve the whole organization and enable it to carry out its mission more effectively, not to allow some faction to emerge as the winner. Sometimes outside consultants and facilitators can help address issues of the personalization of recommendations. They are not vested in the content of the change as much as helping make the process work toward the organization's desired ends.

11. *"They say one thing and then do another."* They usually refers to upper management or supervisors above the organizational level where the change is to occur. Inconsistency between bold plans and real actions opens chasms. Changing plans in the middle with little advance notice (even if justified) can cause people to react in this way. Acting in ways that are inconsistent with the plan serves to undermine the credibility of those who want to lead the change. Leaders should model the behaviors and attitudes that they want others to adopt.

Asking for feedback and then applying it consistently is a powerful example for others to follow. A good plan for change must include assessment according to specific criteria to measure progress. Sharing these criteria in advance can demonstrate that many units are working toward a common goal and strengthens the system's accountability for progress and staying on course.

One of the most important roles for all nonprofit leaders is to act as a catalyst for needed change and demonstrate the new approaches in their own behavior. This includes listening to others, getting their views and feedback, and correcting future efforts to take the feedback into account.

Change agents should expect to encounter the complete spectrum of reactions, ranging from those who embrace the ideas to those who are actively resisting them. In between are the covert saboteurs and others who are just cautious. Still others may remain neutral and must be shown the why and the how before committing. With participation comes greater involvement, which results in investment in desired actions. Leaders should resist impulses to criticize those who are afraid of change and instead demonstrate positive regard for and engagement with everyone in the organization.

It is helpful to remember that in its purest form, resistance is indeed energy. A leader's role is to understand these concerns, harness their energy, and use it to achieve the organization's goals, quality services, and programs. But this will not happen in a few weeks or months. Long-term change requires several years if it is to alter an organization's culture, establish new ideals of quality, and cluster diverse programs under a common umbrella. Patience and persistence complement each other, and both are needed in equal parts. The old saying remains true: "The biggest room in the world is the room for improvement."

In planning and implementing change, give employees a reason to change. Then give them the tools to adjust. Third, give them time to adjust. Finally, give timely feedback. People can move from resistance to being just uncomfortable with the new ideas, from being stuck in place to moving to new levels of action. Education, training, resources, communication, participation, involvement, support, and direct feedback are the principal ingredients. When leaders share clearly stated plans and provide effective supervision, success is more likely to result.

Dealing with Conflicts Constructively

Unfortunately, not all change comes about easily and smoothly. Whenever there are two or more people, the potential for conflict exists. The goal is not to eliminate it; that is impossible. Instead, effective leaders learn how to recognize potential conflicts and develop appropriate responses. Start from the premise that conflict is not always bad, an idea that departs from the conventional wisdom that conflict results from poor management. Instead, conflict can be constructive and productive if it is handled well.

There can be benefits from conflicts and their resolution. Conflict is energy that can be channeled into positive action. Conflict raises problems to the surface where they must be addressed instead of avoided. It can actually strengthen relationships when successfully resolved. Effective resolution illustrates that not all issues should be allowed to smolder. A greater understanding of how the system works and how it can adapt may also be an important long-term benefit. New ideas and greater job satisfaction may also provide incentives for conflicts to be aired and resolved.

It is through conflicts that organizations learn about problems, find solutions, change policies, and ultimately move forward. Conflict certainly helps avoid stagnation. Effective conflict resolution approaches empower all staff members to offer creative ideas and demonstrate a willingness to be flexible. The win/lose approach tends to be divisive, so win/win approaches that involve employees are far more productive. The leader's goal is to maximize the positive aspects of conflict and minimize the destructive elements of conflicts.

What causes conflict in the first place? Generally, people or groups disagree about either the means to accomplish a task or the purpose of the task itself. Conflict can result from a clash of values. For example, some people believe that the poor need services because they have become dependent on them. Others believe that services help people become less dependent. Opposing views like these have no simple resolution, but they do represent fundamental differences that will either support or hinder programs and services. Even where there is agreement on values and goals, conflicts can arise on how best to work on them.

One thing is clear: communication in conflict situations decreases and becomes distorted. Generally, people in these positions avoid one another, assume that the other party is out to get them, and use critical attacks and distortions. Conflicts can easily escalate when the parties involved distort, manipulate, and misstate what the other party wants. The reasons differ. First, it is natural to think that we hold the right position and that the other person is obviously wrong. But when both groups have this view, resolution is almost impossible. Second, we assume that the proper resolution is our own position and that others are biased, uncooperative, full of innuendo and false statements, and just out for themselves. But that is how they characterize our team and us. This is called *tunnel vision*: we see only what is right in front of us and nothing else matters. In this realm, conflict resolution means "do it my way or else," but this is more a threat than a solution.

Third, who would argue that someone else wants to reduce quality programs and services? Why would anyone want to do that? In this scenario, the ideals of the nonprofit's mission are brought in as armament. They serve not only as a goal but also as a block to resolving conflict, since the natural assumption is that other party wants to take away quality.

Finally, alliances form and others, often uninvolved neutral parties, are drawn into the conflict. Or colleagues may find creative ways to avoid both parties.

Conflicts can be intensely competitive, with winners and losers. This type of conflict comes from one approach to rationing or distributing limited resources: someone wins and others lose. The benefits, resources, money, space, tasks, office awards, and other results that we value (and thus cause the conflict) are a zero-sum game because there is only so much to go around. The more one party wins, the less there will be for others. The main strategy here is to gather and use power, resources, and aggressive tactics to win.

Alternatively, win/win strategies dominate when two people or units in conflict are dependent on each other. Successful work in one unit helps others meet their goals and expectations. This collaborative approach maximizes favorable outcomes for the larger system, uses resources more effectively than distributive conflicts do, and generally connects people, departments, and programs.

Aggression may deepen a conflict by creating its own backlash and its own resistance and impeding effective communication by making the recipients of the aggressive behavior more defensive and less interested in resolving the conflict. Assertive positions may be grounded in data, rules, procedures, or values that must be defined in ways that can be communicated to others before they can be resolved. Assertive conflicts tend to be resolved faster than aggressive groups or individuals are.

What should one do when confronted with conflicts in organizations? Effective conflict resolution focuses on the future. Little is accomplished by dwelling on the past, as it serves only to keep the conflict stuck in its present form. Focusing on possible solutions and future goals is more productive. An effective mediator should ask each party, "What are you willing to give?" "What do you need in this situation?" This helps avoid making the conflict completely personal, which is the toughest problem to resolve, since egos dominate facts and personality trumps rational approaches.

There are many ways to approach dealing with a conflict that has surfaced, and it is indeed possible to adopt more than one of these tactics simultaneously.

Power wins through positional authority and access to or control of needed or valued resources.

Negotiation is finding a way through the conflict by using trade-offs, that is, getting something and giving something.

Collaboration is finding the win/win options, creating new approaches and solutions. Since most of the problems were created in the organization, the same people who contributed to its formation should be expected to help find creative solutions.

Smoothing it over is downplaying the importance of the conflict.

Going separate ways refers to exiting the conflict, living to fight another day, or using energies in other, more productive ways.

Mediation is finding a mutually acceptable third party to help open the lines of communication.

Giving in means letting the other party have its way, perhaps earning credits for the next conflict situation.

Maintenance refers to allowing the conflict to fester a bit longer, providing time to explore options and possible responses.

A legalistic solution uses existing rules, policies, procedures, regulations, or laws to resolve the conflict, without either side really giving in.

Fleeing is resolving the conflict by leaving the job, organization, or situation. Sometimes leaving is much easier than finding an appropriate way to return.

Arbitration is agreeing to let a third party listen to the issues and having both sides agree in advance to abide by the arbitrator's decision.

Thomas and Kilman described five different styles of conflict resolution. No one approach works all the time, nor should anyone be limited to using only one style.[11] The *competition* style is one person asserting that his or her position is the right one, the better approach, or the one best suited to the issues at hand. It is a win/lose approach that leaves little room for movement. *Avoidance* is the approach that sees other things as more important than this conflict at this time. Some people may choose to avoid the conflict because they realize they cannot win or even be heard, in which case avoidance is a smart tactic.

Compromise is in the middle; it builds on the premise that there is a solution or an approach that allows both parties to gain something and at the same time give something. Resolution benefits the people involved and the system as a whole. *Accommodation* is the opposite of competition; here one party decides to downplay his or her own position and find ways to allow the others to have their way, to implement their plan. It is not the same as losing, since the accommodators choose to take this approach. Ultimately, the more successful approaches involve *collaborating* with others, in which both sides state their views and work together to find ways to use all of them. This is how integrative, longer-term solutions can emerge.

Effective leadership while resolving conflicts is deciding on the appropriate mix of strategies and their implementation. The following are some useful principles for these steps:

1. Managers and supervisors need to communicate clearly their goals and objectives for each unit and employee. Without these, staff may not work efficiently toward the proper end points, thereby creating problems for others and increasing the likelihood of conflicts.

2. Establish the ground rules for conflict. Examples are no name-calling, no swearing, taking time to reflect on ideas before responding, and summarizing conversations.

3. Be sure to get facts before reaching conclusions. Too often, the excitement and energy created by a conflict stimulates rapid discussion and problem solutions. But these may not be the best options, just the first ones offered.

4. Avoid conflicts that are not yours. Sometimes supervisors should stay away from small, interpersonal conflicts and insist that those who are party to the difference try to settle it themselves before involving others.

When addressing a conflict, it is important to begin by getting as much relevant information as possible before deciding on the next steps. Relevance is sometimes hard to assess. When asked, all parties to the conflict will have their own view of the issues involved and generally present them in the light most favorable to their perspective. "We were treated unfairly" may not be the actual words used, but they certainly convey the message. There is almost always more to the conflict than initially revealed. Leaders should not take the issue personally, for if they do, they will risk allowing the conflict to escalate far beyond its initial boundaries.

Allowing some time to pass may help people settle down and remove some of the emotion that undercuts thoughtful conversation. An effective leader knows how to use active listening skills to make sure each side feels it has at least been heard clearly. Active listening means reflecting and restating the issues as conveyed by the speaker. Done without editorializing or adding added perspectives, these listening skills help calm frayed nerves.

In instances of less extensive conflict, just listening as one party explains a conflicting situation can lead to insights and possible solutions. Venting and letting off steam can be both cathartic and allow new ideas to emerge. Conversely, if handled poorly, it may harden the positions, since there are no countervailing forces or other information available.

Serving as a devil's advocate can help each party understand a conflict. If a mediator or the supervisor can enable each party to take the other person's perspective, this sometimes will free people up to see new ways of resolving differences. Thus, instead of finding new arguments to support one position, individuals are asked to restate the other person's or group's concerns and discuss them from that vantage point. This tends to help find solutions rather than asserting right or wrong, blame or accusation.

In situations involving a large number of people, sending them off to resolve interpersonal conflicts can be counterproductive. Without a neutral mediator, the people involved usually lack the skills to resolve problems. Some managers ask subordinates to work out their differences and let the boss know when this has been done. But this "you-can-resolve-it-yourselves" is a dubious practice in larger conflicts and rarely is successful for more than a short period of time.

Drawing on existing rules, regulations, policies, and procedures can help guide and resolve a conflict. This approach builds on the fact that some of the organization's processes have contributed significantly to the current situation. The main advantage of this model is that no new rules need to be created and the leader does not have to choose based on more subjective criteria. It always is advisable for supervisors to be believed not to "play favorites." On the downside, using existing rules may not really get to the heart of the conflict, which can eventually resurface in some other form.

Some conflicts are so severe that they may require a mediator or, more formally, a negotiator. An effective mediator is someone who does not actually take sides on the issues but instead asks questions to help clarify issues, listens equally to both sides, finds out what the more salient issues are, determines what each party really wants, and helps them find common ground. In this way, the win/lose tactics of unresolved conflict are replaced by possible win/win approaches. If both sides can find that common ground, the organization will probably benefit. The mediator can be someone from the personnel department, another manager in the system, a counselor. or an external resource person brought in for this process.

Negotiation is a more formal process and requires the help of a third party who should not have any direct connection to the issues, departments, or individuals involved. The negotiator has more freedom than a mediator usually does to propose and push solutions. The goal is the same, however, to find a way thorough the problems.

In summary, effective conflict resolution requires the following steps:

1. *Stop arguing.* This will help prevent escalating the conflict and allow reason to prevail. Often it is not the "head" that causes the conflict; it is the heart, the emotion, the subjective.
2. *State the problem.* Invite each party to define the causes of the conflict and what it wants as a desired outcome. This can be a risky step, but articulating one's aspirations can contribute to finding solutions.
3. *Start listening.* Learning what the other party says it wants, how it defines the issues, and what constraints it sees in the situation can move the process along more effectively than can merely elaborating old arguments.
4. *Seek mutual solutions.* This requires finding issues and aspects on which both parties can agree. Often, starting with the smallest area of agreement provides a basis for moving to more complex tasks and issues. An effective mediator should ask each party, "What are you willing to give?" "What do you need in this situation?" This helps avoid making the conflict personal, the toughest situation to resolve.

5. *Focus on the future.* Little is accomplished by rehashing the history; the conflicting parties are likely to disagree on that, too. Dwelling the past will serve only to keep the conflict stuck in its present form. Discussing possible solutions and future goals is more productive.

In conclusion, organizations go through stages of development, from birth to maturity, and along the way they encounter a variety of common problems. Transitions are difficult, especially that from leadership by the founders to a new director. Organizations can go into decline if they value self-maintenance more than their mission. Organizational development offers a number of approaches to renewal. Even successful organizations encounter resistance and conflicts, but if handled effectively, they can contribute to their growth and health.

Keep in mind the following guidelines for organizational renewal:

Renewal reminds us of why the nonprofit exists and the importance of its mission.

Renewal rejects apathy and mediocrity.

Renewal regards external voices as important information to be understood and used in decision making as appropriate.

Renewal reaffirms the need for openness and organizational self-awareness.

Renewal removes built-in obstacles to successful planning and programs.

Renewal recognizes conflicts as energy that can be harnessed and used constructively.

Renewal redefines leadership as both a process and a position.

Renewal reinforces the roles and contributions of all members of nonprofit organizations.

Renewal responds to the reality that nonprofit organizations do change; the issue is whether these changes are proactively planned or reactively forced on the system.

10

Strategic Planning

This chapter explains how to develop a strategic plan to help nonprofit organizations make the most effective and efficient use of their resources. The material in this chapter enables the reader to

1. Understand the basic components and processes of developing a strategic plan.
2. Analyze the internal organizational strengths and weaknesses and opportunities and threats of an organization's external environment (SWOT analysis).
3. Learn key principles for effective strategic planning.
4. Analyze and use the organization's mission statement to guide strategic planning.

Strategic planning is a systematic process that leads to basic decisions, goals, and actions to position an organization for future success. It states what the organization will become, what goals it will attain, and what it will do to accomplish them. Strategic planning is an ongoing, inclusive process that an organization uses to decide on a desired future state and then to select those actions that will move toward these desired goals. The planning process examines the organization's environment and the trends that will affect the ways in which it will work in the future.

Plans determine the changes that the organization will make to better fulfill its mission. They show how the organization will build on its strengths, take advantage of opportunities, and overcome internal weakness and external threats. Strategic plans begin with what the organization is and why and then state what it wants to become in the future and how it will get there.[1]

"Evolution without a sense of our own purpose is likely to leave us directionless and powerless."[2] This statement means that purposeful change is possible and that it provides energy and direction for people to work toward important goals. Random or incremental change without a strategy and specific resources can lead to organizational drift and decline.

Strategic planning is necessary to ensure that an organization is aligned with its environment, meets community needs, establishes and sustains effective programs, and uses its resources in the most effective manner possible. Ultimately, the board of directors or trustees should approve the plan, but its development requires input from many voices, from both the organization and the broader community. This chapter explores the components and procedures of successful planning and the changes that can result.

W. Edwards Deming (1900–1993) showed the world how organizations could productively use quality circles, which led to the quality improvement movement in the late twentieth century.[3] Indeed, Deming's work helped move Japanese industry into a leadership role in the world's economy. As he stressed, "It is not necessary to change. Survival is not mandatory." That is, if an organization fails to adapt to changes in its environment, it will decline and eventually die. Other organizations will come to fill the void by shaping their activities for success in the new environment. Many new business entities go bankrupt every year, and many nonprofits are unable to obtain the resources necessary for survival. Finding effective strategies for the future helps ensure an organization's survival and growth, allowing it to pursue its mission in the community.

An organization's operational decisions are either programmed or nonprogrammed. Programmed decisions tend to be routine, repetitive, subject to rules and procedures; to rely on defined criteria; and to be heavily documented. Intake forms gather needed information in predetermined categories. Travel vouchers must include required receipts and signatures. The complexity of admission forms in health facilities and educational settings rivals only that of insurance forms. When reviewed and updated, programmed decisions can be delegated, allowing supervisors to monitor and respond to any exceptions.

Nonprogrammed decisions are made in response to unusual challenges. They require complex problem-solving processes, drawing on information from a variety of sources and weighing alternative potential solutions. Strategic planning, then, is a systematic, nonprogrammed series of decisions involving the whole organization, which is why it can be both a vital and a frustrating process for those working there. Strategic planning predicts the future and positions the organization in the best place in that future.

Strategic planning cultivates and enhances excellence throughout the organization, often according to Peters and Waterman's classic principles of organizational excellence.[4]

Excellence Comes From

Being biased toward action	Not being paralyzed by analysis
Staying close to the client	Not dwelling on the organization's history
Gathering external data	Not using past evaluations exclusively
Value-driven decisions	Not actions taken for expediency or politics
Effective self-analysis	Not believing the organization's own propaganda
Testing new approaches	Not adhering to "the way we always do it"

When employees are very busy and things seem to be going well, some people may ask, Why bother with strategic planning? This question misses the mark by undervaluing the short- and long-term benefits of such efforts. There are numerous reasons both to have a strategic plan (the result) and, more important, to conduct organizationwide strategic planning (the process). These benefits are not limited to just having an administrative rationale for allocating resources and providing a basis for periodic program evaluations. Instead, there are positive outcomes both inside the organization and outside in the external community.

The benefits of strategic planning are

- Improving the organization's effectiveness in carrying out its mission and purposes.
- Increasing its efficiency in using resources for maximum results.
- Strengthening decision making by clarifying the direction of all the organization's components.
- Improving public communications by means of consistent messages and intended position in the community.
- Gaining political and financial support.

The strategic plan itself provides a framework for decisions about what the organization will and will not do in the future. It may be broken down into a series of annual plans, each subject to revision as circumstances change. A plan is not inviolable; rather, it is intended to build on the past by offering effective programs today and tomorrow that are designed to build a strong future. Since circumstances may change in unanticipated ways, the plan should be revisited at least annually to determine whether it needs to be modified.

A good plan lays a strong foundation for recruiting staff, volunteers, and board members. The planning process also highlights areas for professional training and staff development (both to compensate for deficiencies and to help prepare for future changes). Finally, effective strategic planning helps ensure that internal processes (budget preparation, recruitment, programs, services, and personnel evaluations) are aligned with the external world.

As the planning process proceeds, it provides an opportunity to educate the public and to learn from it. By demonstrating its accountability and commitment to use funds efficiently, the nonprofit organization can use the planning process as a basis for grants, contracts, and philanthropic efforts. The planning process also uncovers areas of concern, the threats. A structured process provides needed feedback on a range of issues, like the organization's reputation, competition, and prospects from different constituencies. And at a minimum, strategic planning prevents outsiders from accusing the organization of not having a plan of action. A clear focus for organizational decision making serves the community well: it serves donors, recipients, and those engaged with the organization in any way.

A strategic plan may have several parts, each dealing with a major issue facing the organization. One such part is the *program plan*, which defines what the organization is doing and plans to do in the future. It focuses on the following concerns:

What services and programs does the organization currently offer?
What does the assessment of these efforts reveal in terms of strengths and areas for improvement?
What programs or services will be needed in the future? What documentation supports these needs?
Which areas of possible growth and change will become priorities in the next three to five years?
What specific changes should we make in our programs?
What will these changes produce?
What are the key steps for accomplishing them?

Another part is the *human resource plan*, the organization's way of dealing with important issues related to its personnel. It addresses such issues as

The number of staff needed for current programs and future growth or changes as well as for administrative and other supports.

The percentage of full-time, part-time, and contract employees; volunteers; and consultants.

The acceptable vacancy or turnover rate.

The organization's plans for recruiting and retaining staff.

The appropriate salary and benefit level for the local area and how the organization will match it.

The changes in the organization's personnel policies and practices.

The differences that these changes will make.

The implementation of these changes.

The plan's *facilities and equipment* component asks questions like

What are the organization's space needs?

What steps are needed for repairs and renovations over the long term?

What are the staff's technology needs for hardware, software, training, and infrastructure?

What changes should be made in these areas?

What results will they produce?

How should we go about implementing them?

The plan's *financial* component considers how the system will pay for carrying out the plan.

How much money is needed to meet these challenges for the next three to five years?

What are the organization's current revenue sources?

What income levels are needed to support growth and change?

Are there appropriate reallocations or efficiency measures that can help meet these financial goals?

What new possibilities are there for additional restricted and unrestricted revenue?

What changes should we make in our fund-raising efforts?

What results can we expect?

How should we go about achieving them?

Basic Steps of Planning

The first step in strategic planning is to secure the agreement and commitment of the organization's leaders to undertake the process and use the results. After they have done this, they then should negotiate the overall purposes of the strategic plan, the steps to be taken, the timetable, the resources to be used, and the other people to involve. The leaders may form a group to guide and oversee the planning process and designate a manager for it.

That group should begin its work by examining the organization's mission statement. A clear, concise, and inspiring mission statement is the foundation for the entire planning process, as it explains the reasons for the planning. The group's examination should include judgments about how well the current mission statement

- Expresses the true purposes for which the organization currently exists and its values.
- Specifies the ends sought, not the means or actions to reach them.
- Describes what the organization aspires to be.
- Identifies the distinctions of the organization and its limitations.
- Allows people to understand quickly and fully what the organization stands for and why it is important.
- Inspires and motivates people to pursue a shared vision.

If the current statement of mission already fulfills these conditions, it may not need to be changed. However, if it is outdated, ambiguous, or overly wordy, the group should begin obtaining input from others in the organization and its board regarding improvements or refinements. Once a new statement has been drafted, it should be circulated widely for feedback to be used for further improvements. The following are some examples of nonprofit organizations' mission statements:

"City Year's mission is to build democracy through citizen service, civic leadership and social entrepreneurship."[5]

Lehigh University provides an education that lasts a lifetime.[6]

The North American Deer Farmers Association's "mission is to foster a greater association among people who raise deer for commercial purposes. NADeFA® is dedicated to the promotion of deer farming and ranching as an agricultural pursuit and serves its members through its educational programs and publications and by providing leadership in setting and maintaining quality standards."[7]

The NAMES Project Foundation's mission is "to preserve, care for, and use the AIDS Memorial Quilt to foster healing, heighten awareness, and inspire action in the struggle against HIV and AIDS."[8]

The Georgia Aquarium's mission is "to be an entertaining, educational, and scientific institution featuring exhibits and programs of the highest standards, offering engaging guest experiences, and promoting the conservation of aquatic biodiversity throughout the world."[9]

Exercise

Analyze the above mission statements using the standards cited earlier. How well does each statement meet each of the standards?

Some organizations go further by identifying the values underlying their mission and purposes, which make up their central culture. Values become an organizational personality, forming the spoken and silent boundaries for all decisions. The following are some examples:

American Library Association's Core Values of Librarianship

The foundation of modern librarianship rests on an essential set of core values that define, inform, and guide our professional practice. These values reflect the history and ongoing development of the profession and have been advanced, expanded, and refined by numerous policy statements of the American Library Association. Among these are:

Access
Confidentiality/privacy
Democracy
Diversity
Education and lifelong learning
Intellectual freedom
Preservation
The public good
Professionalism
Service

Source: www.ala.org.

City of Dublin, California, Social Responsibility Values

Building community

Promote locations and events that bring people of all ages together.

Provide more venues for family-based activities.

Foster heritage and cultural development.

Ensuring a safe community

Provide high-quality police and fire services to ensure the safety of the citizens living in the community.

Provide education and training to residents and businesses that would promote public safety.

Guiding development

Ensure that development contributes positively to the City's fiscal health.

Support pedestrian-friendly development, transit-oriented development, green building, and environmental responsiveness.

Respect our neighborhoods, their identity, image, and aspirations.

Believe that no part of the community is better than another.

Promote high quality design and architectural standards in development.

Governing

Be open to the public and community.

Operate at all times with honesty and integrity.

Exercise fairness in consideration of issues—we listen to all sides; we respect every opinion; and we treat all individuals with dignity.

Provide a high level of customer service and responsiveness, from City staff to citizens.

Strive to build an informed community through communication.

Encourage cooperation with other communities on issues of mutual concern.

Relating to Other Communities and Entities

Respect the right of each individual community and entity to determine its own destiny.

Cooperate with other communities and entities, but do not interfere.

Acknowledge that we will not direct the work of another elected body.

Source: http://www.ci.dublin.ca.us/index.cfm.

University of Medicine and Dentistry of New Jersey Values

PEOPLE and DIVERSITY, treating all with compassion, dignity and respect for individual beliefs. ETHICAL BEHAVIOR, professionalism, integrity and accountability in all aspects of our academic, scientific, clinical and administrative work. EXCELLENCE, encouraging achievement in all endeavors of the University family, fostering collegiality and maintaining high academic standards, through a productive, scholarly faculty and a talented student body. KNOWLEDGE, its creation, dissemination, synthesis and application. SERVICE, demonstrated through our commitment to effectiveness, accessibility and affordability in our education, research and health care programs. COLLABORATION within the University family and through partnerships with others to enhance the fulfillment of our Mission and attainment of our Vision. INNOVATION and FLEXIBILITY to meet the ongoing societal needs and challenges of the future. Approved by the Board of Trustees, June 21, 2005.

Source: http://www.umdnj.edu/presweb/president/strategic/ProposedVisionand ValueStatements.htm.

SWOT Analysis

The next phase in the strategic planning process is examining the organization's internal strengths and weaknesses and its external opportunities and threats. This process has come to be known by its acronym, SWOT:

Strengths: What are the organization's strengths? These provide the foundation for the future.

Weaknesses: What are the organization's weaknesses? These are points of vulnerability.

Opportunities: What changes are occurring in the external world that can help the organization fulfill its mission?

Threats: What issues loom in the environment that could undermine the organization's progress or deflect positive results?

Internally, strategic planning helps the organization recognize its strengths and weakness. Knowing these can be both exhilarating and painful; not knowing them is dangerous; and avoiding the process of learning is foolhardy. Staff, supervisors, managers, and board members are asked to point out what they see as the organization's important strengths, to describe them, and to suggest how to build on them and improve them further. Professional staff, board members, and community leaders can help identify trends in the external environment that may represent opportunities or threats to the organization that the strategic plan should address.

Conducting such an analysis can help identify the programs' interconnections as well as ways to increase the organization's efficiency and effectiveness. By seeking the views of people at all levels in the organization, the process demonstrates that it values their perspectives, ensuring both a wide range of views and enhancing teamwork and collaboration. It can also provide information that may be helpful in bridging splits or misunderstandings in the organization.

IDENTIFYING CHOICES

Based on the findings from the SWOT analysis, the next step is to identify the fundamental challenges and policy choices facing the organization. These choices may relate to the direction of the whole organization or any of its parts. People should be asked what issues they see as important to the organization's future, how each issue relates to the findings of the SWOT analysis, and possible ways of addressing each. These issues should be ones the organization can feasibly address, not those beyond its control. Likewise, they should be separated into short-term operational tactics and longer-term strategic goals. The most frequently mentioned strategic issues and possible responses should be marked for further work.

FORMULATING GOALS

The next phase is to formulate goal statements for each of the frequently mentioned issues. A *goal statement* describes the condition the organization could realize in the future, such as having strong support among some population in the community or attaining national certification for a major program. Goal statements should be examined for their importance to the future of the organization and their potential for making it successful in the community.

Then the steps to take to reach the goal should be decided. These steps may involve major changes for the entire organization or its components. They may address programs or services or the organization's functional divisions. Deciding what the organization should do should build on the ideas offered in the previous phase but take the analysis deeper. Goals should be determined, and then alternative approaches to accomplishing them should be considered, the components of the organization needed to act on them, the resources and barriers relating to each, and how each approach could resolve the issue.

For example, a nonprofit that offers family-counseling services identified a major ethnic group in the community that seldom used its services. Overcoming that gap was important to the organization's communitywide mission. One option was to establish a branch office near the geographic center of that group's housing or businesses. Another was to conduct a neighborhood survey with interviews to better understand the concerns and interests of the members of that group. Yet another was to add staff members from that group. Note that the proposed approaches to addressing this issue were not necessarily mutually exclusive, although each required different resources and actions.

In this phase of the planning process, the major issues, proposed goals, and strategies for addressing them should be discussed with people from all parts of the organization. The objective of these discussions is to settle on a few goals and one or more ways of dealing with them. It often is tempting to include several goals for fear of missing anyone's pet issue. But no organization can do everything and so must set priorities. Some projects should be undertaken soon, whereas others may wait until the next cycle of planning. Arriving at such conclusions is difficult and requires all the skills of leadership discussed in chapter 6.

Often, strategic plans offer a series of interim objectives leading to the overall goal; some plans set time lines for achieving each of the objectives and goals; and some even specify the people or groups responsible for accomplishing each, including the criteria for monitoring progress and steps for evaluating results.

The next phase is to present the plan formally to the board for adoption. This is the culmination of all the work and commits the organization to acting on it in the years ahead. This is followed by constructing a detailed action plan to implement the strategic plan, allocating responsibilities for all the tasks, setting timetables for completion, and specifying the steps to be taken when the tasks are not completed. A procedure for monitoring progress and reporting results helps ensure that successes are recognized and celebrated and that problems are addressed promptly and not allowed to derail the plan.

Here is an example of one plan.

Alzheimer's Association 2006–2008 Strategic Plan

The Alzheimer's Association Long-Range Strategic Plan provides a common vision and mission for the national office and chapters and serves as a roadmap for future development. The plan expands the Association's mission to include reducing the risk of dementia through the promotion of brain health. All the goals emphasize the inclusion of diverse ethnic populations.

NOTE: All references to Alzheimer's disease include related disorders.

Our vision: A world without Alzheimer's disease.

Our mission: To eliminate Alzheimer's disease through the advancement of research; to provide and enhance care and support for all affected; and to reduce the risk of dementia through the promotion of brain health.

Our core values: The core values of the Alzheimer's Association are the standards that drive our priorities, commitments and organizational decisions. They guide our behaviors and judgments, including how we carry out our mission and determine our goals and objectives. They inspire us to act.

Integrity: We seek and embrace the truth, and fulfill the trust others place in us.

Commitment to excellence: We lead through innovation and constant improvement in all we do.

Inclusiveness: We search out and welcome the power that comes from diversity.

Consumer focus: We seek always to understand, learn from and meet the needs of individuals with dementia, their families and caregivers.

Accountability: We keep our commitments and make measurable progress to achieve our mission.

2006–2008 Goals and Objectives

Goal 1: Advancing research
Together we will accelerate the progress in Alzheimer research.

Objectives
1. Increase federal funding from diverse sources, through advocacy and other efforts, to a minimum of $1.4 billion annually.
2. Increase the Association's research funding for basic science, prevention and care, with special attention to diverse ethnic populations.
3. Be the convener and catalyst for collaborations with investigators in industry, academia and other organizations to promote basic and applied Alzheimer research.

Goal 2: Providing and enhancing care and support

Together we will provide and promote quality Alzheimer care, support and services, and empower consumers in diverse communities to access them.

Objectives

1. Increase the number and diversity of people the Association serves.

2. Continuously improve the quality and consistency of our services and innovate in response to consumer need.

3. Advocate for integrated systems of healthcare and support that are effective for people with Alzheimer's disease and their families (e.g., disease management strategies, practice guidelines, community/home-based care, hospice care, chronic care management).

4. Develop and deliver evidence-based best practices on dementia care to consumers and providers.

5. Increase and diversify the Association's funding for care, support and services.

6. Investigate national strategies to certify services and individuals.

Goal 3: Mobilizing public support

Together we will alert the public to the growing millions affected by Alzheimer's disease and the importance of brain health, and mobilize them to join our movement.

Objectives

Increase recognition of the Association's brand and public awareness of our messages.

1. Extend and amplify our voice through collaborations, partnerships, appropriate technologies and consistent messaging.

2. Expand our reach to engage underserved populations and those not yet directly affected by Alzheimer's disease.

3. Increase and broaden our advocacy for those affected by Alzheimer's disease with business, care providers, consumers, media, pharmaceutical companies, policymakers and regulators.

Goal 4: Building unity and capacity

Together we will build organizational unity and capacity to achieve our mission.

Objectives

1. Be unified in our mission and message.

2. Increase revenue from both philanthropic and nonphilanthropic (e.g., grants, fee for service, business opportunities) sources.

3. Generate the majority of philanthropic revenue across the Association through joint and collaborative fund-raising while preserving chapter autonomy.

4. Build and strengthen national and chapter fiscal health through improving infrastructure and operational efficiencies; staff and volunteer competencies; and management and governance capabilities.

5. Ensure that the Association is culturally competent and that volunteers and staff reflect the diverse communities that the Association serves.

Source: http://www.alz.org/AboutUs/StratPlan.asp.

Principles for Planning

There are no rules that must be followed in developing a strategic plan, but there are a number of important principles that should be remembered (see figure 10.1).

1. *Ultimately, the board is responsible for the plan and the planning process.* It must approve, support, use, and evaluate the organization's strategic plan. Without visible top support, the plan is doomed to occupy space on someone's shelf. Some members of the board should be involved in each phase of the process, from concept to data collection and from analysis to developing options for the future.

2. *Value-driven strategic planning begins with a clear vision or mission statement.* The Reverend Theodore Hesburgh has received more than one hundred honorary degrees from academic institutions across the globe. A theologian who once served as the president of Notre Dame University and chaired several important presidential commissions, he is familiar with the high and low points of leadership in numerous contexts. He maintains that "the very essence of leadership is that you have to have a vision." In addition to having a clearly and succinctly worded vision statement, it is important to pay attention to how that statement was constructed. Long-term successful implementation requires input from those who must live with the statement, for example, the nonprofit's stakeholders.

The first step in establishing or refining a mission statement for a nonprofit organization is to define the values that underlie all its programs, services, culture, budget priorities, and managerial decision making. Although some practitioners distinguish among statements of mission, values, and vision, they all are closely related. A short, crisp statement about the organization's purposes frames and guides the strategic planning process and its outcomes. The mission does not describe *how* the organization will fulfill its aspirations, nor does it specify near-term goals,

Figure 10.1
Principles for Strategic Planning

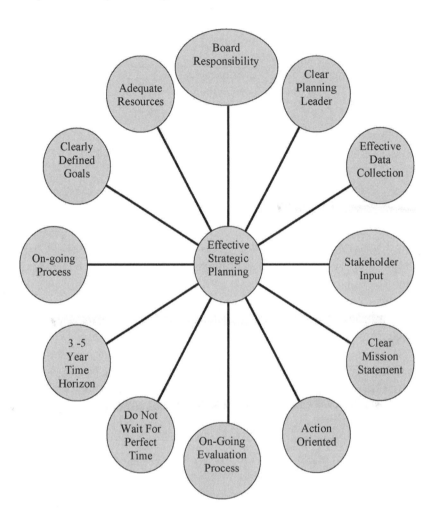

objectives, and activities. These come later. Reaching agreement on the mission statement may take more time than anticipated, since stakeholders will want to emphasize different elements of the organization's work as being essential to its mission and vision. In the end, these concerns must be reduced to a short statement that will guide the organization and its plans.

3. *There is no "perfect" time for planning.* The middle of a deep crisis is not a good time to make a long-term plan. A better time to plan is when the organization may need it most, such as during key personnel transitions, significant

changes in programs, alterations in the organization's services, or major changes in the community (like a large corporation relocating to the city or finding that another organization has decided to provide similar services). If there is extensive board turnover or a new CEO, a strategic plan can help recruit new people who are committed to the plan's values and goals. Being in transition means that people are uncertain; this can hinder strategic planning or it can help the system prepare and commit to a common purpose. It is a better approach than just reacting or wandering along.

4. *Effective plans project goals for three to five years.* This differs from annual operating plans and budgets allocating funds for immediate expenditure. Yearly plans should define tasks and connect these to needed resources; six to ten years is too far long a period for a strategic plan. It is useful to think about the long-term future, but anticipating changes ten years ahead may not be realistic with the environment changing so rapidly. Microsoft's founder, international philanthropist, and citizen-of-the-world Bill Gates once remarked, "We always overestimate the change that will occur in the next two years and underestimate the change that will occur in the next ten."[10]

5. *Strategic planning should be an ongoing process.* There is no single answer to how long this process should take; usually six to nine months should suffice to develop a thoughtful plan. But this depends on several factors, such as the organization's size, complexity, available time, previous experiences with planning, willingness of key people to engage, information needed, and available resources to conduct the planning process. The plan should be reviewed every year or two to make sure it is still valid, and as conditions change, the plan must be revised to take them into account.

6. *Goals should be clearly defined.* A readily understandable statement of goals allows everyone working toward them to see what is being sought and then to decide on the steps needed to get from here to there. Clearly stated goals enable people to focus their attention and energy. They allow them to communicate more easily with one another and the public, and they enable the organization to monitor progress toward the goals. These goals should be challenging and achievable, quantifiable and measurable. Strategic plans that include interim objectives and action steps have a better chance of succeeding than those that cite only long-term goals. Although the plan should specify steps along the way, any successfully completed step should not be taken as a rest stop. Rather, it is an opportunity to celebrate movement toward the larger goal. Such positive reinforcements renew commitment and provide fresh energy for the next phase of change and the actions needed to make it successful.

7. *Gather as much data as you realistically can.* Find appropriate ways to connect with each group of stakeholders: funders, donors, suppliers, venders, clients, staff, board members, former trustees and retired leaders, elected representatives, company executives, national association leaders, and volunteers. The Internet can

help you reach people and gather information, as can surveys, focus groups, interviews, videotapes, and conference calls. Documentation is critical and should include records of meetings, ideas, suggestions, assessment data, community trends, and social indicators.

8. *One person should be charged with overseeing the entire effort.* Organizations often form a strategic planning committee or task force to connect and involve key people in the process. Planning requires staff support and the participation of many individuals and organizations across the organization's service area. This group must have a clearly designated leader to guide and coordinate all phases of the effort. The group may also want to use a facilitator or outside consultant to help with the process. This should be someone with relevant expertise in strategic planning and no vested interest in the specific decisions made by this group along the way.

9. *Strategic planning costs money.* The organization must allocate sufficient funds to support the planning activities. Some organizations have obtained additional resources through grants from foundations, corporations, and governmental agencies. Some communities have low or no-cost resources that can help, such as executive loan programs, RSVP (Retired Senior Volunteer Program), United Way, and religious groups. In addition, faculty members and students at local colleges and universities might help as part of their academic programs.

10. *Assume that everyone involved in the process has knowledge that is important to the project.* Members of the staff provide the perspective from the front lines. Board members bring commitment to the organization, a sense of its history, and an awareness of the community's concerns. Community leaders can help decide what may be needed in the future. Donors can speak about the aspects of the organization's activities that motivate giving. Clients and participants in programs can help judge the quality of and congruence between programs and their needs. All these perspectives contribute to identifying the issues needing attention and to formulating goals to be given priority in the plan.

11. *Effective plans provide well-developed directions for change.* They offer specific recommendations for action that will lead to the major accomplishments emphasized in the plan. Plans also should include steps for revising the plan when needed. Discovering the right direction may mean confronting circumstances that were not known at the outset, so adjustments in the plan are likely to be needed along the way.

12. *Evaluation along the way is essential to documenting successes.* A well-developed plan should include criteria for assessing the completion of each step and for indicating the successful accomplishment of each goal. Procedures for monitoring progress and reporting results should be part of the plan. These procedures can provide early warnings about aspects of the plan that are lagging behind expected deadlines, thus allowing participants to look for ways to deal with barriers and get

back on track. They also are useful for documenting results and reporting them to others both inside and outside the organization.

13. *There is no perfect plan.* Expectations for a perfect product can paralyze action. Remember that the process is as important as the document it produces. The goals identified should stretch the organization but not overwhelm it. They may lead to creative and risky changes, or they may reaffirm or fine-tune current approaches, programs, services, and structures but do so with current data, not old assumptions and recycled information. The written plan, once approved, should be disseminated widely across the organization and the community of stakeholders. Media coverage can inform the public of the organization's future directions and strengthen the community's understanding, input, and support.

Web Assignment

Go a company's Web site and find "goals" and "objectives." When you consider these against the criteria of specificity, challenge, resource availability, and evaluation methods, what do you find?

Web Assignment

Search for several examples of nonprofit organizations' values statements and strategic plans. How well do they convey the importance of their work? Are the goals credible and persuasive? What impacts do these statements and plans have on you as an objective observer? As a potential donor? As a community member if you resided near the organization?

In conclusion, strategic planning is a process that enables an organization to identify the most important changes it should make to maximize its success in the future. It states what the organization will become, what goals it will attain, and what it will do to achieve them. It is an ongoing, inclusive process that an organization uses to decide on a desired future state and then to select the actions that will move toward these desired goals. The planning process examines the organization's environment and the trends that will affect how it operates in the future. Plans show how the organization will build on its strengths, take advantage of opportunities, and overcome weakness and threats. Making basic changes in an organization is difficult for most people, so unanimity on goals or action steps is unlikely. Strong skills of leadership are vital to the success of plans, and the reader is referred to chapters 6 and 9, which discuss those skills in more detail.

Art in the Shelter?

The last thing PJ said as he hung up the telephone was, "Yes, we'll talk about working with you." As executive director of the local homeless shelter, he had an inquiry from the director of community programs at the local art museum. The idea was to explore possibilities for providing cultural arts programs (painting, sketching, photography, ceramics, etc.) to the adults and children in the shelter. On the surface, PJ had never heard of anything like that and was intrigued. But quickly, numerous problems became clear. There was no space. Transportation would be a problem. Money was always in short supply. What about liability concerns? But he had promised to explore the possibility.

1. What steps should PJ take next?
2. What principles would help PJ in this conversation?
3. What are three benefits that the shelter could gain? The museum?
4. What local or national organizations might be interested in creative programs like this?
5. Conduct a SWOT analysis of this proposal using your home community as the location.
6. Under what circumstances would you recommend "yes" or "no" to the board?

Suggestion: Have two teams develop a role-play strategy, and then begin the first meeting of the two organizations with a fifteen-minute session.

Community Relations

This chapter addresses nonprofit organizations' relationships with their communities. Applying the relevant principles of marketing, political science, and public relations will help build and sustain connections with those whose engagement is vital to the organization's effectiveness. Understanding the material in this chapter will enable the reader to

1. Connect the concept of social responsibility to nonprofit organizations' community relations initiatives.
2. Know how to use marketing principles to increase a nonprofit's visibility and reputation in the community.
3. Develop and maintain an effective media relations program.
4. Know how to use advocacy and lobbying efforts.
5. Understand the concepts and principles needed to form mutually beneficial partnerships with other organizations.

Successful community relations programs follow a wide range of principles and activities. At the broadest level, they demonstrate how an organization practices its social responsibilities. Community relations programs are targeted at the macrolevel, the community-at-large and specific segments of it, whereas customer service efforts are focused at the microlevel, the individual, a client, a patron. These connections shape the ways in which an organization presents itself to the wider community. In this chapter, we examine how nonprofits can market their services and analyze their audience to guide program planning, media relationships, advocacy, and interorganizational partnerships.

A somewhat humorous place to start this discussion about community relations comes from an article in the *Journal of College and Character* by a college president reflecting on his experience observing students in a service-oriented corporate environment: "As one of the professional trainers told us, 'a sick guest is not a happy guest.'"[1]

Community relations programs start with the organization's strategic plans and values. The following list is of some of the values defining an organization's culture. It is not meant to be a comprehensive or exclusive list; rather, it shows the range of values and core beliefs underlying an organization's programs, services, and decisions. These values should guide the strategic planning, assist in recruiting, aid in preparing grant proposals and all forms of fund-raising, form the basis for program assessment and accountability, and define effective community relations programs.

> *Continuous Quality Improvement:* Monitoring all programs and services to maintain current strengths and improve where necessary.
>
> *Change:* Improving programs and activities so the nonprofit can meet its mission more effectively.
>
> *Integration:* Connecting goals and programs to make sure that comprehensive information is available to all providers.
>
> *Integrity:* Making sure words and actions match both the community's needs and the organization's values.
>
> *Professionalism:* Providing quality programs and services in ways that meet professional standards, codes of ethics, and applicable laws and regulations.
>
> *Quality:* Offering the highest level of performance in all services and programs.
>
> *Respect:* Treating others in the same way that we would like to be treated.
>
> *Timeliness:* Providing the highest-quality services and programs at the times when they are needed and in an effective manner, using current, accurate, and complete information.

In a provocative essay, Robert Putnam mourns the loss of community and uses the bowling alley as the metaphor for an indoor place where people used to come together and share community ideas, a theme that is similar to the notion of the commons from colonial times.[2] Putnam notes that membership in service organizations is declining while support for advocacy organizations is increasing, a good example being the growth of professional associations and lobbying groups in Washington, D.C., and every state capital. This trend also is reflected in the Rotary International's own pledge: "Every Rotary club and every Rotarian assumes a responsibility to find ways to improve the quality of life for those in their communities and to serve the public interest."[3] Many nonprofits may finally have figured out what corporations have known for years, that community relationships matter.

Are these community and public relations programs really necessary? We believe so. The nonprofit sector seems to be under an uncoordinated attack on several fronts. The drop in public support through governmental programs has caused cutbacks, downsizing, mergers, closings, competition, and even client dumping from one organization onto another. These are unhealthy signs. Although competition may be a strong motivating force in corporate America, it usually diminishes quality and effectiveness in the nonprofit sector. OMB Watch is a nonprofit organization founded during the Reagan administration to ensure public access to government decision making and accountability in fiscal and regulatory matters. Its 2004 report noted that "the nonprofit sector of the economy is traditionally asked to help support the nation in times of economic weakness, and is currently expected to make up for reductions in publicly provided government services. [It] is being asked to do more with less labor input."[4]

How can today's nonprofit organizations be sure that their history, tradition, values, culture, and legacy of service will endure in an environment that seems more concerned about efficiency, accountability, and cost containment than about quality, effectiveness, and the expansion of services? The following are some principles to guide such efforts. Following them will enhance efforts to inform the community, build engagement and trust, and form the foundation for effective community relations.

First, all nonprofits must use their core values to define their mission, their work, their professionalism, and their successes. Leaders should frame their decisions in terms of the organization's service goals, mission, and values. Indeed, the Independent Sector's *Profiles of Excellence* concluded that effective boards and top managers create and support a mission-based culture.[5] Straying from these long-term aspirations almost certainly guarantees failure. Although compromises may meet short-term needs, they will undercut long-term effectiveness and support.

Community relations programs begin with the organization's mission statement, the organization's best and often first chance to state the purposes of its existence and to describe its goals, values, and image. A carefully crafted mission statement informs everyone both inside and outside about the priorities guiding all of the organization's activities. It should be specific enough to help people distinguish this organization from other nonprofits, including those that provide similar programs and services.

A second principle is to learn about and adapt the most effective approaches to delivering services and programs by keeping informed about innovations in the field, incorporating best practices into strategic planning and organizational operations, and making changes that improve quality, energize staff and volunteers, and attract community support. Such steps inform the community, build engagement and trust, and form the foundation for effective community relations. Adopting the best practices from around the world enables an organization to demonstrate its commitment to quality in all its activities.

Another important practice is to seek stakeholders' input when establishing programs, conducting evaluations, and then using these inputs to modify or change as needed. Getting a broad input into designing, evaluating, and changing programs and services expands the ownership of the results. It also invites conversations about possible partnerships or new approaches that can enhance the organization's capacities to achieve its goals.

Finally, leaders should confront the organization's shortfalls or lapses decisively and clearly. They should not make excuses for not doing the right thing.

Marketing

Marketing has become a necessity for nonprofit organizations. Consumer products like automobiles and toothpaste have always been marketed, and now the most successful nonprofits also have complex, if not subtle, marketing strategies. Marketing efforts obtain and use information about an organization's stakeholders in planning and implementing its services in ways that enable it to sustain their engagement and support. The purpose of marketing is to create favorable public awareness, attract consumers, increase donations, and perhaps educate legislators. Each stakeholder group may respond to a different approach from the organization: potential clients need to know about what services are available, whereas potential donors might want to know more about the impacts of those services and programs.

Marketing refers to those activities in an organization that have to do with building the organization's value to the public and thus furthering its mission and goals. It focuses on the organization's external relationships and seeks to communicate to others a consistent, engaging image of itself. Marketing describes the organization's products or services in ways that are attractive to stakeholders, prices them in ways that encourage their use, promotes wide-spread public awareness of them, and makes them available in places that are convenient for the intended audiences. Good marketing requires staying in regular contact with each of the organization's stakeholder groups, under-standing their needs and expectations, and sustaining two-way communica-tion that not only expresses the organization's purposes but also shows how it benefits each group. Tailoring the organization's activities and communica-tions to constituencies' interests results in more extensive engagement with them, stronger loyalty, greater efficiency and effectiveness in use of resources, and ultimately a stronger organization.[6]

Many people working in nonprofit organizations tend to focus on internal activities, the professional quality of programs, and current customers. While internal constituencies are unquestionably important, good relationships with external stakeholders are equally important. For example, the stakehold-ers in early childhood education programs would include families with young children, teachers, referral sources, and donors interested in such programs. Sponsors and donors are a stakeholder group whose interests and concerns must be understood and addressed by the nonprofit. They make possible the organization's survival through gifts and endorsements. Taking the time to understand the interests of these and other stakeholders is essential to engag-ing them with the organization. Guiding these efforts are such questions as

Case Statement

- Are our values, activities, and messages congruent with our stakeholders' interests?
- Are they evident in all we do?
- Are the benefits to them clear and consistent?
- Are there changes that should be taken into account when fine-tuning or modi-fying our programs?
- How well are we meeting their concerns in what we do?

Rather than assuming we already know the answers to these questions, we should look to the organization's stakeholders for this information. Further-more, considering each of its audiences enables the organization to focus on and understand each one's interests. Such knowledge is essential to tailoring its approaches to attract them and sustain their engagement. Public attitudes are changing, and people who were interested in and loyal to a given organization in the past may now find many alternatives around them. Likewise, expecta-tions of accountability are rising, and the demands for custom tailored pro-grams are increasing. Sustaining its responsiveness to the interests of numerous stakeholders is vital to the organization's survival.

Marketing plans should also take into account the activities of actual or potential competitors. For example, many hospitals and nursing homes try to attract consumers to themselves rather than to other health care providers in the region. Health clinics vie with private practices for patients. Museums and orchestras compete for subscribers and donor support. Even local systems like United Way have to show that they are responsive to donors' interests and concerns. Allowing donors to decide which nonprofits will receive their gifts is an important way of honoring specific interests. The United Way also must be concerned about public perceptions that "too much" of their donations go to support causes outside the service area. Religious organizations may have to spell out the reasons for contributing to them rather than to other causes. The main challenge for any organization is to define and shape its programs in ways that are distinctive from others in the environment and uniquely appealing to each of its stakeholder groups.

The organization must remain loyal to its stakeholders in order for them to stay engaged. As a result, the nonprofit must take steps to ensure that it understands their interests and shapes its activities and approaches to them in ways they value and through the media they use. Pine and Gilmore developed the concept of the *experience economy* to describe how the U.S. economy has moved from manufacturing goods and providing services to what they call "theater," explaining that "if you charge for distinctive tangible things, then you are in the *goods business*. If you charge for the activities you perform, then you are in the *service business*. If you charge for the feelings customers have because of engaging with you, then you are in the *experience business*."[7] Nonprofits can use this principle in their marketing efforts so that clients can benefit and at the same time look forward to receiving services and so that donors and volunteers can experience and enjoy the satisfactions of continuing their engagement with the organization and its mission.

The interests of staff and volunteers differ from those of consumers, and each of them from those of sponsors. Likewise, the interests of each may change over time. People in each stakeholder group expect some benefits from their engagement with the nonprofit. Consumers want programs or activities that directly meet their needs. Staff members and volunteers want satisfying work environments, opportunities to apply and improve their skills, and recognition for work well done. Sponsors want the satisfactions of affiliation with an organization that both carries out values they share and uses their contributions efficiently.

Leaders of nonprofit organizations must ensure that the expectations of people in each stakeholder group are being met and that the engagement brings valued results for them. This may require making compromises among all the competing interests and balancing the concerns of one group with all the others in formulating the nonprofit's strategic goals. The challenge to the nonprofit is to tailor its efforts in ways that will continue to appeal to all its stakeholders and sustain their commitment while carrying out its mission.

Segmenting the market starts with the general categories of the organization's consuming publics (consumers or clients), its input publics (major categories of donors), partner publics (other community organizations with whom it collaborates), and internal publics (managers, staff, volunteers, board members). Each of these categories should then be segmented further. For example, donors may be differentiated according to their motivations:

- Personal relationships with the organization's leaders.
- Religious traditions.
- Desire to return benefits to others in the community.
- Family traditions.
- Enjoyment of socializing with others having similar interests.
- Learning new things, getting new experiences.
- Giving in remembrance of a loved one.

An approach that would be successful with one of these groups may be quite different from another. Any such segmentation should be internally compatible with the organization's values and externally distinguished from other segments. Research on each segment will provide information about the distinctive concerns, motivators, interests, and preferred methods of communication. Focus groups are one way of conducting such research, as are individual interviews with leading representatives of each segment.

Exercise

Interview a leader of a nonprofit and ask about the categories of its stakeholders and how their diversity shapes the organization's approaches to engaging them and building support.

Discussion

What benefits have you received from volunteering in a nonprofit activity? What could the sponsoring organization have done to improve those benefits?

The Four P's of Marketing

A nonprofit organization must be able to use the basic steps of marketing to design programs that engage its stakeholders. It must take into account many of the same factors that corporations do: defining their products, programs, or services and deciding on pricing, placement, and promotion. What are the services of your favorite nonprofit organization? Whether they are defined as service programs, information and referrals, education, or art exhibits, these are the nonprofit's equivalent of a business's products. They result from the application of resources and personnel to produce a public benefit. The principal marketing question here centers on how the organization wants to have its work portrayed to and understood by its stakeholders. For example, most United Way campaigns feature children and senior citizens in their advertising, public information spots, and annual reports. Symphony orchestras might focus on the personality of the conductor, who often is the public face and voice of the orchestra. Or it might show the members of the orchestra inspiring young students to practice in pursuit of their dreams.

Pricing for nonprofits does not mean a manufacturer's suggested retail price. Instead, it refers to all those costs a stakeholder group incurs when responding to the organization and obtaining the desired benefits. A consumer may have to invest time and money in transportation to reach the organization and its services. Some nonprofits charge a fee for their services. A donor must invest time in hearing an appeal for a gift and in making it, as well as the amount of the gift itself. A volunteer gives time and energy. A staff member may have invested in higher education to qualify for an open position, and a community may have to forgo property tax assessments on a nonprofit organization. The organization hopes to minimize its costs to all its stakeholders and maximize the benefits in order to attract their participation. Low costs and high efficiency with resources encourage people to become engaged and stay with the organization.

Placement refers to decisions about the location where the organization's services or activities are made available. This can be a building, a network, a delivery partner, direct contact with a person, or something else. Many service organizations find space in large shopping malls to distribute information or provide various health screenings. Art museums often have traveling displays as part of their outreach efforts. A homeless shelter or soup kitchen must have a specific location that is easily accessible to those needing its services. Deciding on where to place a service should take into account the convenience to the intended consumers, such as choosing a building near bus lines. Likewise, convenience of participation by donors will require ready contact via telephone, e-mail, or personal contacts.

These components contribute to the *promotion* strategy for the organization. A *promotion strategy* is all those steps the organization will undertake to ensure that its targeted groups are well informed about its programs or services and are attracted to them. These may be public service announcements on local radio and television stations, endorsements by widely known and respected public figures, brochures in places where people will readily see them, newspaper advertisements about programs and their availability, speeches by leaders of the organization to civic clubs and other community meetings, and repeated references to the organization's Web site. Websites are rapidly becoming an essential medium for promoting organizations' programs, activities, and donation opportunities. For an example, to see an effective Web site where programs and opportunities for giving are skillfully promoted and integrated, visit www.heifer.org.

An increasingly important way to promote an organization is branding. *Branding* is the use of symbols to pull together the collection of messages and public perceptions of an organization in a way that quickly conveys its value and importance to stakeholders. It is intended to build its target audiences' recognition of and trust in the organization. Everybody recognizes McDonald's arches. Another nonprofit organization with an effective brand is the YMCA, using the capital letter Y with a small triangle on the upper right. The large red cross is another well-known organizational symbol. Many universities are working hard to make their brands (often featuring their sports mascots) widely known. An easily recognizable and valued brand is useful in cutting through the clutter of messages bombarding us every day. It reminds us of a specific organization, not just a category of service activities or type of consumer. It reduces the time we need to decide which organization holds our interest and expresses our values. The brand's strength contributes to an organization's competitive advantage, nurtures public trust, and sustains the engagement of its stakeholders.

Effective Media Relations

Nonprofit leaders should develop an organization-wide media relations plan so that the appropriate people can work with the media to reach the desired goals. Connections with the community often are made through print, broadcast, and electronic media. Direct relationships with key representatives are essential to getting out the organization's intended messages. Such relationships can be productive or lead to disasters. Few organizations today can escape reporters' watchful eyes, so to use such scrutiny constructively, the organization must have a plan and gain experience in dealing with media representatives. Not all encounters need to be journalists with cameras catching a person at his or her worst moment.

Finding ways to get through the clutter of information directed at us in the media is a challenge, so tailoring messages and using media effectively are important to nonprofit organizations. An important maxim of effective media relations and public image is that it takes a long time to build a positive community reputation, but a much shorter time to lose it.

An essential skill for any nonprofit leader is knowing how to build positive relationships with the media to reach specific stakeholder groups and the general public. Paid advertising is often a weak form of communication, whereas favorable feature stories and editorials are often much more effective in building public awareness. Press releases can inform media representatives of news that the nonprofit hopes they will pick up and use. Issues or topics that appeal to different audiences should be specifically designed for the particular media used by that target group.

The following are some important skills for working effectively with the media:

Make a list. Find out all the media outlets that are available in your community as well as those farther away. Then choose those focusing on the specific market segments or audiences you want to reach. Consumers and donors are likely to listen to different radio stations and read different newspapers and magazines. Select those media outlets and tailor public awareness messages for each of your intended audiences.

Meet media leaders. Get to know the publishers, editors and reporters, and also their fax and cell phone numbers. Ask them for their guidelines on how they want you to submit material so that it meets their requirements and deadlines.

Help the media. Develop material in the ways and formats that each organization requires. Do not send general announcements to all of them. For example, newspaper articles and public service ads on radio stations require very different formats in style and content. Be aware of their lead times and other requirements.

Avoid jargon. Every organization, profession, and government agency has its own acronyms and initials. Although these may be understandable to insiders, they generally confuse the public and do not help make your key points. Keep the language understandable to the intended audience.

Personalize the message. One good personal story illustrates a point more effectively than does a rigorous program evaluation research paper with numerous charts, tables, and graphs. If you have to cite statistics, keep them simple and relevant to the main point of your message. If you think a reporter might miss the details, have fact sheets available.

Send press releases. Press reports can be released regularly but must conform to the style requirements of each newspaper. Someone should be responsible for obtaining feedback on its usefulness to the reporter writing the story. Although event announcements are important to any organization, what happens at the event or as a result of it is the media story. One problem is that the public may not find out about the program until after it is over, so get the word out well in advance. Likewise, assume that everything you write and say is *on the record.* This includes e-mail messages.

Return telephone calls. If a reporter calls, respond as quickly as you can. Even if you need to end a call before it is complete, promise to call back with more information by an agreed-upon time. Your credibility and trustworthiness are on the line.

Give advance notice. If you are inviting members of the press to an event, let them know well in advance everything they will need to know to participate. This is especially true when photo opportunities are planned.

Know media schedules. The Saturday and Sunday (usually slow news days) editions of newspapers often publish material that they may not use on workdays. Television and radio have different cycles. If you can tailor a public service announcement to their timing requirements, this can become a valued part of a public relations program.

Prepare fact sheets. Be sure to have a handout of names, titles, major achievements, hometowns, and other important information about anyone you want to be included in a story.

Self-promotion is acceptable. Within limits, there is nothing wrong with promoting the good work done by your organization and its members. Media representatives will choose those promotions that they believe their readers will enjoy.

Avoid "no comment." Perhaps it is a sign of the times, but "no comment" has come to imply that someone is hiding something, been caught doing something wrong, or is in an embarrassing situation. If you cannot discuss an issue, explain why you cannot. Or respond to the question with an answer to one that you wish had been asked.

Keep responses short. Emphasize the main point you want to make. If your answer requires more than a few sentences, try a different approach. The longer you discuss an issue or the more details you offer, the greater will be the risk of losing the reporter and therefore the reader or listener.

Refer to individual successes. Testimonials are effective. You have the information, so share individual narratives with a reporter. Think of it as laying a trail of bread crumbs for the media to a good story.

Train staff. Some organizations may have dozens of people who might receive calls from representatives of the media, so they need advance preparation on how to respond. After all, to the public, the source personifies the nonprofit organization. Therefore, the relevant staff members must be prepared, personable, and well informed. Many nonprofits require that all media communications be channeled through the one person in the organization who is best prepared to deal with them.

End with an action step for the reader. An important purpose of getting the media's attention is that it will lead to actions that benefit the organization. So conclude with the steps you want the readers or listeners to take. Buy your tickets at location X. For more information about the event, call this person at this number. Send your check to this person at this address.

Feedback and evaluation are essential to improvement. Watching the ways in which media use (or do not use) material from nonprofit organizations is one way to learn how to improve such efforts. Much more productive, however, are direct calls to media representatives who have used the material from the nonprofit, asking for their advice on how to improve such efforts in the future.

Exercise

Interview nonprofit leaders and ask them how they deal effectively with the media. What has worked well for them? What has not? What lessons have they drawn from their experiences?

LOBBYING AND ADVOCACY

Nonprofit organizations can and should lobby. It isn't difficult. It isn't mysterious. It isn't expensive. It is not an unnatural act. It is a responsibility to those we serve and support, and it is a proper role for nonprofits.

—*Ron Cretaro, Executive Director, Connecticut Association of Nonprofits and Marcia Avner, Director of Public Policy, Minnesota Council of Nonprofits*

Public education and advocacy are key components of many nonprofit organizations' activities. They try to generate support for changes in laws, policies, regulations, and appropriations in ways that help their consumers and programs. Advocacy and lobbying activities must be carefully planned to meet the often-changing federal and state rules and regulations that govern such efforts. Because partisan political action almost always violates both the letter and the spirit of the prohibitions, nonprofit organizations should not endorse candidates for public political office. Individual employees can donate their own energy and money to help elect the candidates of their choice, but they should not do so on the nonprofit organization's time, use its services and facilities, or appear to speak for the organization. In addition, the nonprofit's top management and board should refrain from endorsing a candidate for elected office. But if their advocacy focuses on public education, policy or regulatory changes, governmental roles and responsibilities, or other issues of interest to the public, nonprofits can be effective forces for community change.

One important place to start when dealing with your elected officials is to figure out where they stand on issues of concern to your organization. This may not be as easy as it sounds. Whether in your local community or on the county, state, or national level, nonprofits can engage with members of all three branches of government. Elected officials must remain responsive to their constituents, and government departments usually are required to hold public hearings on regulatory actions, proposals, and modifications. In many municipalities, commissioners and judges must stand for election and thus can be educated on the issues.

Information about the views of those in positions to influence policy changes reveals the forces in the community that are aligned for and against the nonprofit organization's interests. Some people are passionate *advocates* for the organization's programs and services. Sometimes referred to as *champions*, these core supporters can be counted on to help in many tangible ways. They can work on fund-raising campaigns, speak at meetings, and connect your leadership to the right people in the public sector. They must be cultivated, educated, and recognized as needed and appropriate.

A middle group represents the *undecided* public officials. These may be legislators, county commissioners, executive branch heads, and senior staff. Their decisions and perspectives will eventually have a direct impact on your nonprofit. Complementary approaches should be tailored to those who need to be persuaded. Information is almost always a necessary part of the approach. While some people are persuaded by data and research findings, others would prefer the anecdote that shows how a person or a family was affected by a rule, law, or policy. While the nonprofit can certainly approach the undecideds on its own, it generally is wiser to meet personally with an ally.

Unfortunately, there will always be the *opponents*. It makes a huge difference if an opponent is against the values and principles of your services and programs or is resisting a specific issue. For example, if an official thinks that schoolchildren should be exposed to the arts, extensive statistics or research on the costs of these services is unlikely to change his vote. But that same official might be persuaded that it is appropriate for public schools to charge a fee for transportation to a museum. If that same official were passionate about the need for better highways, then few arguments would persuade a change in her position to support lower gasoline taxes to help the poor. And all these issues might be wrapped into the same legislative proposal.

Whether it is worthwhile to try to contact and discuss issues with hardcore opponents is a judgment call. Some people believe that it is a waste of time and energy that could backfire. Perhaps it is better to use your limited time and resources to build support and strengthen your existing supporters and to persuade those still undecided about your issue.

If a nonprofit organization is skilled enough, providing testimony at public hearings and submitting written materials can be effective both directly and indirectly. Expert testimony can be persuasive and can lead to local media coverage. If testimony is not an option, staff members can use the facts, current materials, and policy alternatives to inform and persuade the undecideds.

In order to be effective, the leaders of nonprofit organizations must know what their goals are as well as what they will settle for. Since the policymakers and the executive branch usually have to make compromises, few ever get all they ask for, want, or demand. It is acceptable to oppose a specific idea or proposal, but it is always more productive to present workable alternatives.

A central question facing nonprofits whose leaders want to become effective advocates and lobby for issues pertaining to their clients, services, staff, and programs is how to do so in ways that comply with the IRS's requirements. Section 501 (c) 3 defines two alternatives: the expenditure test (section 501h) or the substantial part test. Recently, the IRS has encouraged nonprofits to use the expenditure test rules. (For current information, see http://www.irs.gov/pub/irs-pdf/f5768.pdf.) In simple terms, the IRS allows a nonprofit to spend limited funds on these activities. There is a formula for figuring allowable amounts to be used and penalties for overspending these limits as well as for underreporting. It is advisable to consult with appropriate counsel on all these matters to make sure that the organization's planned activities comply with federal, state, and local laws; reporting requirements; ethics commission mandates; and other regulations.

Partnerships

Leaders of nonprofits should cultivate and refine their abilities to negotiate and work collaboratively with other organizations to meet their desired goals. Many nonprofit organizations find it helpful to develop formal partnerships with others in order to fulfill their missions. No one organization can meet all the needs of an entire community. In the 1990s the number of national public/private partnerships increased rapidly. Part of the reason was the greater demand of federal and state departments to use their funds most efficiently for the greatest public benefit. The higher number of partnerships also reflects the reality that advocacy, human services, and the arts depend on many others for success.

A growing practice in the field is to form partnerships with businesses. Called *cause-related marketing*, these are alliances between a nonprofit and a business to develop and offer a service that benefits both partners. Businesses want to be perceived as being good citizens in the community, and nonprofits can show them how to do that. For example, in several communities, nonprofits have asked restaurants to offer a small portion of their net returns on a special day to the nonprofit, and in return the nonprofit will publicize the event and contact its participants and friends to urge them to patronize that restaurant on the designated evening. One large chain of bookstores contributes to literacy programs in return for free advertising on their printed program materials. Several years ago, American Express launched a fund-raising campaign to support the foundation that was restoring the Statue of Liberty.

Or such partnerships may be an alliance of nonprofit organizations themselves to reach goals that each could not achieve alone. For example, symphony orchestras now spend about 15 percent of their budgets on educational outreach programs to schools in rural areas and inner cities. These programs include musicians-in-residence, individualized lessons, after-school concerts, and instruments for talented youth. They do not replace the school system's music or band curriculum instruction; rather, they augment these in a highly professional manner. The orchestra, school, students, and community all benefit as a result.

Partnerships between any two organizations can strengthen the impacts of each. In an alliance between a nonprofit and a business, the nonprofit gains by receiving more financial support. Partnering with a respected corporation can increase the public's trust in the nonprofit and lead to more contributions. Conversely, the risks of such efforts are having the corporate partner exploit the nonprofit and diminish its public trust. Public attitudes toward the company then may change, harming its nonprofit partner as well. The business may discontinue its support with little warning. Since the nonprofit is usually the financially weaker of the pair, it may be used by the stronger business in ways it did not foresee. Such partnerships may damage public credibility if they are perceived as compromising the nonprofit's objectivity.

From the company's perspective, partnering with a nonprofit may enhance the company's reputation and strengthen its trustworthiness, and thus sales, in the community. Partnering can improve the recruitment and retention of employees and may offer opportunities for staff members to extend their skills. Many companies encourage their employees to expand their involvement in the community by volunteering in local nonprofits.

The disadvantages of such partnerships from the company's perspective are declining public perceptions of the nonprofit which, by association, also can hurt the company. Embarrassing publicity about the nonprofit can wipe out positive gains for the partner company. The company's stockholders may see the corporate contributions as supporting causes they do not approve and as lowering net profits that should be divided among them. In tight financial times when staff may receive little or no raises, they may resent having the company's resources go to an outside, nonessential organization.

The Independent Sector developed the following guidelines for nonprofits considering forming partnerships, in which the partners should[8]

1. Have excellent community reputations.
2. Develop mutually acceptable approaches to meet mutual goals.
3. Offer high-quality programs and services with professional staff.
4. Secure needed resources (time, staff, money, space, etc.) to implement the partnership.
5. Define conditions for continuing and for terminating the partnership.

Discussion

Identify and describe a collaborative project between two or more nonprofit organizations. Ask the leaders about the benefits for each partner in the project. What challenges did they encounter, and how did they handle them? What advice would they offer to other nonprofits considering collaborative projects?

In conclusion, nonprofit organizations depend on outside support to carry out their programs and services. Positive relationships with many segments of the community are vital to success. Demonstrating how the organization is benefiting the community is an essential part of the reciprocal relationship between the organization and its stakeholders. Nonprofits should design their programs in ways that are responsive to the interests and concerns of those stakeholders. Maximizing the benefits of engagement with the nonprofit and minimizing the costs to them are the ingredients of good community relations. Skillful use of the media also is important to increasing public awareness of the organization. Partnerships with other organizations can improve community benefits, but entering into them should begin with clearly stated goals and expectations for each partner and include limitations on their use of each other.

Case for Discussion

Bike Morgan is a small nonprofit in Morgan City, a midsize city that is dominated by Morgan State University. About ten years ago, several members of the faculty, staff, and students came together to press the university to include bicycle lanes when it repaved and relined the streets in the campus. Having had some success there, the group decided to form a nonprofit organization and extend its attention to the county commission for the same purpose. The organization continues to be run by a small group of volunteers from around the campus. Modest dues allow it to conduct studies of alternative transportation issues for use in lobbying the county commissioners. After a few notable successes in getting bike lanes added to some city streets, it lost a major recent battle with Morgan City merchants who saw narrowing auto lanes to allow space for bike lanes as impeding traffic and delaying customers' access to their downtown stores.

The six volunteer board members do all the work of the organization, with each person taking on a project. For example, one member organizes and leads an annual "Tour de Sprawl," in which community members are invited to ride their bicycles as a group to see some of the rapid growth of suburbs. Another heads up a project to rehabilitate old bikes donated by members and by the police (stolen and abandoned bikes). Everyone feels burned out and frustrated by limited participation in these projects by people in the community. They wish they could generate more interest in their projects but do not know how to do that.

Questions for discussion:

1. Who are the stakeholders in this organization?

2. What segments of Morgan City are not involved?

3. How might the organization learn more about the interests of people in those publics?

4. Name three public segments, and figure out how the people in them would view this organization and its projects.

5. What other approaches to its mission might the organization consider that may make it more attractive to people in those groups?

12

Principles and Practices
of Effective Fund-Raising

While some people would prefer not to discuss financial matters outside the privacy of their own home, money nonetheless drives nonprofit organizations. This chapter focuses on how to get the results needed to continue offering quality programs and services. By reading this chapter, participants will learn how

1. To describe different revenue and income streams.
2. To write grant proposals to public and private organizations.
3. To ask donors to increase their philanthropic generosity.
4. To identify the essential ingredients for successful annual campaigns.
5. To cultivate major donors.
6. To take care of all resources, no matter their source.

This chapter identifies the main principles for nonprofit leaders to raise funds from individuals, government, corporations, and foundations to support needed activities.

The Center for Effective Philanthropy reports that concerned residents in the United States donate billions of dollars each year to nonprofit organizations.[1] In fact, even a huge tsunami, devastating hurricanes, and earthquakes in 2005 did not overwhelm people's willingness to help. Despite the extensive attention of the media, donations for tsunami relief accounted for less that one-half of 1 percent of all donations that year. Much more went to other causes, disproving the notion of "donor fatigue." Planning their fund-raising from all sources makes a significant difference to most nonprofit organizations.

In 2004, donations to nonprofit organizations in the United States reached almost $259 billion, the highest on record until then, according to Giving USA Foundation.[2] The 2005 data showed that another record was set in the following year. Religious organizations are the primary recipient of the U.S. largesse (almost $80 billion in 2004), followed by education programs ($34 billion). Of special note to nonprofit organizations of all sizes and missions, more than $190 billion of the total (75%) comes from individual donors and fees for services, not from philanthropic foundations.

Charity does truly begin at home. Since about 80 percent of Americans give to at least one charity, there is a donor pool in every community. The organization's goal is to make friends to raise funds. Increasingly, nonprofit organizations depend on these funds as other sources of revenue decline or fail to keep up with inflation. Even the major government programs such as Medicare and Medicaid have dropped in real dollar terms over the past several decades, and these trends show no sign of reversal.

The marketplace for nonprofits is becoming more competitive, thus requiring new approaches to clients, vendors, supporters, and others who know even less about the organization's mission and programs. Regardless of the nonprofit organization's services, securing its future is a top priority for every board member, leader, manager, volunteer, staff member, client, and stakeholder.

There are many ways that nonprofits get income (see figure 12.1).[3] Some charge user fees for their services, and others generate income from sales of services or materials. Many nonprofits submit grant proposals to governmental departments and private foundations, and many directly solicit gifts from individuals through letters, telephone calls, and face-to-face requests. Many also hold special events, such as banquets, marathons, sports tournaments, or other such activities for which a contribution is expected. Some nonprofits hold joint ventures with private businesses to generate income, while others have for-profit subsidiary businesses. In-kind gifts are another way of generating support, such as asking a computer company to donate its surplus equipment or requesting restaurants to donate unused food to a shelter. Many nonprofits use several of these approaches to raise funds to support their programs.

Figure 12.1
Sources of Nonprofit Organization Income

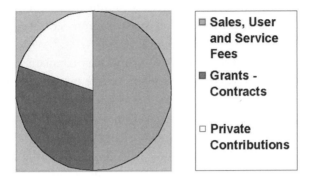

The sources of income for nonprofit organizations have the following characteristics:[4]

1. Fees for services constitute, on average, about 50 percent of their income. Of course, this varies widely, from professional associations that rely almost wholly on membership fees to churches that receive little of their income from fees.
2. Grants and contracts from governmental organizations make up about 30 percent of the income of nonprofits, which usually is restricted to specifically identified projects.
3. Private contributions constitute the remaining 20 percent. These include gifts from individuals (the large majority of contributions) as well as smaller amounts from foundations, corporations, and endowments.

Sales and User Fees

Many nonprofits count on direct sales and fees as sources of income. For example, many museums have entrance fees and gift shops where merchandise related to the exhibits is available for purchase. Job readiness programs contract with local businesses to provide supervised services as part of their training programs, such as those that prepare workers for custodial or food preparation jobs. Professional associations have membership fees. Scout troops sell uniforms, equipment, and supplies. Bake sales are a staple of many PTA groups and others. The profitability of such efforts varies widely, so at least once a year managers should conduct cost-benefit comparisons of several sales efforts.

It is a common assumption in our society that people pay for goods and services that benefit them. Of course, some people have very limited resources, so many organizations use sliding scales for fees, in which charges for more affluent users offset losses from undercharging those with fewer resources.

Nonprofits may also set up for-profit subsidiary companies whose activities are not directly related to their mission. The net gains or profits from such businesses go to the nonprofit as income. Such for-profit subsidiaries are subject to corporate income taxes, just as any other company faces, which is often referred to as unrelated business income tax (UBIT), but the after-tax profits are designated to go to the nonprofit as the sole owner or shareholder of the business. The IRS has specific regulations for such for-profit subsidiary enterprises, so check them carefully before getting involved in such activities.[5]

Market analysis and planning are crucial to the success of any projects that are intended to produce income from sales or user fees. The nonprofit considering undertaking any such project should take time to understand the needs and interests of those it hopes will become its customers. The nonprofit's views of appropriate products or services, fee rates, methods of delivery, and preferred avenues for information are necessary for the planning and operation of all its income-producing ventures.

Grants

Grants from governmental agencies and foundations are another important source of income for some nonprofits. Federal, state, and local governments make grants to nonprofits and also enter into contracts with them to deliver some public services. *Grants* are awards to organizations to carry out projects designed by the nonprofit within broad guidelines from the granting agency, whereas *contracts* are restricted to explicit purposes and actions specified by the grantor. Grants often are made to research or field-test an innovation in service for particular populations. Rarely do grants fund a nonprofit's ongoing operations. Contracts include operational support for only those activities that directly carry out the granting agency's purposes for a specific period of time. Proposals are expected to define a new service or activity or to extend or modify a successful program. Generally, the organization's core budget is expected to fund its base programs.

Sometimes governments and businesses give money to nonprofits that agree to carry out specified activities deemed valuable by the sponsor. Examples are local community development block grants that support local services for the poor or a corporate gift to expand a sports program for youth.

Information about public grants and contracts often is readily available through public notices and Web sites. To find such information, search the Web sites of funding organizations to learn about their priorities, availability of funds, requirements, and application procedures. Information about contracts with local governments, such as community development block grants, is best obtained from personal contacts at local governmental offices.

Some examples of Web sites providing information on public grants at the national level are

Catalog of Federal Domestic Assistance: www.cfda.gov
Centers for Disease Control and Prevention: www.cdc.gov/funding.htm
National Institutes of Health: www.nih.gov
Substance Abuse and Mental Health Services Administration: www.samhsa.gov
U.S. Department of Education: www.ed.gov
U.S. Department of Health and Human Services: www.hhs.gov
U.S. Department of Justice: www.usdoj.gov
U.S. Environmental Protection Agency: www.epa.gov/ogd

Web Assignment

Go to several of the Web sites just listed and search for grant opportunities that you think could serve a specific population group in your hometown or county. Write a project abstract of less than 250 words addressing a priority of the grantmaker. Be sure to state what is distinctive about what you propose to accomplish with the funds.

Nonprofit managers and interested staff members need to search actively among the numerous sources of information about grant and contract possibilities to find those that fit their organization's mission and goals. Competition is intense for these funds, so careful preparation of proposals is essential (discussed more extensively later in this chapter). Telephone or personal contacts with the granting officers overseeing the programs to which you are applying are excellent ways to learn more about the grantmaker's priorities and expectations, thus leading to a more targeted, stronger proposal. Make sure you carefully follow the guidelines provided by the granting officer. Good writing skills and rigorous compliance with the often highly specific forms and application procedures are necessary. Since the grantmakers receive so many applications, the reader generally stops reading when any type of non-compliance is spotted, so follow the rules. It usually helps to add letters of support specifically for your proposal from people in positions of leadership, particularly public officials who may influence the granting organizations.

Foundations

There are several types of foundations of which the grant seeker should be aware before approaching any of them.[6] First are the *independent foundations*, which may be private (whose capital is contributed by a single individual, such as the Ford Foundation) or public (whose capital is contributed by many individuals, such as the Good Samaritan Foundation). Most of these foundations accept unsolicited proposals, but a few restrict their grants to organizations that they have specifically asked to apply. This information is usually available on their Web sites and in printed materials.

Next are the *corporate foundations*, which are established by businesses to handle their philanthropy by channeling them outside their usual business operations. There are several thousand such foundations, including ones set up by companies such as IBM, AT&T, Home Depot, and SunTrust Bank. Some of these offer in-kind gifts; others make grants only in communities where they have branch offices or stores.[7]

Community foundations receive gifts from many individuals but restrict their grants to nonprofits within an identified geographic region. Finally are the *operating foundations*, which channel endowment income to specifically identified nonprofits. Operating foundations do not accept applications from organizations not on that list.

No less than in individual solicitations, personal cultivation is essential when seeking grants or contracts from any source. People give money to people, not to paper. Finding out the interests and priorities of a granting agency's officers is the first step. Those organizations often make the first level of screening easy by publishing statements about their funding priorities and restrictions as well as the procedures needed to submit an application. The Web sites of many foundation offices are great sources of information about what they are interested in funding. Do not overlook the necessary early step:

getting to know someone in the office, talking with him or her, finding out directly about the organization's interests and priorities, and letting the contact know about yours. Often success at later stages of the grant-getting process depends on a favorable word on your behalf by the grant officer with whom you talked earlier.

Fortunately for the grant seeker, many foundations are members of a national association, the Foundation Center. This organization serves foundations in a variety of ways, not the least of which is to help reduce the volume of grant proposals that fall outside the funding interests of a member foundation. The Foundation Center has branch libraries in many larger cities, where many research resources are readily available, along with guidance on preparing effective grant proposals. The center also publishes a directory of foundations that lists their funding priorities and contact information. It has a national Web site (www.fdncenter.org) that provides an electronic search resource for grant seekers to identify foundations that make grants in the areas represented by the search words the user enters. Entering a term like *music*, *environment*, or *children* quickly leads to a list of foundations that have the same word in their statement of priorities. The Web sites for those foundations are linked, making it easy for the user to click on a specific foundation's Web site for more information about funding priorities, contact information, and instructions on how to apply. Another good source of information about foundations is www.guidestar.org, which gives direct access to the financial reports that every nonprofit must file annually with the IRS.

When you think you may have identified a funding source whose interests match those of your organization, get in touch with the person identified on their Web site for initial contact. This will enable you to get more detailed information about the foundation's priorities, discuss areas of match or mismatch between that organization and your own, begin building name recognition, and start a relationship between you and this person. Ask for further information about how the foundation wants to receive grant proposals, in what format, and by what deadline. Ask how you should show your budget and what expenses are allowable, including how to treat the project's administrative or overhead costs.

Be sure to do your homework in advance of this conversation, and make sure you understand what the organization already says about itself, so you do not waste time or show that you have not taken the time to read the information already available. During the conversation, take careful notes so you can return to your colleagues with useful details about how to proceed. Sometimes foundations want a brief summary letter in advance to which its staff can respond, whereas others want proposals in specific formats, lengths, and components. Some require that proposals come to them along with the completed forms or outlines they already have available online. In every case, send a handwritten thank-you note to the person with whom you talked.

Preparing Grant Proposals

Grant proposals can take many shapes. Despite the many guidebooks available promising to enable you to win grants, it is far more important that your document comply with the guidelines that you obtain directly from the potential funding source. The typical grant application package should include the following components.[8]

- Cover letter.
- Title page, including the nonprofit's contact information, name of the project, and the organization to which it is addressed. For more lengthy proposals, add a table of contents.
- Executive summary.
- Statement of need or purpose for which the grant is sought and the goals the project will achieve.
- Description of major project activities and an evaluation process. This section should be action oriented and explain exactly how the organization will meet the goals defined earlier in the proposal.
- Budget and explanations.
- A description of the organization and what it has accomplished that provide evidence of its abilities to carry out the proposed project. No one wants a helpful program to raise expectations and then to end at the conclusion of the grant period. Is there a way to build in a mechanism for continuing in the organization or in partnership with others?
- A concluding paragraph summarizing the major points.
- Appendices, including letters of support from leaders with name recognition in the field.

The following are suggestions to help clarify the process of developing and writing successful proposals:

1. Sort out your thoughts and write a detailed outline.
2. Compare the outline against the specific issues expected by the grantmaker and modify it accordingly.

3. Write a compelling and persuasive proposal without overstating your case. Avoid internal jargon by writing simply and clearly.
4. Edit and revise your proposal to ensure maximum impact and compliance with any page limits.
5. Seek feedback on your draft proposal from someone who has not been a part of the conversation to help identify topics or aspects that need further attention.

Your cover letter should refer to any prior contacts between your organization and the funder. It should briefly describe what is in the proposal and specify the amount of money requested. It should indicate that other material will be provided on request, such as annual reports, and offer to answer any questions or meet to address them in person. The top officer of your organization should sign the letter.

The title page should list the name of the project, to whom and from whom the proposal is submitted, the date, and contact information. The executive summary is a one-page umbrella statement of the case for the project, including the problem to be addressed, the solution offered for solving it, the organization's funding requirements, and the expertise of the organization needed to complete the project successfully.

The statement of need and purpose should answer the basic question of why this project is necessary and worthy of support. You may want to include statistics to support the importance of the issue, such as current examples showing that attaining the goals of the project is possible and how these outcomes will affect people's lives. The distinctive elements of the project should be noted as well as its utility as a resource or model for others.

The project description builds on the stated goals and shows how they will be achieved. The major components and steps should be described, followed by a table giving time lines for the completion of each element. The description should identify who will carry out the project, what each one will do, how progress will be monitored and evaluated, and how the effort will be sustained in the future after the grant is terminated. Every proposal must contain an evaluation component, specifying what services or programs will be offered and how the differences or impacts they will have on the recipients will be measured (see chapter 13 for more on evaluation).

The budget should begin by specifying who will be responsible for completing each part of the project, the amount of time each person will require to do that, and the salaries of those individuals plus the costs of fringe benefits. If consultants or outside experts are to be involved, they should be listed separately, along with the time and costs for each. If any staff will work on the project at no charge to the grant, be sure to estimate the value of each as in-kind contributions by the organization. All these personnel costs should be added up to summarize this component of the budget.

After this, detail all nonpersonnel costs, such as travel expenses, workspace, utilities, supplies, and equipment. They must be directly related to the project, and some funders require justifications for the items in this category.. These nonpersonnel costs should then be summarized. Add the allowable administrative or overhead charges (10% to 25% of direct costs may be allowed by some foundations, but public funders may accept higher amounts). Then add up all personnel, nonpersonnel, and overhead costs to arrive at the project's total cost.

The section that offers information about the applicant organization should provide a brief overview of its mission and purposes, date of establishment, its current structure and programs, areas of special expertise in the organization, officers, and information about its board. It should include information about the audience(s) served by the organization and summaries of recent accomplishments that are relevant to the proposed project and demonstrate its capacity to deliver what is promised.

The appendix may include the names and titles of board members, a copy of the IRS letter granting the organization's tax-exempt status, the most recent annual report, a copy of the organization's current budget and most recent IRS Form 990, résumés of people to be involved in the project, and letters of support.

Fund-Raising with Individuals

Philanthropy begins when a donor believes in an organization's mission, programs and services, although this is not enough to secure a steady stream of contributions. Accordingly, a nonprofit organization must carefully define its relevant stakeholders and frame its appeals in ways that attract them.

The vast majority of contributed income for nonprofits comes from private individuals, and about 80 percent of all Americans contribute to some type of nonprofit organization.[9] Clearly, obtaining smaller gifts from many people is important, but nonetheless, about 90 percent of donations come from 10 percent of the givers. You can ask one million people for a dollar each, or you can ask one hundred people for $10,000 and come out with the same total. Going for larger gifts from fewer people is more practical and feasible. The Internet provides useful research tools for looking for these big givers, but the best route is to ask people we know about those whom they know who may be interested in our mission and have the means to make substantial gifts. Of course, donors of smaller amounts should not be overlooked. Networks of personal relationships are essential to identifying potential givers and to cultivating their awareness of your organization and interest in becoming involved with it.

People give to an organization whose values they share and whose purposes they support. They recognize that we should work together to address a purpose that benefits others. Whether that purpose is improving the environment or providing recreational opportunities for children, we know that shared efforts accomplish more than we can do alone. We volunteer our time and money when someone we trust invites us to become involved in a cause we care about. Building that trust takes time; sustaining it requires faithfulness to the purposes we intended to advance. It is no surprise that religious organizations are the most popular beneficiary of individual donations. Moreover, people who give to one nonprofit are quite likely to give to others, provided they are doing work valued by the donor.

Why Do People Give?

The reason most often cited by donors is that they give because they were asked. When asked for further elaboration, most people say, "Because *I was asked to give by someone I trust for a cause that I believe in.*" Other motivations mentioned are the sense of obligation to help those with less, the satisfactions from giving, religious beliefs, family philanthropic traditions, benefits to the community, and gifts in remembrance of a loved one.[10] The cultivation process is learning what motivates specific individuals to give and then providing them an opportunity to contribute through a specific invitation to give. Additional reasons offered by respondents to a survey of their motivations for giving are (in descending frequency) as follows:

"I believe that those with more resources should help those with less."
"I get personal satisfaction from giving."
"I donate because of my religious beliefs or commitments."
"I feel that I benefit when I help others."
"Giving is a tradition in my family."
"Giving sets a good example for others."

"Giving helps my community."

"I gave in remembrance of a loved one."

"My gift is tax deductible."

"Giving is encouraged by my employer."

Another study of donors identified seven types of motivations:[11]

1. Communitarians: "I give to help my community."
2. Religious: "I give because of my faith."
3. Investors: "I give for tax reductions."
4. Socialites: "I enjoy being engaged socially with worthwhile projects."
5. Repayers: "Someone helped me, so I want to help others."
6. Altruists: "This program is consistent with my beliefs and values."
7. Dynasts: "Our family has always been involved with organizations like this."

People give to nonprofits because they want to, because they are asked to do so, and because they find organizations that meet their motivations. They want to know they are making a positive difference in and impact on the community. They give money to people, not to organizations, and certainly not to make up for deficits. Fund-raisers must take the time to learn about each potential donor's interests and match them with specific organizational goals to improve benefits for the recipients of its service.

Nonprofit organizations must sustain themselves by seeking out a number of sources of support and persuading them to become involved with and provide support for the organization's programs. Fund-raising efforts must provide a persuasive case—in terms the prospective donor understands—about why the donor should become engaged with them and donate money to carry out a mutually valued activity.

Support cannot be taken for granted, and it is pointless to whine, "Why don't people recognize the importance of what we are trying to do and just give us the money to do it?" Support must be earned through hard work, demonstrating clearly what the organization is doing, how it benefits the community, how it links with the values of the potential sponsors, how they can become meaningfully involved in acting on shared values, and how they can help achieve beneficial results (not just give away money). Support is offering a persuasive case for involvement and investing the needed time communicating that to others. Honesty, openness, credibility, trustworthiness, and accountability all are required. Such relationships take years to nurture but may be undermined in a moment by poor performance. As in many other parts of life, having some social skills and extrovert tendencies are great resources for building networks of positive relationships.[12]

The stars of every nonprofit organization are its donors. They are the best friends the organization can have. Developing, retaining, and extending its relationships are the primary responsibilities of everyone in the organization. Donors' motivations may vary, so the fund-raisers must seek ways to present the organization's work in terms that are inviting and persuasive to them. These relationships are the lifeblood of every nonprofit. Chief executive officers and board members should establish and regularly use the organization's development committee. The committee could be made up of members who are seen as advocates for the organization and who are willing to fulfill that role in the community. Not only does this committee guide the fund-raising efforts, but it also can help recruit the next generation of leaders for the organization. Professional resources for fund-raisers may be found at www.afpnet.org.

Whatever the method, getting income from any source requires cultivating good relationships with them and building credibility for your organization. Many *fund*-raisers emphasize that the whole process is really *friend*-raising, or establishing good relationships between the organization and those whose support it.

Every nonprofit needs friends to survive. The concerns, values, viewpoints, and interests of other people are crucial to its success, and nonprofits have to spend a great deal of time talking with people to find and cultivate those whose values and concerns overlap with theirs. Most people working in nonprofit organizations are focused on the consumers of the organizations' services, clients, or recipients. In addition, there is another constituency with which they have to operate—those whose gifts make the organization's survival possible. These are the donors and volunteers who support the organization and help it operate. Sometimes the two constituencies overlap, such as in a membership association whose members' dues make it possible for the association to deliver its services to them. Most often, however, the two groups, consumers and supporters, do not overlap, such as in a homeless shelter or soup kitchen.

Leaders of every nonprofit must talk with many, many people in order to find those whose concerns overlap those of the organization. They want to find those people, either individuals or grantmakers, who are interested in its mission, and they must find ways to inform them about this organization in terms that make sense to them.

Building reciprocal relationships is central to success, so donors must feel that they are getting something from the nonprofit that they want. This may be the sense of satisfaction that they are helping support actions that express their own beliefs and values. It may be opportunities to be with others they respect or opportunities for public recognition for their contributions. Different things motivate different people, and the organization's job is to find out what they value and how it can help provide it, in exchange for their support. And the organization's leaders have to thank them often and tell them what great things their contributions have helped accomplish.[13]

A Donor's Bill of Rights

1. To be informed of the organization's mission, how the organization intends to use donated resources, and its capacity to use donations effectively for its intended purposes.

2. To know the identity of those serving on the organization's governing board and to expect the board to exercise prudent judgment in its stewardship responsibilities.

3. To have access to the organization's most recent financial statements.

4. To be sure that his or her gift will be used for the purposes for which it is given.

5. To receive appropriate acknowledgment and recognition.

6. To ensure that information about his or her donations is handled with respect and with confidentiality to the extent provided by law.

7. To expect that all relationships with the person representing organizations of interest to the donor will be professional in nature.

8. To be informed whether those seeking donations are volunteers, employees of the organization, or hired solicitors.

9. To have an opportunity to have his or her name deleted from mailing lists that an organization may intend to share.

10. To feel free to ask questions when making a donation and to receive prompt, truthful, and forthright answers.[14]

It never is advisable to contact people cold, without warning or preparation. Funds come from those who have become friends. Therefore, the organization must draw up a list of friends and want-to-be friends. A good rule is to make at least three personal contacts per year before asking for money. These can range from inviting prospective donors to a program, mailing them newsletters, inviting them to an important event, or asking them to work on a committee or sit on an advisory board or a search committee. The range of options is almost limitless; the point to remember is not to ask a total stranger. That approach is as unsuccessful as are the telephone solicitations that come during the dinner hour.

There are numerous ways to find information about potential donors. You may ask people to list prospects, tell you about their backgrounds and interests, and devise strategies to reach them. The top administrators and the board leadership should carefully read through lists of community leaders and pick out those who might donate money. Within ethical guidelines, you may also use public documents and web searches to help set targets for giving, based on their resources and past patterns of philanthropy.

Leaders of nonprofit organizations should regard any gift as the first in an ongoing process, and so they try to establish long-term donor relationships. Some givers can be encouraged to make larger gifts in the future as they become more involved with the organization. The Council of Philanthropy cites a government report that teenagers volunteer at twice the adult rate. After-school and summer programs can be a new and renewable source of volunteers for an organization that is willing to recruit and train these young adults. The benefits and ripple effects can be enormous. Volunteers often become donors, so the next generation of donors should be cultivated early. Everyone has some friends, so the opportunities to contribute and make a difference can be channeled into effective help in the short term and committed donors or fund-raisers in the longer term.

You should begin seeking donations from those who are already involved in the organization, such as board and staff members, volunteers, former service recipients, and alumni. Then you should enlarge the circle by asking whom else they know who might be interested. Find opportunities to talk with people in this expanding group about the organization and its mission, sharing your excitement, and listening for indications of their interest in getting to know more about the organization's mission, services, and needs.

Some people in nonprofit organizations try all sorts of ways to get around this relationship-building process, relying on letters, brochures, videos, and ads. But these impersonal means are far less productive than face-to-face conversations. A big event like a banquet or a small event like a personal letter is never as effective as a simple, direct conversation. There is no substitute for a relationship, no quick and easy way to raise money.

Some people say things like "I'll do anything here except ask for money," claiming to be too busy or not good at asking. But there are no special talents or secrets for raising money apart from ordinary conversations with people you get to know, discussing the values and concerns you both care about. For example, if you genuinely believe that the Girl Scouts organization is an important community resource that helps girls become more successful as they go through school and become young adults, then you should be able to talk easily about that with people you know. If you see a specific opportunity to extend the benefits of scouting, you will naturally want to help it be realized. The first step is making your own contribution, putting your money where your mouth is. Then you will want to invite others to join you in extending the organization's programs and services. You might say to a friend something like, "You know, we've been talking about some of the great things Girl Scouts here are doing. We have an opportunity to offer participation to a group of girls in a low-income part of our community, and I'm excited about that step. I've contributed $100 to support that move and hope you'll consider giving that amount too." No pressure and no arm-twisting, just excitement about a great opportunity to make a difference in the lives of people who will benefit greatly by this support.

Asking becomes easier with practice. Accompanying someone who is already quite comfortable making asks is a good way to get over the anxiety of doing it yourself. It can be quite satisfying to know that you are helping others support a worthwhile cause. Another way that some people get started is by asking people to become volunteers, contributing their time to a specific service program or activity. This enlarges the scope and effectiveness of any nonprofit, and it lays the groundwork for additional forms of involvement, including money. Taking the time to discover people's interests and then trying to match their interests with opportunities are necessary steps before inviting them to help with any specific activity, whether it is volunteering or contributing.

Making the Case for Giving

Before beginning any solicitations, the people in a nonprofit must formulate a clear, persuasive case for giving. Written case statements may be offered to potential donors either before or after conversations with them about the organization and what their contributions will enable it to do. The case statement itself is a brief, clearly written document that communicates the organization's purpose, programs, and financial needs. It should provide a persuasive answer to why you are asking for money and why your organization warrants support. Many nonprofits already have good case statements for the novice to model. The case statement should include both rational and emotional elements, and it can be used to train solicitors to offer consistent information about the organization and specific requests for gifts that allow it to grow.

In no more than two or three pages, an effective case statement should succinctly present the following components:

1. Begin with the why: What is the mission? What is this organization, and why does it exist?
2. Then state the what: What does the organization want to achieve? What is distinctive about that?
3. Then state the how: How will the donor's gift meet this need and help the organization fulfill its mission?
4. Then state who: Who are we, who are our beneficiaries, and how well have we been serving them? Selected data that are clearly presented can illustrate major points.
5. Demonstrate how donors can become involved and why they should. What is in it for them?
6. Describe the particular action that you want the readers or listeners to take. What should they do, and how should they do it? Offer choices about levels of giving and uses to which their donation may be applied.
7. End by offering clear and specific contact information, including a name, address, and telephone number at the organization's site.

The internal process of developing the case statement also can help members of the organization resolve internal differences regarding goals, priorities, and needs. Writing a good statement should involve the board, staff, and volunteers in reaching shared conclusions about its priorities, content, and format. It should focus on the specific needs of those in the community who would benefit from extending the organization's efforts. Finally, the case statement should be externally focused, emphasizing benefits to people in the community and not just asking people to help sustain the organization for its own sake.

The case statement may have longer and shorter forms, and some versions may be tailored to various target audiences. Case statements should not be printed in multicolored ink on expensive, glossy paper, lest the recipient think that the organization already has more than enough resources. Photos, graphs, and tables may be used (but sparingly) to emphasize certain aspects of the message.

Annual Giving

Each year, every nonprofit organization should seek contributions from donors, both individuals and local businesses. This is the foundation for all other forms of fund-raising and provides substantial resources for carrying out the organization's ongoing operations. The purpose of annual campaigns is to acquire new donors, bring back lapsed donors, encourage previous donors to increase their giving levels, strengthen donors' loyalty, and help them become more involved in the organization.[15] The process begins with soliciting those already involved with the organization and then moving outward to others.

Records of annual gifts become an excellent place to find people who might give more money. New donors not well acquainted with the organization are unlikely to make substantial gifts initially. This means that fund-raisers should track the giving records over time and to engage givers more extensively with the organization while monitoring the frequency and magnitude of their gifts. Doing background research on donors and spending time with them to understand their interests are crucial to this cultivation process. Several years of work is required to establish a broad base of predictable annual donors.

As the annual campaign becomes well established, the number and size of gifts tend to take the shape of a pyramid. About a third of the total raised usually comes from the top few sources. Another third comes from the middle-range donors, and the largest number of gifts is small amounts from many people.

There are many ways to approach givers, from personal conversation to impersonal advertising. One extensive study ranked the effectiveness of various fund-raising techniques, from most to least effective:[16]

Personal solicitation.

Personal letter with follow-up telephone call.

Personal telephone call with follow-up letter.

Personal telephone call with no follow-up.

Special fund-raising event.

Direct mail of impersonal form letters.

Door-to-door solicitations.

Sales of products.

Impersonal telemarketing calls.

Media advertising.

Clearly, there is no good substitute for individual conversations. Fund-raisers should take the time to get to know their prospects, beginning with their interests. Some fund-raisers convene focus groups of current donors at each level of giving to get ideas about other possible donors and good ways of approaching them. Giving opportunities should include several levels or amounts sought and several projects or uses of gifts, so donors have choices.

Personal telephone calls can be useful, especially if preceded or followed by a personal letter. Personal conversations can provide useful information about current and prospective donors and are good ways to involve board members and other volunteers. Case statements and coaching are important to ensure consistency in the organization's message.[17]

Although many nonprofits hope to raise money through mail solicitations alone, very few succeed.[18] Letters may reach the largest number of people, but such campaigns often net only slightly more money than was spent to prepare and send the letters. Letters sometimes are useful to remind current donors but seldom persuade them to increase the size of their gifts. Many companies now sell mailing lists of people who have given to similar programs, but compiling one's own list is far more effective, especially if telephone contacts or personal conversations are included in the contacts.

Web Assignment

See if you can find nonprofit organizations that use external consulting firms to handle their annual campaigns. Try the *NonProfit Times* (www.nptimes.com) for information about consulting firms that help nonprofits raise money. Some of them proudly list their clients in marketing materials, and some specialize. Do any of them seem appropriate to your organization? What principles or issues helped you reach this conclusion?

Learning How to Ask

Many people are anxious about asking others for money, so they make up all sorts of excuses for avoiding or delaying it. But an organization's survival requires that at least several people on the board and staff actively solicit money.

Getting ready to ask for gifts begins with understanding the organization, its case for giving, its annual budget, and the costs per customer served. You should know something about the people you are going to solicit, including whether or not they have given in the past and in what amounts. Conversely, they should already have been given opportunities to learn about the organization. You should have some basic information about the prospect's interests and potential size of donation. Be prepared to ask for a specific amount and for a specific purpose. Askers should show enthusiasm about the organization and those it serves, and they should already have made a gift to the organization. A necessary component of any request is inviting another person to join you in a great opportunity to make a difference in this community, making things better for people in need.

With this information at hand, call the prospective donor and arrange a time to meet him or her. Offer to go to the person's office or meet at a mutually agreed-on location, perhaps a restaurant. State in this call your name and role in the organization and that the meeting is to offer more information about the organization and to seek ways to engage that person in its work, including making a gift. Once you are together, briefly repeat the case statement. Ask about the person's interests and listen to his or her responses. Maintain good eye contact, show your enthusiasm, and respond to any questions. Questions are great opportunities to better understand the person's motivations and concerns, and your respectful responses bring you closer to securing a gift.

When you feel that you have established good rapport with this person, then ask for the amount and use that you planned, unless the conversation indicates that a different amount or use would be more appropriate. Don't be afraid to ask for larger amounts, as many people are flattered that you would think they could afford such a large gift. But once you have made your request, be quiet. Don't fill the silence with chatter, and don't offer excuses. Maintain eye contact, and simply wait respectfully for the person to respond. He or she may have more questions or ask about other aspects of the organization or its possible uses of gifts. The potential donor may suggest a different amount than asked. In any case, respond graciously and clearly. If the person agrees to give, thank him or her immediately and make certain you both are clear about the specific steps to follow (for example,

"Shall I take your check now, or would you prefer to send it to our executive directly?") Ask how he or she would like the gift to be recognized.

If the person decides not to give, ask politely for the reasons. This may be an opportunity to clarify misconceptions about the organization or the uses of gifts. Or it may be an opportunity to find out about the person's interests and limitations, leading to the possibility of suggesting different uses of the gift, another amount, or another time.

Regardless of the outcome, write a personal thank-you note to the individual very soon after the meeting. Then make sure that the contact information, amount, purposes, preferred recognition, concerns, possibilities of recontact, and other important facts are entered into a central record of donors. All that information will be useful when preparing for subsequent contacts with that person.

Stewardship of Gifts

Having made a gift is the best predictor of making another gift. Any donation should be seen as the first step in many years of giving. The nonprofit should increase its donors' level of engagement and sustain their trust and involvement. One way to do this is to thank the donor, starting with a simple, handwritten note from the person who obtained the gift and also from the board's chairperson or executive. Finding additional ways to recognize a donor should include asking that person what forms of recognition are preferable. Some people want to see their names in published lists of donors; others prefer personal recognition at an annual event, and still others want to remain anonymous. Make sure the organization knows the donors' preferred forms of recognition and follows them.

Another ingredient of good stewardship is to make sure the gift is used as the donor requested when making it. Periodic letters should go to those who make larger gifts, and newsletters and annual reports can include information about specific projects that givers supported. They should be invited to events, open house receptions, or other occasions where they can be recognized and thanked and learn more about the organization.

Special Events

Many nonprofit organizations raise funds through a variety of events to which the public, as well as current and previous donors, may be invited. Examples are sports events (golf tournaments, marathons), banquets, auctions, or fairs where participants are asked to make contributions to the organization. Often such events cost a great deal of seed money and volunteer time to organize and run, and unfortunately, many of them do not produce net gains for the several years it takes to build a reputation. For that reason, an organization considering starting a new special event may view it as an occasion to build public awareness rather than expecting it to generate much money. Such events can be evaluated to decide which parts worked better than others, so as to improve subsequent events. Managers may invite local business leaders to collaborate in planning and sponsoring the event in return for publicity about the business.

Arguments in support of holding special events are

- Raising the organization's visibility and the public's awareness of it.
- Offering opportunities to identify and begin cultivating new prospects.
- Socializing among members of the board, staff, and volunteers.
- Putting on a fun and memorable event.

Arguments against special events are

- They usually require huge amounts of time, energy, and people and may leave some feeling burned out.
- The rate of financial return usually is disappointing, especially in the early years.

Organizing a special event requires careful planning with realistic goals. So many organizations hold them that the competition for attendance is usually quite strong, so finding some new niche or distinctive appeal is important to attract people to participate. Knowing and building on the interests of your current donor base are crucial to ensure their attendance. You should have contingency plans for everything from bad weather to not enough food. The nonprofit should also supply receipts that differentiate the value of benefits received, such as a banquet meal, from the amount that is a gift directly to the organization for its programs apart from the event. This is a requirement of the tax code for philanthropic contributions.

One important feature, regardless of the type of event or its level of financial success, is to find a way to get the names, addresses, and phone numbers of everyone who attends. Registration and sign-in sheets are useful for this purpose. People who come to the event have thus demonstrated some interest in the organization, on which subsequent contacts may be based. Thank-you notes may be sent to participants. Adding their names to the distribution list for announcements or newsletters is another way to continue cultivating donors. Personal invitations to subsequent events will enhance the relationship. The contact list can extend the database of potential donors who may be contacted at later points in the organization's yearly cycle.

Capital Campaigns and Major Gifts

Efforts to encourage donors to make larger gifts will produce some who emerge as major supporters of the organization. The difference between "ordinary" and "major" gifts varies among organizations. As noted earlier, the range of gift sizes and numbers usually takes a pyramid form. There are many who give small amounts, somewhat fewer who give larger amounts, and even fewer who give the most coveted gifts. Over time, the nonprofit fund-raiser hopes to see some smaller givers make larger gifts. Those who indicate the potential for such upgrading may become the focus of more extensive cultivation.[19]

The organization may decide to involve these larger givers in campaigns to provide capital expansion, such as a new building, the establishment of a new service or branch, or the creation of an endowment fund for the organization's future. Certain major donors should be included in planning such a campaign, and their gifts in an early "quiet phase" will allow the organization to open the formal campaign with encouraging announcements of a substantial percentage of the goal already in hand.

Planned Giving

At the pinnacle of the giving pyramid are those few people who agree to name the organization in their wills or estates. They may simply designate a specific amount to go to the nonprofit, or they may set up a trust that eventually will provide substantial capital to the organization following their own or their dependents' deaths. Such trusts may also be arranged to provide interest income to the nonprofit while the donor is still living. There are several approaches to arranging trusts to benefit family members and nonprofits. The nonprofit leader who anticipates becoming involved in such plans should make sure to consult with an attorney or estate planner with expertise in this field.

In conclusion, people give to people they trust as a way of helping other people. Nonprofit organizations must have supporters to allow them to carry out the programs and services that they want to offer to those who need them. Supporters make their decisions based on relationships and the extent to which the appeal responds to their values and interests. Supporters want to know that their gifts will have an important impact on others in need. It has been said that successful fund-raising is the right person asking the right prospect for the right amount for the right project at the right time and in the right way. Those six "rights" are critical to the success of any fund-raising campaign.

13

Program Evaluation

Chapter 13, "Program Evaluation," describes the components and steps of assessing the impacts of nonprofit programs on their users. The continuing public outcry for greater transparency and accountability means that nonprofits must conduct more open and rigorous self-evaluations or outsiders will do it for them. The thesis of this chapter is that nonprofit organizations should take the initiative in program evaluation and work cooperatively and collaboratively with others. The objectives of this chapter are to enable readers to

1. Understand the uses and benefits of program evaluations in nonprofit organizations.
2. Identify the components and steps of a sound evaluation.
3. Specify a program's goals and ways of measuring them.
4. Understand the basic designs used in evaluations.
5. Apply principles and skills of leadership in planning, conducting, reporting, and using findings to improve an organization's performance.

This chapter examines the tools and procedures for making objective, rational assessments of nonprofit organizations' programs in order to improve their quality, effectiveness, and/or efficiency. These programs or services may cover a wide range of activities intended to help people, such as education, health care, artistic performances, and economic development, or they may try to improve people's lives or change their attitudes. *Program evaluation* is choosing a standard by which to assess actions and then collecting information to see how well the activity is meeting this standard. To collect that information, we may use interviews, questionnaires, observations, focus groups, existing records, and data files.

Standards for everyday evaluations may be intuitive or impulsive or personal opinions, but making them objective and open increases the likelihood of agreeing on the conclusions reached. Credible findings help identify those activities or aspects of programs that need to be changed. Evaluation measures the results of a program against the goals it was intended to achieve. An example of an evaluative study conducted by a nonprofit organization comes from the Big Brothers / Big Sisters of America, which examined a program to strengthen intergenerational relationships in a sample of elementary schools. Parents, volunteers, and teachers reported increases in the participating students' grades in all subjects as well as improvements in their social and emotional growth.[1]

The evidence from evaluations is important to planners, managers, staff, consumers, and sponsors, as they want to know whether their efforts and resources are producing what they are supposed to do. Is this sequence of treatment steps producing the results intended? Is the local high school graduation rate rising as a consequence of this mentoring program? If not, then how can the program be modified so it will become more effective?

Considerable resources have been used to produce negligible results in the United States' health, education, poverty, economic development, and other important fields. The human needs in areas like these are great, so eliminating waste and finding the most productive ways to address them is crucial to success, even if that comes in small steps. Resources are not unlimited, and applying them efficiently and effectively is key to maximizing results.

Evaluating the results of programs is an important part of policymaking, but such findings are by no means the only consideration in deciding where to focus energy and resources. Rationality is important, but there is no way to avoid the more political and emotional aspects of decisions about programs. Other factors that must be considered are the public's reaction to a program, the responses of those participating in it, the availability of people and places to carry it out, the interests of potential supporters, and possible alternatives to the way of delivering it. Existing ideologies may prevent starting a program that has been effective elsewhere or stopping one that has not produced the intended results. Systematic evaluations can contribute greater clarity of the costs and benefits of decisions about programs and better knowledge of the alternatives.

So, why wouldn't nonprofits embrace assessment efforts? There are many reasons why managers and staff avoid evaluating their own programs and services. Although each of the following is indeed a real concern, coping strategies are necessary, since evaluation is indeed an organizational reality. It is a major step toward accountability and one that can come from inside the system rather than being imposed from the outside.

First, some administrators avoid assessment because they are afraid of what it might reveal. When an organization feels that it is doing the "best it can under these circumstances," managers may want to avoid bad news in the form of data that show problems.

Second, some organizations want to avoid being evaluated because they are fearful that the results will require changes. Several factors combine to create blinders to the real benefits of effective program evaluation: limited resources, satisfaction with the status quo, unwillingness to define expected results before initiating programs and services, and an inability to see other options.

In addition, many organizations have had unfortunate experiences with how the results of an evaluation have been used, misinterpreted, or made to fit someone's political agenda. Although this is not an abstract concern, how others will use the information cannot be controlled completely. People biased against a nonprofit will still pursue their agendas with or without data. Even so, a nonprofit is in a stronger position with assessments over time than without them. Expectations of transparency and effective accountability endure, but goodwill without supporting evidence does not last long.

Just as there are many kinds of programs, so too there are many approaches to evaluating them. Programs vary in scope, size, length, goals, and complexity. It is simpler to evaluate a short-term, highly specific, and well-defined project, such as a new approach to teaching how use a software package, than one that is larger, even national in scope, and extending over a number of years, such federal antipoverty programs. In this chapter we examine the methods of evaluating a variety of programs.

Because the expectations of each stakeholder group may be different, the politics of undertaking an evaluation can be quite complex. Before getting under way, it is important to make sure that the expectations of everyone using the conclusions are clear. Staff members who deal with the public often see themselves as the best source of information about participants' and clients' interests. But recently, evaluation studies have asked the clients or customers of nonprofit organizations to offer their own views of how well a program serves their concerns and meets their needs.

Staff also tend to believe they best understand the professional knowledge of and standards for good programs and services. Because managers oversee the whole organization and are concerned about its future viability, they may emphasize the programs' potential costs and benefits. Policymakers usually attend to similarities and differences across organizations and the possible ways to shift public allocations to support the more effective ones. Donors and taxpayers are concerned about raising more money to fund activities of unknown or distant benefits. Because it may not be possible to reconcile all these views or attend to everyone's interests in a single large evaluation study, choices and limitations are often necessary.[2]

Evaluation studies are either summative or formative. *Formative* studies look for information about a program while it is under way and feeds back that information to those carrying it out in order to improve their efforts. *Summative* studies look at a program after it is completed for information about its overall effectiveness in achieving its goals. Formative studies intend to help staff do better work along the way, and summative studies answer questions about whether the program should be continued, modified, stopped, or tried elsewhere.

Nonprofit organizations can evaluate many aspects of their programs and services, such as

- Documenting how consumers benefited from receiving a service.
- Showing how funds were used.
- Assessing what services have been provided and to whom.
- Understanding the views of staff, consumers, donors, and community leaders.
- Evaluating the professional quality of services delivered.
- Pinpointing issues of concern (such as staff morale, motivations, and satisfactions).
- Comparing stakeholders' views of a program.
- Gauging the congruence between resources and needs.
- Finding out the views of consumers and other organizations about a program's accessibility, timeliness, courtesy, responsiveness, benefits. and gaps.

A noteworthy distinction is the difference between inputs and outcomes. *Inputs* are used in carrying out a program (such as staff time, facilities, materials) and also are the characteristics of the activities themselves (such as numbers of participants, clients, appointments, attendance, follow-up contacts). Inputs are necessary to conducting any program or service, but information about them says nothing about the results of those efforts. *Outcomes* are the documented benefits or changes for participants that resulted from their involvement in a program.[3] These changes may be the participants' knowledge, skills, attitudes, behaviors, or living conditions. They may be realized quickly, as in learning a new application of a software package, or over a longer term, such as higher rates of graduation from high school or lower rates of delinquency.

Evaluating inputs can be important to a nonprofit organization. The management team may want to better understand how consumers see its programs or how other organizations assess their usefulness. It may want to compare views of staff in various parts of the organization regarding how well the organization is supporting their efforts. Monitoring the staff's morale and satisfaction with their work can tell a lot to leaders, just as the staff's views of the work climate and supervisory practices can. Just trying to understand the stakeholders' views sends the message that they are important.

Many nonprofit organizations keep records of some of their inputs, such as clients' application rates and appointments, completed service cycles, and employees' attendance and hours. These are relatively easy to document and record and are useful in demonstrating how hard people are working and how much programs cost. Documenting outcomes is much more difficult, since they often are harder to identify and measure. Donors are becoming increasingly interested in the results of expenditures, not just the amounts. Many national associations have developed (or are developing) resources to help their member organizations document the results of their efforts. Examples are the United Way of America, Girl Scouts of the U.S.A., Goodwill Industries, YMCA, Child Welfare League of America, and Girls, Inc. Public agencies and foundations also expect evidence of the results of their investments in nonprofits and often require evaluations to be included in grant proposals.

Exercise

Go to the Web sites of several national nonprofit organizations that interest you and look for their resources for program evaluation. Note the components, standards, and tools used in the project.

Nonprofit organizations gain a number of benefits from evaluating their programs' results. They include helping the organization and its participants focus on specific results and reducing tangential efforts and expenditures. Assessments help an organization better align its strategies and operations with the results expected by stakeholders. Understanding the current outcome provides a basis for tracking improvements and for planning. It motivates people to decide how to use their time and resources, and it also informs decisions about the staff's training. Documented outcomes help justify budget changes and fund-raising purposes. Such information positions the organization for success, which leads to greater public recognition and financial support.

The principal steps of conducting an evaluative study are

- Securing a commitment to address an important issue in the organization.
- Engaging representatives of the groups needed to carry out the evaluation and act on the findings.
- Negotiating shared purposes, goals, and implementation steps.
- Specifying what will be evaluated, why, and how.
- Communicating expectations with all those expected to participate in the project.
- Collecting the relevant information.
- Interpreting the findings in ways that are understandable and useful for action.
- Distributing the findings and recommendations.
- Engaging participants in refining action plans and implementing them.[4]

Build Ownership from the Start

For any evaluative study to be productive, those expected to act on its findings must support it, beginning with the leaders of the organization. The board and senior staff must be openly supportive and enthusiastic about the effort and committed to using the findings to improve the organization. They must believe that the study will lead to changes that will improve performance and satisfaction, and they must persuade others to join in this commitment. They must believe that the organization's mission will be better served by addressing these issues rather than keeping things the same. Ambiguous statements by leaders at the beginning indicate problems later on. Many staff members feel that they have participated in too many busywork projects in the past and resent being told to do one more without good reasons to do so.

Probably several other stakeholder groups will be important to using the results, such as supervisors, front-line staff, donors, and perhaps even leaders

Figure 13.1
The Evaluation Process

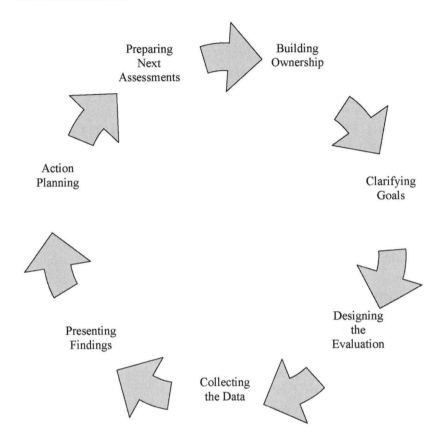

of other organizations. Their views should help shape the project if they are expected to take its results seriously. Since these stakeholders' views and interests can be quite different, it is important to ask them at the start to help plan the evaluative study. People who have helped design the project, formulate its goals, and collect the data are much more likely to believe in the findings, want to use them, and advocate for them with others.

A productive step at the outset of an evaluative study is to bring together a small group of representatives of those constituencies who will be important to implementing the findings. This group should decide on the purposes of the study and how it will be carried out. Agreeing on the design of the project will require careful negotiations and compromises, but the investment of time up front will pay off throughout the project and especially at the end, when acting on the findings will be important.

Clarify Goals

Not only will this group encounter differences among its members about expectations and purposes of the project, but they also are likely to confront challenges in identifying the goals of the program(s) to be evaluated. Program goals may be ambiguous, divergent, or statements of values more than intended results. What is meant by a goal of "improving citizenship," for example? How would anyone recognize that? Moreover, a program may have several goals. What is "improved study habits?" In whose view? Programs may have results different from those the designers hoped. Programs are carried out by people who are likely to have different interests, motivations, levels of skill, and concerns for implementing them. Clarifying a program's goals is essential to a helpful evaluation of its results.

Since stakeholders may disagree about what they want a program to produce, reaching a mutually acceptable statement of goals may take considerable negotiation. Those who are planning an evaluation study often face multiple demands and inconsistencies, and the failure to resolve them will damage all subsequent efforts. They may just ask staff or other stakeholders to reconcile their differences and agree on goals before anything starts. But even this may take a very long time and still not be successful. A more productive approach is to set up a small group representing the stakeholders and offer them sample goal statements from other, similar programs. The ensuing discussions will help focus and refine the final product.

Some programs are intended to produce several goals, some leading to other goals and then to others. Such sequences of goals can be seen as a series of "if–then" statements. For example, if a program provides nutrition education to expectant mothers, the mothers will have a better knowledge of good nutrition. Then, with such knowledge, they are more likely to select and consume healthier foods. If they do that, then they are likely to have healthier babies. Such a logical flow of results may be seen as a chain: inputs lead to activities that lead to initial outcomes that lead to intermediate outcomes that lead to longer-term outcomes. Of course, the more the outcomes are stretched out, the more likely it is that other factors will influence the circumstances and the more difficult it will be to argue that the inputs and activities were the sources of these changes.[5]

Programs may have multiple goals, and those planning the evaluation study will disagree on those they believe to be the most important. In that case, it is best to reduce the number of goals to be examined to a feasible few. A helpful criterion is the practicality or feasibility of obtaining information about the issue. Interviewing people who left this homeless shelter over the past five years may be interesting, but the chances of actually locating many of them are limited. Of course, it is tempting simply to measure what is easily available, rather than what would be the most useful, so the goals should be both important and feasible to address.

A goal's relative importance is another criterion. What is the relative importance of this goal in comparison with others? How important, for example, is a goal of satisfying volunteers in a mentoring program compared with tracking the attendance and grades of schoolchildren? Should we try to measure the impact of participating in an art course on their participants' skills or on their attitudes? Examining several dimensions of a program can reveal *why* a program produced results, which is often more useful than just whether or how well it worked overall.

Another consideration is the importance of long-term versus short-term goals. Managers work within annual budgets, so evidence of a program's impact over a twelve-month period is more useful than the impact that can be achieved over three years. Staff may be more interested in overall results for clients or patients in a program, even if those results take a long time to be realized.

Yet another criterion is the limits on time and money for the evaluation project. Even though a number of goals may be important and feasible to examine, some are likely to be quite expensive, perhaps even beyond the project's resources. It may be necessary to acknowledge that even though a particular goal is important, it simply cannot be addressed within the limited available time and resources. An example may be trying to get information about the impact of a mentoring program on past participants who are now adults.

Designing the Evaluation

Most of the many ways of developing good program evaluations use basic methods of scientific research. Using a representative sample of participants, not just those who are easily available, increases the likelihood that the findings will be helpful beyond the specific study. Clearly defining the intervention or activity improves the chances that the conclusions can be used elsewhere. A systematic measurement of the relevant characteristics before and after the activity increases confidence that the activity itself and not other events were responsible for the changes observed.

Once the goals and targets of assessment have been identified, the planning group's next task is to decide on the methods of gathering information about them. Each of the many designs for evaluation studies follows steps intended to estimate what changes can be attributed to the project being evaluated rather than to outside influences. The purpose of these steps is to compare what actually happened with what would have happened if nothing had changed and the project had not been implemented. But because this is impossible, the challenge is to provide plausible substitutes, like the following:[6]

1. *Before and after comparison*: This approach compares data on the participants from just before a program was implemented and soon afterward. The program's goals are specified and measured before the program is begun, and the same measurement is made again when the program ends. The differences are taken as evidence of the program's results. This approach assumes that the levels before the program are acceptable estimates of what they would have been without the program.

Although this is a relatively inexpensive approach to evaluation, it has several problems, especially with regard to other possible influences besides the program that may have caused the changes. Other things may have taken place while the program was under way, from personal changes to social and political events. People who agreed to participate may have been interested in or concerned about the issues addressed by the program so were more likely to attend to its content than were other people without such interests. The before-and-after comparison therefore should be used only when time and resources are limited, when the program is short and specific in scope, and when external conditions are stable.

2. *Time trend comparisons*: This approach compares data gathered after the program's completion with data gathered several times before it began. It attempts to determine the participants' stability before the program or whether changes were under way that would have been missed with just a single assessment. For example, children in a standard reading education program ordinarily would be improving in their skills. Therefore, an innovative new approach should not be evaluated just on the differences in their skills before and after the trial run, since they would have shown some improvement even if they had not been in the program. Instead, the rate of change in their skills should be measured by several assessments before starting them in the new program. Only if the rate rises faster than otherwise expected can the new program claim to have had an impact on the children.

This format for an evaluation is appropriate if there is an underlying trend upward or downward that may influence observed changes in indicators of the program's impacts. It is slightly more expensive than the before-and-after method, since time and resources must be invested in several assessments before the program begins. This kind of evaluation also is vulnerable to the possibility that other influences also affected the participants' experiences while they were in the program that may have modified their levels in the postparticipation assessment. In addition, it is possible that the several measurements taken before the program was instituted were unstable and hence were not good estimates for projecting expected rates of change. Nevertheless, this format improves on the previous one in that it compares the differences between the projected rates of change with those after the program has been completed.

3. *Comparison of people participating in a program with similar people not participating*: This approach to evaluation addresses the problem of extraneous influences that may confound a logical conclusion that the program was responsible for the changes observed. It requires identifying and getting access to people who are highly similar to those participating in the program. The same assessment tools are used to measure their levels according to criteria relevant to the expected program outcomes as well as those of participants in the program.

These same measures are used for both groups before and again after the participating group completes the program. The amounts of change found among the nonparticipants by proxy become the best estimate of what the participants would have shown if they had not been in the program. So if the nonparticipants changed by twenty points on a measure and the participants changed by thirty, the program had a greater impact than did any external circumstances or influences. For example, students in a standard reading program may be compared before some are moved to an alternative program and then again afterward. The reading skills of those in each of the two groups are compared. If the scores of those in the alternative program improved more than the scores of those in the standard program, the alternative program may be argued to have been responsible for the differences.

This approach is more expensive than both the previous ones, due to the inclusion of multiple assessments of members of the two groups and the step of finding people who are similar in most respects to those in the program. If the children selected for the alternative program already are improving at a faster or slower rate than those remaining in the standard program, the comparison will not be valid. If the selection is made up of volunteers, then whatever factors motivated them to participate in the study make them different from those who did not. Even with the best of efforts, there still may be unknown differences between the people in the two groups that are relevant to the program's impacts. Dividing participants into two groups may be difficult, since many organizations want to provide the best services they can to all their consumers equally and not select some for the unknown benefits of an alternative approach.

4. *Controlled experimentation*: This is the most powerful approach to evaluation and is also the most difficult and expensive. It addresses the problem of similarities or differences between those not participating in a program with those who are, after having created the two groups by means of random selection. Random selection is intended to ensure that there are no relevant differences between

the participants in the two groups. One group participates in the program and the other does not. Both groups are measured before and after the program. The randomization protects against the confounding influences of extraneous factors and buttresses the conclusion that any differences observed are due to participation in the program.

This is the most rigorous and costly approach to evaluation. The step of randomly choosing two groups and analyzing the data requires additional technical expertise. Furthermore, it requires an opportunity to carry out the randomization. Many organizations resist such arbitrary differentiation of their consumers, especially if a service is to be withheld from some of them. However, the findings from such an approach are the strongest and most credible foundation for concluding that a program actually produced the benefits it intended. To ensure fair treatment, those in the control group may later be given the service.

Other approaches to carrying out evaluative studies are designed to be useful in a variety of program circumstances.[7] They all attempt in one way or another to address the problem of extraneous influences on changes and to strengthen the credibility of any conclusions that a program was actually the source of those changes. Like the four preceding approaches, they vary in expense and complexity. A nonprofit organization planning an evaluative study should use the most rigorous approach it can afford. The simple before-and-after approach is the least expensive, but it is also the weakest in that it is highly vulnerable to the charge that extraneous influences produced any changes observed.

Note that a sound summative study is almost impossible to conduct after a program is already under way. Often the idea to conduct an evaluation arises after a program has begun, but by then it is too late to accurately assess the participants' characteristics. Retrospective estimates are notoriously inaccurate, unless the aspect or characteristic being measured has already been well documented in past records and the same information will be used at the end of the program.

Data Collection Tools

Each goal selected for study must have at least one valid and reliable indicator. If we were to decide that "improved citizenship" was an important goal of a youth program, what specific evidence would reveal it? Would self-ratings be credible? Would better indicators be the number of civic clubs a person joined, the frequency and duration of active participation, or the assessments of peers regarding that person's leadership performance? Would joining three new school or community activities mean the same thing to a person who formerly was active in none compared with another person who already had been active in five? Credible standards of judgment should be set so the findings will be persuasive to the consumers of the evaluation.[8]

Obtaining trustworthy assessments of conditions or characteristics relevant to program goals requires both accurate indicators for each of them and careful data collection. Among the several approaches are using existing records and statistics, direct interviews, self-administered questionnaires, and ratings by staff or observers. Some information relevant to a program's goals may already have been collected. For example, a youth program intended to reduce delinquency rates and increase graduation rates may be able to obtain, from schools and courts in the region, such information from the past and after the conclusion of the program. Make sure that the definitions or categories or reporting procedures have not changed, as that would cause inconsistencies in the records.

Relying on existing records is usually not sufficient for conducting an evaluation study. The goals of many programs are complex enough to require tailored methods to obtain the data relevant to the evaluation. The most frequently used method is a survey, using a standard set of questions administered in face-to-face interviews, over the telephone or Internet, or by mail. When there are a very large number of people to contact, a sample may be drawn randomly to obtain a smaller and more feasible number for responses. Finally, direct observations may be appropriate when behaviors are to be examined or rated.

A measuring tool should provide systematic information about participants through sets of statements or questions asked of everybody in the program (see table 13.1). Sometimes it is possible to find well-written questionnaires about the characteristics that a program is addressing. A search on the Internet can find appropriate tools, thus saving the project staff a great deal of time. Some sites you might explore (URLs may change) are

www.surveyconsole.com/community-survey.html (click on free survey templates).
www.upstatealliancenp.org/assessments (click on assessment tools).
www.pomp5.net (outcome measures for programs serving older adults).
www.eval.org/evaluationlinks/surveylinks.htm (a variety of tools).
www.pic.org/toolkitfiles.htm (tools for assessing outcomes of legal aid programs).
www.nlm.nih.gov/nichsr/hsrr_search (descriptions of client assessment tools for a variety of health and human service programs).
http://searcheric.org (type in the desired topic or issue).

Table 13.1
Methods of Collecting Data

Strengths	Weaknesses
A. Records Review	
Uses existing data	Time often is short
Builds a culture of record keeping	Data often incomplete
Should be on file in system	Data collected for another purpose may not be useful
	Review limited to what is accessible
	Categories may have changed over time
	Definitions of different activities may have changed over time
B. Observation	
Provides actual live data	May be intrusive
Uses experts or trained observers	Can be difficult to interpret
	Can be difficult to categorize observations
	Can change what people do if they know they are being observed
	Cost may be a factor
	May be time-consuming
	Finding experts may be difficult
	Training observers may be difficult
C. Focus Groups	
Content and interactions provide valuable data	Require trained facilitator
Gather lots of information	Can be misinterpreted
Obtain nuances about issues being reviewed	On-the-spot opinions may differ from data or more thoughtful answers
	May be tainted by group process
	Group composition can bias process and content
D. Self-Assessment	
Staff know how effective they are	Staff has tendency to skew toward the positive
Staff can get a high response rate	Staff may fear how data will be used or misused
	Staff may have difficulty creating a system of honesty
	Staff may have concern for anonymity

Table 13.1, *continued*
Methods of Collecting Data

E. Interviews (in person or telephone)	
Offer broader information	May be expensive
Interviewer can tailor questions to ensure clear communication	Are labor intensive
Are more personal	Interviewer may get sidetracked
Are focused on what both parties want and/or need	Interviewer may be biased (intentionally or unintentionally)
Interviews can clarify unclear answers	Data may be harder to analyze
Interviews allow fewer nonresponses (once interview begins)	May not offer comparable data even if using standard interview guide
	Nonagency people may have different standards or expectations

F. Questionnaires	
Can be anonymous	May produce sloppy responses (remember the hanging chads??)
Cost relatively little	Can be impersonal
Allow detailed analysis	Have limited ability to go beyond numbers
Can use large sample size	Must be pretested
Can cover many topics	Nonagency respondents may have no sense of history or of the organization's mission and programs
Can use existing forms	
Have proved to be reliable and valid	
Can be filled out by computer	Samples of large cohorts may not reflect total population
Can be accessed online	

www.centerpointforleaders.org/toolkit_org_home.html.
www.learningcenter.net/library/management.shtml.

If it is not possible to locate an existing tool to evaluate a program, then try inventing a new one, tailored to the goals of that program. Most goals concern the effects on the people who participate in the program, which may be changes in attitudes, values, behaviors, or skills. The program's intended changes may be short term, intermediate, or longer term. Likewise, the indicators for some of them may be self-reports by participants, and others may involve observational ratings by experts on the topic.

To create a measuring tool, start with the goal(s) and write short statements of the goal's indicators. For example, a health education program may want to improve the participants' understanding of communicable diseases, warning signs for them, appropriate treatments, preventive steps, sources for help, and the frequency of their visits to health clinics. A descriptive statement may be something like "Covering your mouth when you cough or sneeze can reduce the spread of germs." The respondent is given answers to check, such as True, False, and Don't Know. Similar statements apply to the program's other goals. Each is a partial picture of a small piece of the program's results. Multiple statements covering various aspects of the program's goals forms a fuller picture of its attainment than could any one question or statement.

Adding up the correct answers provides a score for each individual, and averaging the scores for all those in the group indicates where the group stands at that time on the conditions (knowledge or skill) addressed by the program. A low group score before the program begins followed by a high group score after completing it may show how well the program achieved its goals.

Different measurement tools may be used for the various levels of a program's goals. A short-term goal of improving knowledge in a topic area may use a list of statements pertaining to such knowledge. An intermediate goal may be to change attitudes, so a series of attitudinal statements would be appropriate. A longer-term goal may be to change behaviors, so statements about the participants' behavior in areas relevant to the program's goals would be used.

Early drafts of a new measuring tool should be examined first by the staff involved in the program and by experts in that field to make sure that each statement is relevant to some aspect of the program's goals. This input allows the designers to fine-tune the tool, clarifying some items, eliminating some, and adding some. A useful next step is to test the tool with people who are very much like those who will be participating in the program. Their views and comments can be quite helpful in further refining the tool. Issues to look for in these pilot tests are awkwardly worded or confusing questions or statements, ones to which almost everybody gives the same answers, aspects of the program's goals that may have been overlooked, and resistance from respondents.

Collecting the Data

Once the project's steering group is satisfied that the tool(s) are ready for use, the next phase is administering them, collecting responses from those in the program (and from a matched group of nonparticipants, if that is the project design). Whether administered by face-to-face interviews, via the telephone or Internet, or self-administered paper questionnaires, the approach should be the same for every contact. The respondents should receive a prepared explanation, either in writing at the top of a written questionnaire or an oral introduction for interviews. The purpose of this is to reduce the respondents' anxieties about what is expected of them and how the information will be used. The other reason for offering the same introduction is to avoid influencing the respondents' answers by varying the explanations of the purpose of collecting the data.

The planning group should decide on all the steps in the data collection, including how, where, and when the completed forms or questionnaires will be returned. Then the group should make an outline of the final report, leaving spaces where the results of tabulating the data will be entered. When the results have been tabulated, they are entered into the appropriate spaces in the report. Then the group drafts suggested explanations or interpretations of the findings, writing in a style that is easily understood and credible to its readers. The group may recommend specific ways of using the findings to modify the program's aspects and improve it.

Presenting the Findings

If the entire process began with strong commitments by the organization's leaders and the extensive involvement of representatives of those who will use the findings to make changes in the organization, then the presentations and discussions of the report are more likely to be well received. Nevertheless, resistance should be expected, regardless of how well the early stages of the project were handled. Most people are comfortable with how things are going in their program and confident they have carried them out well. Therefore, suggestions that familiar things need to be changed can make them defensive and even angry, which often is expressed by attacking the bearers of the news or criticizing the report itself as flawed. Although the technical questions should be resolved before proceeding, the more emotional reactions should be heard respectfully but should not be allowed to block the findings. Acknowledging that change usually provokes anxiety is appropriate. Comments that personalize the issues should be avoided, and the focus should be kept on the results and the ways to use them together to improve the programs. It may be useful to assign small groups of staff to work on improving the project team's recommendations. The program's strengths should be emphasized, and specific issues or areas needing change should be framed in terms of helping the program become more successful and contributing to the organization's mission.

From Reporting to Action

Not every recommendation is likely to receive unanimous support, with some more widely accepted than others. The project leaders should begin with those that are more acceptable to the staff and designate people to decide on the specific steps for implementing the changes. The leadership skills addressed earlier in this book will be needed to make the changes suggested by the evaluation. Managers and supervisors should oversee those recommendations affecting their staff. People's strengths and interests should be matched with tasks as much as possible. Sometimes managers will need to talk with individuals to determine how they can fit in with the changes and find acceptable roles in the new ways of working. Emphasis should remain on the organization's mission and the ways in which the recommended changes will strengthen the organization in carrying that out, and not on trying to make everyone happy. Sometimes recalcitrant opponents of change may have to be encouraged to seek more satisfying jobs elsewhere.

The action plan should include reasonable timetables for action, ways to record and document the steps taken, and ways of dealing with challenges or obstacles that show up as the changes are made. There will be surprises, barriers, unexpected delays, and problems along the way, so ways of responding to them should be decided in advance, without allowing the process to grind to a halt. It also is important to recognize successes, communicate them widely, and celebrate them, to help build momentum for further changes and reinforce efforts to continue improving the program.

In conclusion, program evaluations can make important contributions to improving an organization and its programs when old ideas and old ways of working are not producing the promised results. Outdated theories about why some action should lead to some desired results may be misconceived and inappropriate, even if they seem to have worked in the past. Organizations get into ruts and often ignore changes in the environment that may make old ways of working obsolete. Finding ways to open the organization and its people to new ways of thinking and working are crucial to the organization's health and growth. Program evaluation is one way of looking at an existing program or organizational component and seeing whether it is producing the intended results or it needs to be modified to improve its performance. An evaluation can identify gaps in services, redundancies, and opportunities for improvement. It is an important means for improving nonprofit organizations and demonstrating their accountability for the resources entrusted to them.

Exercise

On the Internet or in your library, find some reports of evaluation studies carried out by organizations whose programs interest you. See how the program's goals were described and measured, how the data were collected and reported, and the steps taken to apply the findings to improve the program. Then use those ideas to sketch out an evaluation plan for another program that interests you.

For Discussion

How can a nonprofit measure a program's overall effectiveness when its success depends so heavily on the efforts of individual staff members?

14

Accountability

According to a recent publication of the Harvard Business School, "Non-profits have been able to avoid the hurdles of accountability that for-profits must confront on a regular basis," hence the importance of accountability to nonprofit organizations.[1] Criticism of their performance and demands for their greater accountability are growing rapidly. Public scandals such as those noted in chapter 3 have fueled calls for increasing scrutiny of non-profits' performance, for tighter regulations, and for fewer tax exemptions. Because they are dependent on the public's trust and credibility, nonprofits have no choice but to make their policies and practices as transparent and open as possible.

This chapter focuses on the issues related to accountability and what steps nonprofit organizations and their leadership must take to meet these challenges. A thorough understanding of this material will help readers

1. Describe the steps that employees, departments, organizations, and boards can take to demonstrate their accountability.
2. Differentiate process accountability from structural accountability.
3. Discuss important federal legislation designed to increase accountability.
4. Understand when public advocacy (acceptable) becomes political lobbying (problematic).

5. Be aware of the consequences of failing to meet these rising expectations for greater accountability.

Public trust in nonprofits is undermined by media stories of wasted funds and violated trust, such as using donors' funds for things they did not intend, paying executives too much, using large proportions of raised funds to pay for the fund-raising efforts themselves, retaining a board that does not exercise oversight of the organization and its finances, failing to live up to a code of ethics, and using funds for questionable ventures, loans, or partnerships. Donors understandably want assurances that their donations are being used as promised. Consumers want to know about the quality and accessibility of services, and competing organizations may challenge a nonprofit's education programs, asserting that they cross the line into political lobbying.

Building and sustaining public trust is crucial to every nonprofit. Being *accountable* refers to its responsibilities for using its resources as promised to those who provided them. It begins with identifying those constituencies to whom the organization owes compliance in exchange for their support and then moves to specifying the expectations or conditions under which their support was provided. The next step is collecting and reporting accurate information to the nonprofit's constituencies about how their resources were used in advancing the mission of the organization, as well as modeling or demonstrating integrity in all the organization's decisions and actions.

Clarifying the sponsors' expectations may be hard, since contributors may have different interests in the organization's programs and services. Understanding and reconciling those differences may be difficult, especially if the organization accepts contributions for things not clearly and directly tied to its mission. Some desperate nonprofits have later found themselves in trouble because they accepted support from individuals or organizations that wanted the nonprofit to serve their own interests apart from the organization's mission or policies.

Nonprofit organizations should set standards for performance based on their mission and goals. Gone are the days when good deeds, honorable intentions, and humane values were a sufficient basis for reporting to one's stakeholders. Now nonprofits must have a clear mission and apply all their resources to that mission. They now must show how they are enhancing the well-being of communities, how they are exercising responsible stewardship of resources, and how they are maintaining quality and excellence in all their work. Toward those ends, accountable nonprofits set and enforce their expectations for staff, maintain

Too Many Strings?

A well-known museum accepted a very large gift from a donor to expand its building and collections in a category of art that it had not previously held. By mutual agreement, the donor's name was to be prominently displayed at the entrance to the new wing. As the executive began searching for a lead curator for the new collection, he was surprised to hear that the donor expected a specific person to be appointed. Furthermore, the donor stated that he expected to approve all purchases of artwork for the collection. Such strings on gifts had never been discussed and constituted a violation of the museum's policies. Negotiations failed, and with considerable pain, the museum had to return the gift.

organizational structures to abide by those standards, and use assessments and audits to ensure and demonstrate compliance.

Consider the following quotation from *Forbes Magazine* in 2005: "Motivated in part by an uncertain economy, nonprofit organizations have become more results-driven by developing new ways of creating revenue, increasing employee specialization, and enhancing marketing techniques."[2] Nonprofit leaders believe that they must meet new challenges more actively, and regulators and legislators are concerned that these organizations need more rigorous oversight and control. These are responses to the growing calls for accountability.

Some organizations have a "watchdog" whose primary purpose is to make sure that nonprofits perform their proper roles and do not exceed their legal mandates (see ngowatch.com). This group's philosophy is best summarized in its slogan "to bring clarity and accountability to the burgeoning world of NGOs."[3] The Better Business Bureau also assesses the larger nonprofits, using sound criteria for organizational practices (www.give.org).

Staff and Board Accountability

Developing and following policies for selecting members of the staff and board, assigning them specific duties, and making their responsibilities clear are the beginning steps of an organization's accountability. Before interviewing applicants to any staff position or nominees for the board, the organization must have in place personnel policies, job descriptions, performance standards, reporting requirements, and evaluation criteria for assessing work. The organization must then use these objectively to screen applicants and make hiring decisions. The staff are the first line of accountability, and their supervisor is responsible for ensuring the staff's compliance with the expectations of the positions they hold. Many boards prepare job descriptions for their members to improve their performance and become more accountable.

Annual work evaluations are a common, though often poorly used, means to secure the staff's accountability. These evaluations summarize the employees' work at various intervals, along with feedback on how to improve. Many supervisors do not pay close attention to the work of those reporting to them unless their work indicates a problem. Hence, they miss opportunities to offer feedback and suggestions that could raise the employees' productivity, enhance their career development, and help them advance the organization's mission.

Effective boards go beyond requiring only that the executive evaluate staff to also evaluating themselves.[4] They periodically assess their own performance, by means of either self-evaluation questionnaires or external reviews, and use the findings to determine how they can add greater value to the organization. Commitment to excellence in the board's leadership is one of its responsibilities, and finding ways to carry out that commitment can be enhanced by board assessments. Brief discussions at the conclusion of a board (or staff) meeting can point out aspects that went well and aspects that need improvement. Annual performance appraisals can provide useful information to the board regarding its own work and can help establish realistic yet challenging goals for the next year or two. Such goals should be focused on the board's own work and complement the organization's strategic plans. This practice enables the board to be an integral part of the organization and guides its efforts to become more accountable.

Supporting any evaluation system, whether focusing on board or staff, must be an organizational commitment to becoming more effective and a stronger contributor to the organization. Habits are very hard to break, and it is difficult to hear that one is not working as well as one could. Exploring new ways of achieving goals is awkward and often produces anxiety. For these reasons, the executive and the board should model the use of evaluative feedback to make changes that will strengthen performance. They must show that ongoing learning and improvement are everyone's responsibilities. Rather than punishing mistakes, they should encourage creativity, taking reasonable risks, learning from mistakes, and finding better ways to achieve their goals. Boards that set such a tone in their organizations will find their credibility rising among staff and external constituencies. When their accountability improves, their stakeholders' trust grows, and the organization becomes more successful.

This does not mean that the board should micromanage the staff and the organization's programs, services, and activities. That is the role and responsibility of the executive director and the managerial staff. The cartoon in figure 14.1 illustrates what micromanagement looks like to staff and outsiders. Such an approach detracts from the board's fulfilling its role, undercuts the managers' authority, and serves little purpose.

Another form of accountability comes from the professional associations that certify or license professionals for practice. These associations have codes of ethics and standards of practice that their members are required to meet. Violations may be reported to the association, which then investigates the member's actions and determines the appropriate sanctions. Likewise, many nonprofit organizations belong to national associations, which usually have policies and standards for their member organizations. Some of these associations require periodic assessments or self-studies to provide information that may be used to improve the organization's effectiveness.

Challenges to organizational practices come from many external and internal sources. In any organization, employees can bring their concerns to the leaders about actions of others that violate the organization's own policies and standards or those of professional associations or national associations of nonprofits in the same field. Such "whistle-blowers" expose practices that supervisors have ignored, thus initiating changes intended to improve the organization's accountability. Of course, many people in the organization may have a stake in continuing the familiar old practices going and may retaliate against those who expose them. For such efforts to work well, therefore, the organization must have in place policies, ethics, and standards of practice for identifying actions that are not in compliance. Likewise, it should have safeguards for those who bring violations into the open.[5]

One policy that every nonprofit should have and follow pertains to conflicts of interest. Many organizations have boilerplate statements buried somewhere in their files, and few staff or board members ever recall having seen them. Only when some self-serving action draws attention is the policy statement dug out, but by then the organization has already been hurt. Instead, the organization should review at least annually its policy regarding what constitutes a conflict of interest, how disclosures should be made, what someone in such a conflict must do and not do, and the possible penalties for violation. An example of such a policy is given in chapter 3.

Figure 14.1
Accountability?

Process Accountability

Maintaining responsible procedures and accurate records is another important part of an organization's accountability. This includes formulating policies and procedures to guide activities and record keeping and then ensuring that the organization complies with its own policies. An example is the annual financial audit. An audit analyzes the financial records and transactions of those in the organization who receive and spend its money to ascertain whether they have followed generally accepted accounting procedures (often referred to as GAAPs). A management letter may accompany the audit, detailing the recommended changes to resolve problems and prevent them from occurring in the future.

Another aspect of financial accountability is compliance with federal and state regulations pertaining to the disclosure of a nonprofit's financial records. The IRS requires that nonprofits complete and submit a 990 form every year and to make those reports available to anyone who requests a copy. Copies of these completed forms for all nonprofits are available at www.guidestar.org. In addition, many states now require nonprofits engaged in fund-raising to report annually the amounts raised and the proportion of the sums that actually went to the nonprofit, as distinguished from the amount that was spent to raise money. Having such information publicly available allows everyone to examine the nonprofit's financial records.

Accountability also means that every organization should have written policies and procedures to guide its internal financial controls. Not only do they protect the organization from fraud, abuse, waste, and inefficiency, but they also educate the staff and the public about the nonprofit's compliance and accountability. Some of the areas in which internal controls make a difference are the following:

- Preparing and reviewing financial statements.
- Developing and adjusting annual budgets.
- Making timely deposits of cash and checks.
- Reconciling bank statements.
- Managing accounts receivable.
- Managing accounts payable.
- Accounting for bad debts.
- Monitoring petty cash transactions.
- Maintaining and controlling inventory and expenditures.
- Recording, verifying, depreciating, and disposing of capital assets.
- Approving, documenting, and reimbursing employees' travel expenses.
- Managing payroll systems (salary, deductions, withholding taxes).

Another form of accountability is the human resource audit, which examines the organization's practices of hiring, firing, and promotion and its handling of charges of discrimination. The organization's human resource policies must define each job position's responsibilities; the criteria for selection, promotion, and termination; and the procedures for appealing a personnel decision. Fair and impartial policies and procedures do not guarantee that every employee will be treated completely fairly, nor do they preclude legal action against the organization. However, they do provide a strong basis for the staff's understanding of expectations and procedures to follow when any person believes that he or she has been treated unfairly. Having ambiguous policies or failing to follow clearly worded ones are invitations to disaster, and the resulting negative publicity can damage the public's trust in the organization.

Accountability also ensures that board meetings are in compliance with state laws regarding open meetings and open records. Often referred to as "sunshine" laws, these regulations are intended to allow the public to know what is going on in the organization and to raise questions about any issue that may be of concern. Transparency or availability to the public is an important component of accountability.

Another component of accountability is keeping the board's and staff's time and attention focused on the most important issues facing the organization. This begins with formulating specific strategic goals for the organization and then keeping its work and resources directed toward achieving them. Unfortunately, many nonprofits drift along with ambiguous goals and activities that merely carry forward what has been done in the past. After all, setting goals is hard work and the environment seems to change slowly and in ways beyond control. Most people, including both board members and staff, are preoccupied with operational details and neglect the organization's goals and priorities. Even if there was a strategic plan sometime in the past, it usually sits on a shelf, exercising little influence on decisions. Such habits undermine accountability.

We discussed strategic planning in chapter 10. Here the important point is that goals must be shared and that everyone must use his or her energy to achieve them. Accountability is strengthened when all participants understand how their actions are tied to goals and lead to their attainment. Internal operations become more productive and efficient, and communication with constituencies becomes more credible when everyone in the organization can clearly describe how his or her efforts are contributing to the organization's successes.

Legislation and Lobbying

A significant advancement in public regulation to improve government accountability was PL 103-62, the Government Performance and Results Act (GPRA). The main purpose of this legislation is explained as follows: "Waste and inefficiency in federal programs undermine the confidence of the American people in government and reduces its ability to address adequately vital public needs." Drawing on practices from successful corporations, this law connects budget processes to organizational performance. Rather than just relying on inflation or incremental increases, the law seeks to reduce fraud and abuse while strengthening successful programs and new models of work. It underscores the expectation of transparency by requiring that all plans and actual results of efforts to achieve them be made available to the public. The law also requires that all federally funded programs and services include rigorous assessment processes and documentation of results. Because many federally funded programs have contracts with nonprofit organizations, these changes have directly affected those individuals and organizations that receive federal funds.

Exercise

Use the Internet to find GPRA reports from two government agencies. Examine the connections among their strategic plans, performance plans, and actual results reported. How were the results measured? Are the findings credible? If you were a legislator, what questions would you ask regarding whether to continue funding these programs?

The federal government's increasingly active role has stimulated nonprofit organizations to become more politically active. Nonprofits must be careful not to cross the line between effectively advocating for their consumers as part of the organization's mission and lobbying versus actively campaigning for political candidates. When a nonprofit tries to influence government rules or regulations, its actions can be considered advocacy. If, however, the goal is to influence elections, then it becomes political lobbying, since influencing votes is the ultimate target.

Section 501(h) of the Internal Revenue Service's tax code states that lobbying can include those communications to a legislator, a staff member, or other connected employee that express a specific point of view about a piece of legislation. But nonprofits cannot endorse or campaign for any candidates for public office.

This is the critical distinction. Lobbying does not exclude contacts with public officials and their staff members. Any organization may seek to protect itself from changes in the law that will directly affect it. For example, if a proposed section of a bill will affect your organization's programs, you and your advocates can try to justify keeping these specific provisions, and if asked, you can respond by providing information and professional advice.

There are guidelines for work in this area. For lobbying or advocacy to be effective, managers must understand how the legislative process works. The process on the national level may differ greatly from that on the state and local levels. Effective advocacy requires persistence, since passing legislation is greatly different from an appropriation to fund programs.

The organization's public position should reflect the majority of the board's views. Nothing undermines successful work as much as dissenting voices from within. But you should be prepared for people on the outside who disagree and make their feelings known. Public policy issues always have many sides. Thoughtful tactics should guide responses, and countervailing opinions must be anticipated and considered. Criticism of the people doing the lobbying, the processes they use, or the products of their work (information sheets, advertising and such) are common.

There are financial concerns regarding public advocacy efforts. Nonprofits' tax-exempt status is contingent on their abstaining from political campaigns for or against any candidate. Accordingly, any voter education efforts must be conducted in a nonpartisan manner. Nonprofits must be careful not to use restricted funds for lobbying or advocacy purposes. Government grants and contracts often spell out these conditions, and foundations almost always describe such activities as being beyond their scope, since they too want to maintain their nonprofit status.

Growing public awareness may lead to backlashes against nonprofits' advocacy and lobbying. When board members, chief executive officers, and other employees become involved in public policy, they have certain rights as citizens. But they may not participate in political campaigns when they are acting as representatives of the organization. Being accountable means not letting advocacy efforts turn into political campaigning.

The American Association of Retired Persons (AARP) came under close scrutiny in 2004 as Congress debated various proposals for Medicare's Part D, Prescription Drug Coverage for the senior citizens. Because AARP contracts out its group insurance policies, the organization stood to take in millions of dollars in new revenues by supporting one of the hundreds of competing insurance plans. Thus, the same question arose: Are these relationships appropriate to nonprofits?

As IRS Commissioner Mark Everson pointed out in a speech, "We are strengthening enforcement in the tax exempt sector."[6] He asserted that stricter enforcement would weed out those "individuals and organizations which should be taxed [but] masquerade as charities." Even though the past may have been characterized by less enforcement in the nonprofit sector because of legal ambiguities, limited IRS budgets, or other priorities, those days are gone. Everson cited for specific attention nonprofit credit-counseling organizations, many of which use their status to reap huge surpluses, as well as any organizations that engage in "prohibited political activity."

As noted throughout this text, accountability can take many forms. The Internal Revenue Service has several ways of meeting this standard of excellence: by enforcing laws and tax rulings, requiring more detailed reporting of a widening range of financial matters to increase transparency, and sharing information with state and local tax authorities to ensure compliance and follow-up. The transparency ideal was a major catalyst in the government's decision to require nonprofit organizations to allow public access to the IRS's Form 990.

Because the current Internal Revenue Service regulations require nonprofit organizations to submit Form 990 annually, let us consider what this means for the nonprofit and the public. The form and the process do provide a wealth of information about the organization's finances, which should help increase their accountability and transparency, in other words, to make its work clear(er) to the public.

Form 990's major categories are

1. A revenue and income statement, with categories like salaries, postage, and rental revenue.
2. A balance sheet, with categories like cash and accounts receivable.
3. A statement of functional expenses, in which all expenses must be allocated to program services, fund-raising, or operations.
4. A report of total expenses and also those for each program or service, like educational mailings and seminar programs.
5. A support schedule detailing the organization's sources of revenue, with categories like charitable donations, membership fees, and investment income.

Mandating public disclosure of this required annual filing can actually help a nonprofit organization build (or rebuild) public confidence in its mission and its uses of funds for worthy purposes. But IRS Form 990 does not cover everything; in fact, it has been called a "weak link" between the regulatory requirements and full disclosure.[7] Some people believe that more rigorous accountability means more extensive disclosure, and we expect such changes will be made in the future.

Practical Steps to Improve Accountability

Nonprofit leaders who want to strengthen the accountability of their organization can follow a number of steps to do this. First, they must recognize that better accountability leads to greater credibility for the organization and wider support for it. Commitment to improving accountability is essential. Then the executive or board chair can discuss ways in which this organization might work toward that goal. Several common events may be used to identify possible improvements. For example, these discussions can examine a recent turnover in a key staff or board position, a change in revenue patterns (such as loss of an income source), the completion of some difficult but important task or the failure to complete it, expressions of dissatisfaction about meetings, or decisions reached (or not reached) in them.

These discussions should take place in a trusting and open environment so that the participants know they can be honest and free in exploring options. They may ask what led to the present situation, what the assumptions were going into the events and decisions leading up to it, how the ensuing actions and conclusions influenced the process, what was missed or misunderstood, what other aspects should have been given attention, what other sources of information or insights should be sought in similar future circumstances, and what ideas or lessons could be used to handle such situations more effectively in the future.

Even if the organization is not undergoing some problem or transition, productive discussions can address challenges that the organization may face in the coming year and what it might do to deal with them more effectively. Instead of waiting for someone to provide a solution for every challenge, groups can reflect together about emerging issues and possible ways to address them before they become problems.

One conclusion may be that we need to learn more about such issues from others who have faced them before we try to come up with our own solutions. Another may be to take time to learn more about how the organization's sponsors and external constituencies look at such issues. Steps like these can help board and staff members become better partners in guiding the organization into the future.

Formulating strategic goals is complex, but if the participants are accustomed to reflective discussions about lessons to take into the future and to staying informed about how others view and are dealing with challenges, they will be better prepared to carry out those steps. Instead of seeing problems or goals as someone else's responsibility, mutual engagement in working on them builds commitment to implementing mutually acceptable solutions. Instead of resisting change, participants can embrace new goals and priorities and then focus on them in their work.

A special panel formed by the Independent Sector recently issued a number of policy recommendations to Congress as part of a collaborative effort to increase nonprofit organizations' transparency and accountability. The presidents of some of the United States' largest and most prestigious foundations and nonprofit associations accepted invitations to serve, and their ideas and ideals will form the basis for future legislation and standards in this field.[8]

1. There should be more vigorous enforcement of national and state laws, tightening the requirements on nonprofits and penalizing those nonprofits that fail to comply.
2. The requirements on nonprofits in reporting to the Internal Revenue Service should be expanded. The present situation is that those nonprofits with incomes above $25,000 per year must file a form identified as 990. This requirement is treated quite casually by many nonprofits, especially smaller ones. The recommendation is that the components of this form be expanded and greater detail required about the organization's finances. Penalties should be stiffened for those that fail to file or that omit or misrepresent information on their returned forms. Each organization's highest-ranking officer should be required to sign the form and to certify that its contents are accurate. In addition, any nonprofit that submits inaccurate information for two years should have its nonprofit status revoked.
3. The Internal Revenue Service should regularly review nonprofits' status to make sure they are in compliance with all regulations and requirements to qualify for tax-exempt status.

4. External audits of each nonprofit's finances should be mandated, and copies of audited financial statements should be attached to Form 990 every year. Boards should also be required to have some members with expertise in finances and to establish an active audit committee.

5. Every nonprofit should periodically evaluate its programs and services and report the findings to the public through reports, Web sites, and other means.

6. Laws and regulations pertaining to donor-advised funds should be tightened so that donors or related persons do not receive inappropriate benefits from those funds. Penalties on violators should be raised.

7. Congress should extend the requirements for financial reporting to *all* tax-exempt organizations, including those not now required to file Form 990. All nonprofits should be subject to the same extended requirements as taxable businesses, especially with regard to transactions through tax shelter entities. Penalties for noncompliance should be raised significantly.

8. Requirements for estimating the value of noncash contributions (in-kind gifts) should be raised and the penalties for violations stiffened.

9. Any form of compensation to members of the boards of nonprofits should be discontinued without strong reasons for their use. Loans to board members should be prohibited by law. Rules regarding reimbursement for travel expenses should be clear and followed and should not include expenses for spouses or other family members. A copy of the reimbursement policy should be included with the annual 990 form.

10. Nonprofits should be required to disclose all forms and amounts of compensation paid to their chief executive officers and to the five highest-compensated employees. The IRS should specify levels of appropriate and excessive compensation. Boards should be required to have procedures for determining the reasonableness of compensation, and they should be penalized if they do not follow them carefully.

11. Boards should be required to have a minimum of three members. At least one-third of the members of any board must be from outside the organization, have not received any material benefits from it for the past year, and not be related to anyone who has received such benefits from the organization. Boards should demonstrate that their members are complying with their legal and ethical duties and ensuring that the organization is being governed properly.

12. Boards should be required to adopt and enforce a policy on conflicts of interest, consistent with federal and state laws. They should be required to indicate on their 990 forms whether they have such a policy and are enforcing it. They also should adopt policies and procedures that encourage and protect individuals who come forward with credible information about illegal practices or violations of the board's policies.

These requirements are likely to be included in future legislation pertaining to nonprofit organizations and will become another route to improving accountability.

Concerns about accountability are likely to continue rising. A number of public and private approaches address such concerns, and in response, nonprofits should

1. Make sure to follow federal and state laws and IRS requirements carefully.
2. Contract with accountants to conduct financial audits annually.
3. Draw up planning and control procedures for each job and each department, including the board of trustees.
4. Provide ongoing training so all board members and employees know what is expected of them.
5. Require compliance with policies regarding conflicts of interest.
6. Develop and disseminate whistle-blower policies so that employees feel free to report concerns without fear of reprisal or retaliation.
7. Ensure that supervisors act appropriately and responsibly (rather than collude to cover up something because it may reflect poorly on them or their unit).
8. Within the limitations of confidentiality, find ways to report annually actions taken. This demonstrates that the organization takes accountability seriously.

Classroom Activity

Dr. Hammond read the annual report and seemed proud of the accomplishments during the past year. The data showed that services increased by 9 percent, even though gross revenues from all sources fell by 2 percent. Even though the staff's raises were delayed for six months, recruitment efforts succeeded, and the new employees brought vitality and the latest skills. Some of the reserve fund was used to repair the leaky roof and to purchase a new computer server and hardware for the administration. So, all in all it was a good year, according to the director.

Role play: One person should assume each of the following roles: a trustee, the head of the staff council, a long-term employee in the agency, the head of community relations, the associate director, a local news reporter, and a critic of the organization.

Key questions: What is the message that the director wants people to take away from the annual report? What is missing from his report? How would you feel if your raise were delayed for six months? What questions should you ask the director?

In conclusion, accountability is multidimensional and is achieved by clarifying expectations of the board, staff, and sponsors, agreeing on goals and criteria for monitoring the organization's progress toward them, getting feedback to improve its performance, and reporting its accomplishments openly and truthfully. Accountability uses clearly worded goals and commitments to continue improving all aspects of the organization. Consistent delivery on mutually agreeable promises increases the value of the organization and its credibility both inside and outside. Neglect of these important responsibilities leads to disaster for the organization, and complacency can put the organization at risk of conflicts, abuses, and mistrust. In such times, most people want to shift the blame to others rather than face the consequences. Accordingly, nonprofit boards, executives, and staff members should make an effort to understand their constituencies' concerns, set high goals and explicit standards for themselves, monitor their progress, use feedback to improve, and report their results to the community. They should provide credible evidence that the organization warrants greater trust and support.

False Expenses

On a Friday afternoon, the department supervisor was approached by one of the unit's secretaries, who told him that Chris had been filing false expense reports. Even though she did not offer any proof, the secretary shared specific information about two trips, one more than a year ago and the other two weeks before this meeting. She also wanted this conversation to be "off the record" and expressed concern that she could suffer retaliation if it became known that she had "tattled" on someone in the office.

1. What are the possible action steps that the supervisor should consider?
2. Identify the pros and cons of each approach, and explain what you would do in this case.

15

Financial Accountability

Most people in the nonprofit field are continually torn between what they would like to be able to do in their programs and what their resources can support. Accordingly, the organization's priorities must be based on its mission and on what it promised its supporters it would do with their contributions. The organization owes them periodic reports on how it spent their money and for what purposes it was used. Maximizing benefits to the organization's consumers entails controlling its costs and targeting its expenditures efficiently to its highest priorities.

The objectives of this chapter are to enable readers to

1. Identify the relationships between income and expenses, priorities and cost controls.
2. Understand the principles of accountability to donors regarding the organization's income.
3. Understand the importance of setting and following the organization's priorities.
4. Use the organization's basic financial documents, including budgets and financial reports to its sponsors and the public.

Budgets

Budgets are internal tools that every organization uses to plan how it will spend its money. They reflect its leaders' decisions about how to use the organization's resources and thus serve as a good indicator of what has been decided about the organization's priorities for the year. Budgets are then used to guide expenditures and to track *actual* income and expenses against *planned* income and expenses. Month-to-month reports document this movement toward obtaining and using up the available resources for the year. Expenditures in any category that are well over or under the budgeted amount serve as red flags to managers, who should then look for explanations of why the rate of spending is exceeding the projected amounts and what can be done to get back on track.

Budgets are usually drawn up annually and show what the organization will spend its money on in the coming twelve months. They include the expected sources and amounts of income from each category and the planned expenditures and amounts of each. Often, for comparison, budgets show the organization's expenditures for the previous year. Table 15.1 shows an example of one organization's budget.

In addition to the organization's commitments for the current year, this illustrative budget includes what this organization used last year as its planned budget and how it turned out at the end of the year. Note that the projected budget included a $900 deficit but that the money actually spent during the year reduced that deficit by $195, to $705. The projected budget for the coming year shows a $50 surplus.

Since none of us has a foolproof method for predicting the future precisely, there usually is some difference between what we planned and what actually happens. Changes in the external environment, such as an unexpected new funding source or negative publicity about a program, can lead to large fluctuations in actual income. When income or expenses depart widely from expectations, managers should examine the explanations for the changes and take action to get back on course. The example budget indicates that this organization received slightly more in fees and individual donations than projected but substantially less in grant income than expected. It spent more in several categories, ending the year with a deficit of $705. Examining the reasons behind those differences can also serve to inform and improve program and budget planning for the coming year.

Budgets are the results of negotiations concerning the interests of those

Table 15.1

Woodhaven Community Center Budget for Year 200x

	Last Year Projected ($)	Last Year Actual ($)	Coming Year ($)
Revenues ($)			
Membership Fees	8,750	9,410	9,600
Program and Activity Fees	19,860	20,745	22,000
Grants	82,000	80,000	82,000
Individual Donations	36,000	37,980	39,000
Corporate Support	24,500	24,020	26,000
Totals	171,110	172,155	178,600
Expenses ($)			
Payroll			
salaries	98,000	98,000	99,580
taxes	18,750	18,900	20,150
benefits	19,980	20,100	21,600
Lease	24,000	24,000	26,000
Supplies	1,350	1,465	1,300
Printing	1,990	2,185	2,100
Postage	810	890	890
Telephone	1,200	1,185	1,250
Travel	2,480	3,480	3,080
Meals	1,600	1,420	1,400
Purchased Services	1,850	1,195	1,200
Totals	172,010	172,860	178,550
Surplus (deficit)	(900)	(705)	50

who have a stake in the organization and its success. The views of staff, donors, consumers, and managers are likely to differ, and so their interests should be heard at the beginning of drawing up a budget. Then the process should turn to addressing the difficult questions about which needs and interests will take priority and which will be postponed. There always is a wide range of positions on how money should be used, generally adding up to far more than the available and expected resources. These competing interests often vie for inclusion in the final priorities and commitments that will guide the organization in the coming year. A budget represents the conclusions to those difficult questions about the organization's priorities.

Most organizations approach projections of income and expenses for the coming year by making incremental adjustments in each category from the previous year's experiences. So if a category of expenses saw a modest increase last year, the estimates for the coming year would indicate a similarly modest increase. If the organization planned to make substantive changes in programs, such as a cutback on one and major expansions of another, the commitments for the coming year would show these larger changes in the two programs' budgets.

The problem with this traditional, incremental approach to budgeting is that outdated expenditures continue to be made long after the organization's internal and external environments have changed. A more radical approach to budgets is called *zero-based budgeting*. This process intentionally ignores last year's experiences and starts over by reviewing the mission and strategic goals the organization has set for the coming year. The basic question to be answered is, If we were starting completely over and had this mission and these new goals, how would we divide up our resources to achieve them? The basic components needed to attain a goal are identified, and cost estimates are formulated for each. Then the costs for each component of a program are combined to form a program budget, after which they are combined with all the other programs' budgets to form an overall organizational budget.

This approach can result in budget commitments that are substantially different from those of the past year and is useful for new organizations and for larger ones that need extensive overhauling and change. The principal problem with the zero-base budget model is that so many of the organization's costs are fixed. Personnel cannot be fired unilaterally without due process. Rent, insurance, utilities, and other expenses continue even if the activities change to meet new program priorities. Thus, the actual percentage of funds available for reallocation may dwindle to only a small amount.

A budget is a good tool for managers to use in monitoring and controlling spending and keeping the organization within the limits of its income. Salaries have to be paid, and workspace and utilities cannot be avoided, however much staff may want a new program. The expenses of sustaining the organization are *fixed* or *nondiscretionary* expenses. The organization must plan ahead to ensure that its reserves in good months are large enough to cover its expected costs in lean months. Most of the organization's contributions come in December or in the weeks following the completion of a campaign, but expenses such as salaries and lease payments must be paid regularly. When expenses begin to run ahead of resources, controls or cutbacks are necessary to protect the organization's health and viability.

Situations requiring management to cut back spending are often regarded as bad news by staff, particularly those whose wishes cannot be supported. As a result, many employees begin thinking negatively of those who develop and monitor budgets, but this "blame the messenger" tactic only postpones the necessity of keeping expenditures in line with income and preparing for the future. It is easy to overlook the long-range protections that budgets provide for the organization. Honest exchange is important among those who bring in the money, those who spend it, and those who monitor it, as it enables the organization to continue to pursue its mission, even though many participants may see it as falling short of its potential. Accountability means using resources carefully to accomplish as much of the organization's mission as possible with the assets it has.

Budgets may be further broken down into subbudgets for each of the organization's programs. For example, a neighborhood center may have a camping program, an adult literacy program, an after-school tutoring program, and a food pantry. Each of these areas should have a budget showing its expected income and expenses. Subbudgets can be used to track the income and expenses for each program, which can be used when planning a new budget for the coming year. For example, the illustrative budget in table 15.1 could have been expanded by adding more columns, one for each of the organization's programs. Each program can show its expected income and expenses, with the sum of each row adding to the overall budget allocation for that category of expense or income.

Program budgets may also allow coordination among program managers or even negotiations, in which one running low expenses in one budget category may negotiate with another program running higher expenses in another category. For example, program A finds that it doesn't need as much as projected for supplies but needs more than projected for public relations. The leader of that program may propose a trade with another program to offer some of its surplus for the other's deficit in return for help later, all within the organization's overall budget. The organization's executive may negotiate with program directors for short-term transfers across programs, so one program's surplus is used to cover another's deficit and is paid back later in the year. If that does not work, the executive is faced with the undesirable choice of borrowing money from the outside to cover a deficit. While borrowing to cover deficits may seem to solve problems in the short term, the practice can lead to annual deficits, which undermine contributors' support for the organization and result in downward spirals and eventually bankruptcy.

Unexpected new discretionary income is always welcome, but unanticipated lower income or higher expenses (such as the recent and dramatic rise in energy prices) require lowering the expenditures in other areas of the organization. Close monitoring of income and expenses against the budget figures can provide early warning of approaching financial problems and allow the organization to address them before they become crises. Conversely, growing surpluses allow the organization to reconsider proposed expansions that were postponed in the earlier budget negotiations.

Internal Controls

In addition to monitoring income and expenses against the projected budget, every nonprofit should pay attention to the steps in receiving money, depositing that money, paying its expenses, and keeping detailed records of every financial transaction. The organization should have written policies and procedures to strengthen its internal controls. Not only does this protect it from fraud, abuse, waste, and inefficiency, but it also tells the staff and the public on how the nonprofit ensures compliance and accountability. These controls are an integral part of making sure that the various financial statements reflect actual operations. Accurate financial records are essential to trustworthy financial reports, and table 15.2 shows some aspects of the organization's financial activities that warrant attention and accurate records.

Table 15.2
Areas for Strong Internal Controls

Preparing and reviewing financial statements	Making timely deposits
Developing and adjusting annual budgets	Reconciling bank statements
Managing accounts receivable	Payroll
Accounting for bad debts	Recording assets
Maintaining and controlling inventory expenditures	Monitoring petty cash
Developing depreciation	Inventories
Disposition of fixed/capital assets	Accounts payable
Accounts payable records	Aging of accounts payable
Paying the bills	Employee advances

Misplacing One's Frustrations

Your assistant, Jamie Ross, has been pushing for a new computer to help her perform all the tasks needed to be an effective administrative assistant. She now spends most of her time on correspondence, the Internet, spreadsheets, and e-mail, not all of which is related to her work. Recently, whenever people ask her about something, instead of directly offering to help, she whines and says, "I would be glad to help as soon as this old computer finishes saving this document. I wish I could get a new one."

After several months of this, people start to mention it to you. Not wanting to upset her more than necessary, you do remember telling her that the budget did not allow for this purchase and that the agency's technology replacement fund has criteria that put the administration's needs lower on the list than those of the direct service personnel.

How should you discuss this matter with Jamie? What are your goals for the conversation? How will you prepare for her possible reaction? What actions might you consider and propose to her?

The Balance Sheet

Several kinds of financial reports are needed for people outside the organization, including donors, foundations or government grantmakers, and the general public. Demonstrating accountability through careful reports of the organization's finances ensures its contributors that their gifts are being used wisely and to reinforce their trust and hence their further support. The first kind of report we consider is the *balance sheet*, sometimes called a *statement of financial position*.

Balance sheets are summaries of an organization's financial situation at any point in time. They may be prepared monthly, quarterly, or annually. The summary shows the value of all the organization's resources, all its debts, and the differences between the two. It indicates the value of the organization's net resources at the time of the report. Sometimes the balance sheet shows resources and debts at a previous point in time to allow for comparisons of changes over the interval. Often an organization's year-end balance sheet is included with its annual report.

Table 15.3 is a simplified example of an organization's balance sheet. This is for instructional purposes only and does not conform to generally accepted accounting principles, which are maintained and occasionally updated by a

Table 15.3
Balance Sheet for Oakwood Health Center

	2008 ($)	2007 ($)
ASSETS		
Current assets		
Cash	10,985	9,210
Short-term investments	6,040	6,185
Accounts receivable	1,535	1,840
Grants receivable	280	730
Materials inventory	350	308
Prepaid expenses	680	481
Total current assets	19,870	18,754
Fixed assets		
Investments	22,620	22,535
Land, buildings, and equipment	2,880	2,565
Total fixed assets	25,500	25,100
Total Assets	45,370	43,854
LIABILITIES AND FUND BALANCES		
Current liabilities		
Accounts payable	840	1,290
Grants	2,880	3,500
Acquisition contracts	1,325	1,195
Total current liabilities	5,045	5,985
Long-term liabilities		
Notes payable	160	1,215
Fund balances		
Current, unrestricted	30,255	28,305
Current, restricted	680	605
Land, buildings, and equipment	3,890	3,145
Endowment fund	5,340	4,599
Total fund balances	40,165	36,654
Total Liabilities and Fund Balances	45,370	43,854

national organization, the Financial Accounting Standards Board. Understanding the F.A.S.B.'s rules is useful in interpreting typical balance sheet reports and their limitations. Also note that the balance sheets of many larger organizations round each dollar amount to the nearest $1,000, so the reader must mentally add three zeros to each figure if the report indicates such rounding of its figures.

Income is received and expenditures are made on many days during the organization's operations, and they should be recorded systematically and summed up periodically. These transactions are recorded in the organization's accounting journal and provide the figures used in creating a balance sheet. The illustrative report of December 31, 2008, is a composite of all the financial activities during that year and the final balances at that date. A summary like this provides little detail about those activities, but it does offer an overview of the organization's financial health. More detailed information is available in other financial reports.

ASSETS

The first part of table 15.3 shows the organization's assets, which include everything that is owned by the organization and everything that could provide economic benefit to it. Assets are usually listed in order of *liquidity*, or the ease of converting the asset into cash. Obviously, cash on hand in a checking account is the most liquid, so it is first on the list of the organization's assets. Short-term investments, such as savings accounts, come next, followed by accounts receivable. These are the amounts owed to the organization by its members, consumers, or debtors. Then come all the equipment, materials, and supplies on hand (somewhat more difficult to convert into cash), followed by any expenditures the organization has made that will benefit it in the future, such as credit with a supplier, insurance payments made for an additional year ahead, or advance payments on the lease for the building. All these categories are added together to obtain the organization's total current assets.[1]

The next category contains items labeled as *fixed assets*, those things that are necessary to support the organization's productive capacity. These include the land, buildings, and investments that produce ongoing income for the organization. They can be converted into cash but not very quickly. An example is an endowment fund that generates interest that comes to the organization periodically. Land and buildings are another common type of fixed asset. It is necessary to have some place to do the work of the organization, so turning them into cash would be a last resort.

Most of an organization's tangible assets are being used, are growing older, and hence are becoming less valuable. Cars and computers are good examples of this. Their value declines over time, a feature called *depreciation*. The value of an asset given on the balance sheet is its original cost or donated value minus the accumulated depreciation. There are two ways to estimate depreciation. The straight-line method assumes a uniform decline in the asset's value, so the original cost is divided by the projected number of years of usefulness. The accelerated method assumes that an asset provides better use and benefit in its earlier years, so a higher depreciation is shown in the first few years of its use, with smaller declines in later years. Either way, the cost of a tangible asset is spread over its useful life. Note that the depreciated value is not an asset's replacement value.

One F.A.S.B. rule is that those things the organization purchased are reported at their cost at the time of purchase and that donated assets are reported at their fair market value at the time of the gift, minus depreciation. Such assets (other than land) can wear out or become obsolete, so an appropriate depreciation (reduction) in original cost or value is given on the balance sheet. The current market value of fixed assets may be higher or lower than that figure, so balance sheets often include footnotes citing their current market value.

Another type of fixed asset may be the organization's intangible resources, such as patents on inventions or copyrights on books. If there is any evidence that the organization will realize future benefits from such intangibles, they are reported on the balance sheet at their original cost minus the estimated reduction in value. This process of reducing the estimated future value of an intangible asset is called *amortization* and is parallel to the process of depreciating a tangible asset.

All these current and fixed assets are summed up and then combined to show the organization's total assets. When comparing current and fixed assets, a high proportion of current assets to total assets indicates that the organization has a great deal of flexibility, since many of its resources could easily be turned into cash. If such projected cash requirements are low, then managers may want to convert some current assets into fixed assets, such as moving cash into property or endowments.

Conversely, a high proportion of fixed-to-total assets may indicate the organization's long-term stability (or a capital-intensive technology, such as a hospital has in medical equipment) but a lesser amount of flexibility. Because an organization's leaders want to maintain the right combination of stability and flexibility, they examine previous years' balance sheets and then look forward to expected demands to estimate what proportion of assets should be in each type, current or fixed.

LIABILITIES

The next part of table 15.3 is labeled *liabilities*. *Liabilities* are items that represent claims against the organization's resources, amounts owed to other people and organizations. They are obligations that the organization must settle sometime in the future by means of cash or services. Liabilities increase when an organization buys on credit or borrows money, and they decrease as it pays off its debts or returns borrowed resources. They are divided into *current liabilities* (due soon) and *long-term liabilities* (due later).

The list of this organization's current liabilities shows accounts payable as the first category. This refers to all the organization's unpaid bills from those who have provided it with goods or services. A utility bill and an invoice for an insurance premium due are examples of this category of liability. Another kind of liability is promises to pay something to someone in the future, such as scholarships awarded to participants in a future educational series or camp session. All such near-term commitments are summed together into the category of *total current liabilities*.

Long-term liabilities are those debts the organization has incurred that will take several months or even years to pay off. They include amounts borrowed from banks (such as a mortgage) or suppliers of large equipment (such as a bus or a computer network) that require payments of principal and interest each month until the debt is paid off. They are called *notes payable* because they are documented in a legal form called a *note as evidence of the liability*.

In the next part of table 15.3 is a section labeled *Fund Balances*, which represents the organization's net economic resources. Note that on a balance sheet, the term *fund* does *not* refer to cash or a bank balance, which is information given in the Assets part of the report. Rather, *fund balances* are the difference between the accounted value of the organization's assets and the accounted value of its liabilities. Remember that assets minus liabilities equals fund balances.

Types of Funds

While the best gifts are those that come with no strings attached, some people who give money to a nonprofit organization may want to designate or restrict how their money is to be used. For example, a government or foundation grant is typically given for a specific project, not for the organization's general operation. The gift is subject to conditions set down by the giver and accepted in advance by the organization's leaders. Sometimes, however, the demands are so high that an organization's leaders may decide to forgo the gift.

In order to help the organization's leaders keep track of expenditures and provide complete reports on how each gift was used, many nonprofits use types of funds, such as

- Current funds, unrestricted.
- Current funds, restricted.
- Land, building, and equipment fund.
- Endowment fund.

Current unrestricted funds are those over which the executive and board have discretionary control. They may be used in any aspect of the organization for which they are needed. Clearly, a major goal in fund-raising is to maximize the amounts in this category to allow greater flexibility in spending decisions.

Current restricted funds may be used in daily operations but only for the specific purposes designated by the donor. One may require that her gift be used only to support scholarships for needy youth, while another may specify that his contribution be used only to support staff training. A government grant may be designated for only a specific type of program or service. Contributions like these do reduce the managers' flexibility, but their willingness to accept a restriction often encourages a donor who otherwise may not give to the organization.

A fund labeled *Land, Building, and Equipment* is the organization's accumulated net investment in fixed assets (property, buildings) as well as those unspent resources contributed specifically to acquire or replace them. For example, a donor may restrict the use of her gift to building a new wing of a hospital or art museum.

Endowment funds are the organization's long-term investments that produce income from interest earned by the capital. For example, a contributor may specify that a current gift be invested by the organization and that only the income generated by this investment be used for some purpose, such as providing scholarships or purchasing new medical equipment in the future.

CHANGES IN FUND BALANCES

When a nonprofit organization receives contributions from donors, fees from members or participants, grants from foundations or governmental departments, or any other such income, the assets section of the balance

Smart Budgeting?

Jack Jensen was pleased that his grant from the local Community Foundation was renewed for another year. Certainly the orchestra needed the money to continue the children's concerts. But there was one sentence in the award letter that concerned him: "We require an audit of all the past year's expenses to ensure they meet the proposed budget that was approved when the grant was awarded."

The organization's normal practice was to put all income into a "current operations" account category. Would it even be possible to divide into separate categories the expenses for transportation, food, office supplies, telephone, public relations, musical instruments, and copying? This is how the grant proposal's budget had been framed, and apparently the foundation's financial officer now wants that kind of detailed documentation.

In the short term (next month), what can the nonprofit do to respond to this request without putting the grant renewal in jeopardy? What actions should the director take to prevent similar problems in the future?

sheet shows increases. If the organization's liabilities remain the same, then the fund balances will also get bigger. When the costs of carrying out a program exceed the income it produces, then the organization's liabilities increase and its fund balances decrease. Its fund balances rise when its assets increase, its liabilities decrease, or some combination of these two. The fund balances decrease when the assets decrease, the liabilities increase, or some combination of the two. The balance sheet produces a snapshot of the organization's financial situation at one point in time. Such reports may be compared for several years to track changes in the organization's financial situation. Over time, the leaders of all organizations want to see its assets and fund balances grow.

Statement of Activity

A second major type of financial report is the *statement of activity*, which specify the types of activities carried out by the organization over the year and the volume of each of them. They show the revenues generated by each major category (such as individual donor contributions, membership fees, government and foundation grants) and the types of expenses incurred, usually grouped by kind of program and form of expense. Then the organization's funds are identified, followed by the amount from each fund that was used to support each program. For example, a health organization may have programs in the areas of infant inoculations, health education, pregnancy prevention, and screening for various common diseases. Each of these programs has costs, including salaries and equipment. Then there are the costs for the overall management of the organization and for its fund-raising activities. The funds from which all those expenses are shown, including the amounts from each fund covering each of the kinds of expenses. Table 15.4 is a simplified example of one organization's statement of activity.

The statement of activity shows the organization's surpluses (or deficits) in each of its program categories for the year. Such information provides important indicators of the organization's health and effectiveness in financing its operations. Continued deficits will drain the organization until it collapses and are signals to its leaders that management needs to pay attention to increasing revenues and reducing costs. Conversely, surpluses allow managers to do the more pleasant things like increase salaries, try out an innovative new activity, purchase needed equipment, or invest in staff development. Continued surpluses indicate that the organization's leaders may be able to increase the quantity or quality of its services, pay off debts more rapidly than planned, or move some money into savings for the future. For example, table 15.4 indicates that $300 in endowment income was moved to the unrestricted fund, $95 was taken from the unrestricted fund, another $95 from the land, buildings, and equipment fund to purchase equipment that cost $190, and $40 was returned to a dissatisfied donor.

CASH AND ACCRUAL ACCOUNTING

Tracking income and expenses can be divided into income in cash or check and income in promised gifts and, likewise, into expenses paid by cash or check and expenses that are commitments that have not been fulfilled (such as supplies ordered but not yet paid for). A donor may pledge a substantial gift, payable over several years, or an organization may agree to a contract to purchase supplies over several years. There can be large differences between the actual checks coming in and going out and the commitments promising future income and expenses.

One method of recording and reporting cash income and expenses is called a *cash accounting method*, and another method that tracks promises or commitments (of income and expenses) is called an *accrual accounting method*. Cash payments usually lag behind the actual incurrence of promised expenditures, so a cash accounting approach may not show liabilities that are coming

Table 15.4

Statement of Activity for Year Ended December 31, 2008, and Comparative Totals for 2007

Current funds ($)			Land, building, and equipment ($)	Endowment fund ($)	Total All Funds ($) 2008	2007
	Unrestricted	Restricted				
Support and Revenues						
Public Support						
Direct	30,925	755	380	25	32,085	31,215
Indirect	1,175				1,175	1,500
Grants						
Foundations	400				400	
Government		100			100	100
Other revenues	1,980	35		105	2,120	2,080
Total support and revenues	34,480	890	380	130	35,880	34,895
Expenses						
Program A	6,385	785	10		7,180	6,625
Program B	2,605		35		2,640	2,428
Program C	3,860		30		3,890	2,505
Program D	2,040		60		2,100	2,030
Management and general	2,545		85		2,630	2,190
Fund-raising	3,315		68		3,383	2,830
Total expenses	20,750	785	288		21,823	18,608
National payment	5,225				5,225	4,100
Excess of support and revenues over expenses and dues	8,505	105	92	130	8,832	12,191
Other changes in fund balances						
Equipment acquisition	(95)		(95)		(190)	
Endowment fund appreciation	300			(300)		
Returned to donor		(40)			(40)	
Fund balances						
Begin year	26,805	615	3,245	10,085	40,750	35,515
End year	35,515	680	3,242	9,915	49,352	47,702

Table 15.5

Statement of Functional Expenses for Alston Arts Center, 2008, and Comparative Totals for 2007

	Programs ($)							Total Expenses ($)	
	A	B	C	D	Total	Manage-ment & general	Fund-raising	2008	2007
Payroll	860	1,805	1,005	1,485	5,155	1,850	2,025	9,030	7,915
Fees	00	60	00	40	100	105	40	245	205
Supplies	25	278	205	130	638	175	315	1,128	1,040
Utilities	35	185	160	185	565	220	240	1,025	975
Travel	10	110	105	110	335	125	180	640	560
Conferences	55	128	350	100	633	260	385	1,278	905
Awards	6,280	320	890	785	8,275	00	00	8,275	8,130
Miscellaneous	5	20	30	20	75	80	105	260	220
Total before depreciation	7,270	2,906	2,745	2,855	15,776	2,815	3,290	21,881	19,950
Depreciation	10	25	30	50	115	35	20	170	155
Total expenses	7,280	2,931	2,775	2,905	15,841	2,850	3,310	22,051	20,105

up in the future. Accrual accounting provides earlier warning of impending future financial demands, so many organizations prefer this method. Since both kinds of figures are important, some larger organizations maintain both kinds of records.

Statement of Functional Expenses

Providing even greater detail about expenses for each fund and each program of an organization is the third kind of financial report, the *statement of functional expenses*, in which each program and each fund is identified as a column and each kind of expense is a row. For an example, see table 15.5.

In a statement of functional expenses, each type of expense is tied to a particular program. Staff salaries are shown as payroll expenses for those working in each program, and each other type of expense is shown according to where it was used in the organization. Expenses that cannot be directly located in a specific program are recorded in one of two other categories, management and general, and fund-raising. The report provides full disclosure of the type and amount of expense in every program or unit of the organization.

Statement of Changes in Financial Position

A fourth kind of financial report is the *statement of changes in financial position*, which shows the changes in cash balances over a year, including any changes in the sources and amounts of income during that year and changes in the uses of cash over that same time period. For an example, see table 15.6.

Table 15.6
Statement of Changes in Financial Position of Washington Development Center for Year Ending December 31, 2008

Cash came from	
Excess from operations upport and revenue	$38,455
minus	
Expenses other than depreciation	21,740
Payment to national association	6,120
Increase in accounts payable	35
Increase in deferred revenue	110
net	10,450
Cash was used for	
Increase in short-term investments	150
Increase in accounts receivable	200
Increase in pledges receivable	695
Increase in grants receivable	466
Increase in materials	340
Increase in prepaid expenses	218
Increase in investments	3,800
Increase in equipment	605
Decrease in grants payable	110
Decrease in notes payable	825
Returning contributions to donors	30
total	7,439
Net increase (decrease) in cash	3,011
Cash balance, beginning of year	12,210
Cash balance, end of year	15,221

In a typical statement of changes, the main sources of cash for the year are noted along with the amounts coming from each source. Then the major uses of that cash are identified, such as putting some of it into investments or purchasing additional materials or speeding up payments on a bank loan. The cash balance at the beginning of the year is shown, followed by the balance at the end of the year. Along with the other types of financial accounting reports, comparing cash balances over several years is a good way to track an organization's financial health. The information provided in these reports is also used to complete the IRS Form 990.

In summary, annual financial reports include a range of information about an organization. They provide evidence of its income and expenses, allowing donors and the public to see how the organization used the resources it received. These reports are crucial to the public's image of the organization, whereas budgets represent internal plans that identify the specific amounts that will be spent in each category of expenses. They are most useful internally for tracking income and expenses on a monthly basis.

Applications: Using Financial Indicators

The information provided in the various types of financial reports can be used in many different ways, and we looked at just four of them here. These financial ratios may be used to compare an organization with itself over several years and with other similar organizations. They also can be useful when considering which organization one may want to consider for employment or for making donations.

1. The *working capital ratio*. A major financial objective for any organization is to be able to pay its bills on time. This ability is high when its cash and near-cash assets are high in relation to its liabilities. The working capital ratio indicates how readily the organization can pay its bills on time and is made up of current assets divided by current liabilities. A ratio of about 2 to 1 (or better) is considered good, while 1 to 1 (or less) suggests a high risk of insolvency. A very high ratio may suggest that the organization has some idle assets that may be put to more productive use, such as improving the quality and quantity of services. Using the data in table 15.3, we see that this organization has a working capital ratio of 3.94. It is well able to pay its bills on time and may consider expanding its services or increasing savings.

2. The *debt–equity ratio*. Another important objective of any organization is to be able to avoid bankruptcy, which results when an organization's total liabilities

exceed its total assets and it cannot pay its bills. The risk of bankruptcy grows when an organization increases its dependence on borrowing to finance its current operations. A measure of this relative reliance on liabilities is provided by the debt–equity ratio. It is calculated by dividing the total amount of liabilities by the total fund balances. A ratio of larger than 1.0 indicates the organization could not pay its debts if required to do so; hence it is at greater risk of bankruptcy. Smaller decimal fractions are indicators of greater health. Using the data in table 15.3, we see that this organization has a debt-to-equity ratio of 0.13, indicating that it is nowhere near bankruptcy.

3. The *fund mix*. Another objective of an organization's leaders is to have maximum flexibility in financial decisions so they can easily move money from one category to another. The fund mix is found by dividing the amount of unrestricted funds by total assets. The larger the figure is, the greater will be the flexibility in financial decisions. Using the data in table 15.4, we see that this organization has a mix of 0.67. Two-thirds of its funds are available for reallocation, indicating extensive flexibility in management's decisions about how to use its resources.

4. The *growth ratio*. If an organization intends to grow, a measure of success would be the percentage of change over time in its total fund balances. The growth ratio indicates the growth of the organization between any two points in time. It is composed of the fund balances at time 2 minus the fund balance at time 1, divided by the fund balance at time 1. Larger numbers indicate greater growth over the time interval examined, and negative results indicate an organization in decline. Using the data in table 15.4, we see that this organization has a growth ratio of 0.96, or just over 9 percent growth over the years reported. This suggests a growing organization.

5. The *program emphasis*. This figure indicates how well the organization is keeping its expenditures focused on programs and services versus self-maintenance. It is calculated by adding the amounts spent on "management and general" to those for "fund-raising" and then dividing that sum by "total revenue." Some national standard-setting organizations recommend that a healthy nonprofit use no more than about 25 percent of its revenue for self-maintenance and 75 percent or more for its programs and services. Using the data in table 15.4 , we see that this organization spent $5,860 on management and general plus fund-raising, and its total revenue was $34,480, with a resulting score of 0.17. Seventeen percent of its income was used for management and fund-raising expenses, which indicates that the organization spent a very large proportion of its income on program support.

In conclusion, budgets are internal tools that organizations use to plan their expenditures for the coming year and then track and control the outflow of money to sustain their operations. Income usually does not remain steady over a year, but many expenses (such as salaries or rent) do remain steady.

Therefore, accumulating some surpluses in advance of expenses is necessary to avoid borrowing to keep the organization going. Financial reports are ways in which organizations inform their donors, grantors, and the public about their financial strength and efficiency. The *balance sheet* or statement of financial position provides summaries of the organization's resources or assets, its liabilities or debts, and the differences between the two. The *statement of activity* shows the volume and type of activities carried out, including the revenues generated by each type and the expenses of each. The *statement of functional expenses* provides even greater detail about the amounts spent for each of the organization's programs or components. The *statement of changes in financial position* shows the sources and amounts of cash coming in and the uses of that money to sustain and strengthen the organization. These tools are some of the main ways that organizations plan and track their income and expenses and demonstrate accountability for the resources they receive. They are the principal ways that organizations develop and sustain public trust and support.

Web Exercise

Go to the Web site of a large national nonprofit that interests you and find its most recent annual report. Begin with the balance sheet or statement of financial position and examine its assets, liabilities, and fund balances. What are its largest assets? What are its main liabilities? How do the fund balances at the beginning of the year compare with those at the end of the year? What kinds of restricted funds does it have? Calculate the five financial ratios, and describe what they tell you about the organization. Is this a place where you could work with confidence in the future of the organization? Compare this organization with another in the same general field. To which could you make a donation with greater confidence in the future?

16

Nonprofit Organizations Tomorrow

In this concluding chapter, we predict nonprofit organizations' future issues of concern and opportunity, based on many of the ideas already discussed in the book. Thinking about these issues will help readers to

1. Understand and begin preparing for important political, professional, and policy issues that will affect nonprofit organizations.
2. Develop appropriate responses to meet these challenges.
3. Formulate their own ideas of what the future might hold.

Many people take a reactive stance toward external trends, social movements, economic conditions, philanthropy, and service delivery options. Entrepreneurship and invention, however, are more constructive strategies, as they enable nonprofit leaders to work with valid, reliable, and current information and to create strategic plans. This last chapter describes six major issues that nonprofits will encounter in the coming years. Whether they react or plan effectively will be their critical leadership test.

Trend 1: Accountability

The recent upsurge in demands for greater accountability will not wane anytime soon. We believe that Congress will expand the provisions of the

Sarbannes–Oxley Act to include all nonprofit organizations chartered in the United States as well as those offering services here even if chartered elsewhere. The calls to do this stem from the success of the legislation requiring greater corporate accountability. The top leaders, including nonprofits' executives and boards of trustees, will feel the most direct impact.

Among the act's provisions that we predict will be extended to nonprofits are requirements that they

1. Set clearly stated and specific accounting standards.
2. Conduct external audits annually.
3. Prohibit auditors from providing nonaudit services.
4. Require boards to have an audit committee that selects, compensates, oversees, and discharges external auditors.
5. Have their executives evaluate and ensure the accuracy of internal financial controls and describe these steps in annual reports.
6. Have their executives certify the accuracy of all financial reports, including the expanded IRS Form 990.
7. Have their executives fully disclose all financial transactions.
8. Prohibit loans to executives and board members.
9. Have their boards and executives follow policies on conflicts of interest.
10. Have on their boards at least one member who is financially qualified and also serves on the audit committee.
11. Include in the U.S. Code requirements for criminal penalties for knowingly destroying, altering, concealing, or falsifying records to obstruct investigations.
12. Keep financial and other relevant documents for at least five years.
13. Establish policies that protect whistle-blowers and prohibit retaliation against them.
14. Prohibit the board from incurring debts resulting from fraudulent activities and prevent them from being discharged in bankruptcy.
15. Increase the penalties for fraudulent activities and the limitations on the future employment of violators of these rules.

As chapter 14 explains, these calls for greater accountability have many roots, but mainly they seek to correct what the public believes are abuses. Examples range from excessive salaries for nonprofit leaders to diverting money from its intended uses, from poor quality to the neglect of clientele, from the failure to maintain appropriate records to wasteful management practices, from nepotism to not reflecting community values, and from the failure to correct known problems to outright fraud. Each of these issues requires appropriate action, and together they fuel a movement for reform of the nonprofit sector.

Community service organizations, fund-raising programs and founda-tions, labor unions, political advocacy groups all fall under this umbrella of required expansions in transparency and accountability. Currently, the at-torneys general of most states do not routinely audit nonprofit organizations, relying instead on informed allegations to surface before acting. But when the federal and state governments begin taking a more proactive stance, the resulting greater oversight will lead to more transparency of and public trust in nonprofit organizations.

An example shows how the voluntary sector can craft a productive approach to raising standards. The Maryland Association of Nonprofit Organizations (Maryland Nonprofits) created a certificate program and curriculum whose "Standards of Excellence" include "an Ethics and Accountability Code for the Nonprofit Sector" based on honesty, integrity, fairness, respect, trust, responsi-bility, and accountability.[1] These standards set a high benchmark and go beyond the minimum legal requirements by describing how well-managed and respon-sibly governed nonprofits should operate. They address many of the hot-but-ton topics in today's public discourse and reflect legislative agendas across the country: mission, governance, conflicts of interest, legal and regulatory compli-ance, financial accountability, openness and transparency, fund-raising, policy, advocacy, and public affairs. The Maryland Association has taken the process a step further by listing more than fifty behaviorally based performance standards needed for full compliance. For example, in the section on effective governance, the third standard states, "The board should have no fewer than five (5) unre-lated directors. Seven (7) or more directors are preferable." Although these stan-dards are not yet mandatory, they demonstrate that the state's nonprofit leaders are dealing seriously with the trend for greater accountability.

Additional support for greater transparency and accountability comes from the Independent Sector, which in its testimony to Congress supported the IRS's more extensive and rigorous monitoring of charitable organiza-tions.[2] The Independent Sector called for expanding the IRS's enforcement program for nonprofits, offering more extensive educational resources so that nonprofit organizations better understand the audit process, and instituting harsher penalties for failing to adhere to the higher standards.

Trend 2: Advocacy Backlash

Many nonprofits actively engage in advocacy as part of their mission. Their intention is to serve their consumers both directly and indirectly by helping change the social conditions that limit the resources for them. This form of public education sometimes includes legislative lobbying. Hunger groups, housing advocates, United Way, American Red Cross, educational foundations, professional associations, performing and cultural arts organizations, and religious groups use the protections of their nonprofit tax status to inform legislative leaders and their staff members and to advocate for change. This is seen as democracy in action and represents the best ideals of our nation's heritage.

Nonetheless, events ranging from the National Rifle Association's political stands to AARP's support of Medicare changes have raised concerns that these and other nonprofits are no different from their corporate counterparts. Former House Majority Leader Tom Delay's well-chronicled problems with his own charity allegedly included using nonprofit funds to entertain Republican delegates at their national convention, which led to even more calls for reform.

The leadership dilemma is how the nonprofit can help those members of society whom it is dedicated to serve without crossing the line into partisan politics. Many nonprofits are based on beliefs that the social contract and governmental protections provided by health, education, welfare, social services, and human service programs no longer are valid, owing to formal actions to reduce benefits and tighten eligibility standards and the failure to keep up with inflationary cost increases. Many nonprofits see these changes as calls to action.

Critics of nonprofit organizations claim that nonprofits have violated their articles of incorporation, bylaws, and federal or state tax rules in their advocacy efforts, that such activities are seen as prohibited political action. Efforts to further restrict nonprofits' advocacy efforts are likely to gain wider public support, and so their leaders must devise strategies for dealing with them. They should start by scrupulously adhering to the IRS's rules on this matter and then try to educate the public better about the value of nonpartisan public education and reform.

Trend 3: Professional Education

An emerging trend that will change the way that nonprofit organizations function is the professionalization of their managers and staff. The traditional promotional ladder that selected a top fund-raiser, a highly successful practitioner, or a socially elite community member to serve as the president or as a trustee is gradually disappearing. Now, the expectation for professional expertise has led to numerous training programs on management concepts, issues, skills, and techniques. Many colleges and universities now offer specific courses, academic majors, and degrees in the broad field of nonprofit organizations. Graduates of these programs get priority consideration when vacancies occur in leadership positions in nonprofits. Not only have they demonstrated their commitment to the voluntary sector, but they also bring the skills and abilities needed to succeed in this unique environment. A more extensive form of credentialing system will emerge, through a private national organization, quasi-governmental board, or as part of a government department.

An excellent example of how this trend is developing in U.S. colleges and universities is American Humanics, Inc. (AH).[3] With more than one hundred academic partners, AH provides a rigorous structure for undergraduate students in any major to earn a certificate upon completion of their bachelor's degree. The requirements include practical experience, formal course work, attendance at national leadership programs, and nonprofit internships while a student. This certificate program defines the competencies in the following areas that each student must display and document:

1. Career development and employment skills.
2. Communication skills.
3. Personal characteristics.
4. History of nonprofit organizations and management.
5. Board, committee, and volunteer development.
6. Fund-raising principles, practices, and ethics.
7. Human resource development.
8. Nonprofit accounting.
9. Public relations and marketing for nonprofit organizations.
10. Financial management.
11. Risk management.
12. Youth and adult development.
13. Program planning and evaluation.
14. General nonprofit organization management.

In addition, the concept of service as part of professional education now resides firmly in most colleges and universities. This "service-learning" movement is raising expectations of better linkages between classroom studies and community volunteering. For example, the University of Minnesota notes that its students receive

> direct experience working on the same content, ideas, and issues discussed in class through working at a community organization a couple hours per week, [build-

ing] a real relationship with a community organization. That relationship is reciprocal—you help the organization meet its goals, and the organization gives you the opportunity to develop professional skills and contacts while applying your academic work to real-world situations.[4]

This trend will expand to provide better-prepared professionals for the field.

Trend 4: Closing the Tax-Exempt Umbrella

Because many tax-exempt organizations are in the broadly defined health and educational fields, should these be covered by the same rules as apply to the New York Stock Exchange or to the U.S. Chamber of Commerce?[5] The IRS has proposed new rules that differ from the current definitions of tax-exempt status. These regulations would strengthen "the requirement that an organization serve a public rather than a private interest."[6] Nonprofit organizations already are required to have accounting systems in place to report and pay unrelated business income taxes, even if the surplus income is used for mission-related purposes. It is not a huge step in the same direction to tighten other legal requirements on nonprofits.

The New York Stock Exchange touches the lives of almost every American today, through individuals, corporations, pension funds, investor groups, or mutual funds. What prompted the exchange to get tax-exempt status? "The New York Stock Exchange traces its origins to 1792, when twenty-four New York City stockbrokers and merchants signed the Buttonwood Agreement. This agreement set in motion the NYSE's unwavering commitment to investors and issuers."[7] Does this meet the intent of serving the public? That is a policy question for elected officials to debate, but current trends suggest they will have this conversation and rethink the status of that organization.

The U.S. Chamber of Commerce issues policy statements on a wide range of issues affecting the United States' business interests. Trade reform, immigration, health and medical care, tort reform, and labor relations are a few of the many issues on which the chamber takes public stands. As its Web site notes, "The U.S. Chamber fights for you every day."[8] The *fight* is against other groups representing sectors such as labor unions and many professional associations. The point is not whether you agree with the chamber's stands on various issues. Rather, its work and that of others raises questions about why a nonprofit organization should be able to work under tax-exempt status to help corporations make greater profits or get higher returns on their investments. We predict that the requirements and restrictions for tax-exempt status will be increased.

Trend 5: Partnerships, Mergers, and Consolidations

The distinctions among business, government, and nonprofits have begun to blur. The Independent Sector (I.S.) calls for a new, collaborative approach called the Three Sector Initiative.[9] This perspective on community issues comes from an organization according to whose mission statement the "Independent Sector is the leadership forum for charities, foundations, and corporate giving programs committed to advancing the common good in America and around the world."[10] The I.S. sees more extensive collaboration across public, private, and voluntary sectors as an important trend for the future.

Interdependence is an emerging trend in the nonprofit world. But why would an independent organization with a history of dedicated service and programs that already meets a documented need consider merging or forming strategic alliances with another agency? There are a dozen reasons:

1. They enhance the organization's mission. For example, an art museum offers public educational programs to thousands of schoolchildren each year. What if this museum were to extend its educational mission by forming a partnership with the local university's school of education or art department? In that way, future teachers would gain experience and novice artists could find needed studio space in exchange for their contribution to the school's field trips.

2. Working collaboratively with others can affect the quality of services. Certainly, offering more services means meeting a larger portion of the community's needs. Services can also be improved and coordinated. For example, partnerships between hospitals and rehabilitation centers have been the norm for decades. This benefits patients because many of the interorganizational agreements have been negotiated in advance, thus smoothing their transitions from one facility to the other. Insurance coverage can be designed to facilitate these service programs.

3. Access to new technologies, skills, programs, services, and market share are excellent reasons to consider collaborating with other programs. Even though bigger may not always be better, in the case of nonprofit organization, bigger may allow increased access to a wider range of needed resources.

4. The most important and the seemingly most limited resource is money. Financial concerns dominate much of every executive's and board's time and ef-

fort. Increasing access to added revenue, reducing duplicate costs, improving bond ratings with accompanying lower interest rates, and showing external funding sources that cost controls make their investments go further all are legitimate reasons to consider a merger. The entire community has a stake in the nonprofit organizations' financial stability, prompted by program uncertainties caused by limited financial resources. How many times have we heard that if the local Untied Way campaign does not reach its goal, some elderly people will not have meals delivered to their homes?

5. A new organizational structure can be a positive outcome. Many nonprofits suffer from the same ailments as their corporate counterparts do. Old structures may not fit into today's realities.

6. Governance benefits. New board members can bring fresh ideas and energy, and needed new perspectives can lead to creative new possibilities and directions.

7. Stakeholders can be a force for change. Connecting with another organization can increase community awareness, access, and support. Good reputations can complement each other, especially if the consolidation is not a direct response to a public crisis.

8. Staff benefits. Possible outcomes are increased salaries and benefits, better work environments, more effective recruitment programs, new career paths and job opportunities, and promotion possibilities.

9. "If you cannot beat them, join them." Mergers reduce competition for scarce resources, for years the basis of the United States' economic model for the for-profit sector. But competition is usually not seen as a valued principle in the nonprofit world. In fact, several organizations offering overlapping services can be viewed as unnecessary duplication and therefore creating inefficiency. Mergers directly address such problems.

10. A weak reason for merger, consolidation, or partnership is crisis management. This should be only a last resort, although it seems to be a common one. Many city hospitals have closed or joined other hospitals because of documented scandals, poor finances, challenges to maintaining needed accreditation, or outdated physical facilities.

11. Access to new markets can be an important catalyst for change.

12. Greater political clout can work to the participating organizations' advantage. When it is part of the organization's mission, better advocacy for clients and programs enhances its resources and reputation.

As noted in chapter 11, an organization has several options if it wants to consider new models for organizing and delivering its programs and services. The simplest is, rather than doing it alone, for its leaders to consider *joint programs* in which two organizations come together as equal partners to expand existing programs or offer new programs. This arrangement permits each organization to retain its autonomy, rules, policies, articles of incorporation, and other support structures.

Partnerships can help some nonprofit organizations fulfill their missions more effectively or efficiently. In the 1990s, the number of public–private partnerships increased nationally, due in part to the rising demand of federal and state departments for nonprofits to use their funds more efficiently. Partnerships also demonstrate that advocacy, human services, and the arts depend on many others for success.

No one organization can meet all the needs of an entire community. Partnerships require two or more independent organizations to contribute something to a relationship. Autonomy and independence remain for their other programs and services. Thus the focus of a partnership may be limited.

For example, nationally, symphony orchestras now spend about 15 percent of their budgets on educational outreach programs, many to schools in rural areas and inner cities. These partnerships include sponsoring musicians-in-residence, offering individual lessons, staging after-school concerts, and making instruments available for talented youth. They do not replace the school system's music or band curriculum instruction; rather, they supplement them. The orchestra, school, students, and the community all benefit as a result.

Administrative consolidations can lead to efficiencies while maintaining the institutions' integrity and autonomy. This is not unlike outsourcing. Payroll processing, grant writing, housekeeping, data processing, media relations, fund-raising, and employee wellness programs are examples of consolidations that can save organizations time, money, and space while at the same time allowing experts to conduct these efforts. In Cleveland, Ohio, the Council on Smaller Enterprises provides numerous services ranging from group purchasing to health insurance for those organizations that cannot afford them by themselves.[11] Greater efficiencies for the participating organizations result.

Total *merger* is the most dramatic type of change. In this scenario, one organization is totally subsumed by another. It ceases to exist in its former state, and almost everything changes. This can be good if the organization's quality, reputation, service programs, or facilities are declining. Its independent board ceases to exist, and its articles of incorporation become null and void. A variation of this model is the joining of two systems to create a third, new entity. Both of us have long connections to Case Western Reserve University, which used to be two separate, independent universities with different, though complementary, missions: Western Reserve University and Case

Institute of Technology. After the federation of these two adjacent campuses into one institution, the missions of both were strengthened.

This decision was not easy and revealed some of the major problems that mergers, partnerships, consolidations, or joint ventures face. The following are several important concerns when considering such a decision:

1. Great ideas can lead to trying to do too much too soon. Success comes in small steps. Thus, effective planning for both the short term and the long term is needed.

2. Managing in the new, often larger, system requires different skills and styles than may have been needed in the old, smaller organization. Delegation to informed, competent subordinates frees top leaders to focus on strategic issues. Operational details should be delegated, not controlled centrally. Such transitions, however, are difficult for many people.

3. Duplicate systems must be eliminated, by either adopting the "better" one or creating a new one, which in itself can lead to additional problems. For example, computers, personnel manuals, training programs, salary scales, and control procedures all must be reviewed and probably revised for the new organization.

4. The new system requires policies that must be written, reviewed, disseminated, and implemented. A note of caution is in order here. When even considering partnerships or mergers, the board must be careful to maintain all its fiduciary duties and responsibilities and must adhere to all current policies and bylaws while making the changes.

5. Failure to inform the public and other stakeholders will lead to problems. Most people are not willing to undergo short-term confusion or pain for longer-term gains.

6. Merging two cultures into one takes many years. Long-term employees do not stop telling stories about how things worked in the past. If the employees are resisting the change, these tales will often insist that things were better "before." Training across the organization helps, but the organization's culture will take a long time to coalesce.

7. There are almost certainly unexpected and hidden costs. Even changing computer Web sites and informing vendors and users are time-consuming, and working with financial institutions gives new meaning to the term *paperwork*.

8. Understanding the past does not ensure that the future will be kind to strategic plans. There are always economic uncertainties, clients' concerns, employees' feelings of loss, and new competition from unexpected sources. Flexibility, persistence, and a good sense of humor all help in the difficult transition.

9. Time and professional attention must be paid to legal implications, liability

exposures, regulatory specifications, and licensure requirements. Failure to do so will result in unacceptable consequences for the organization.

10. A hidden concern may be that the new arrangement increases financial obligations, such as the nonprofit's debt, debt service, and accounts payable.

11. The new organization must cultivate new funding sources. Old loyalists may not be enamored with new organization, since it has no history and direct connection to them personally or institutionally, and they may view these new arrangements as diluting or compromising, changes too drastic to keep on supporting.

The final question for board members is, What are the impacts of the changes on the organization's capacities to carry out its mission? While focusing on "why," leaders and community stakeholders must proceed with strategic perspectives. Then they can decide what is best for the system in the long term. If their answers are uncertain, then the changes may not be worth pursuing.

Trend 6: Competencies Needed by Tomorrow's Nonprofit Organizational Leaders

Dedicated shelves in most libraries, volumes in local bookstores, and hundreds of thousands of Web sites proclaim the need for specific managerial skills to meet the challenges facing nonprofit organizations. In this closing section of the text, we describe the competencies that collectively can turn managers into leaders and make leaders more successful. They will increasingly be expected of people in nonprofit organizations. The following list summarizes much of the material presented in this book and can serve as a reminder and means of self-assessment and as a guide to one's further development of skills:

1. Visionary leaders enhance employees' work efforts to implement the approved organizational vision and strategic plans. They define, advocate for, and drive strategic initiatives through words, deeds, and actions, both internally and externally.

2. Results-oriented leaders establish, support, and reinforce a culture that delivers quality programs and produces desired outcomes in a timely manner in the most efficient and effective manner. They use information to constantly monitor and improve quality.

3. Team builders develop teams by becoming involved, sharing information, creating a positive environment, and enhancing loyalty through internal and external relationships. They are open to ideas and sharing power and spend time strengthening the team's functions as well as its members' results.

4. Customer or client-oriented leaders build, maintain, and reinforce long-term organizational relationships designed to meet documented needs. They effectively predict, plan for, and respond to customers' and clients' immediate needs and learn from experience how to adapt programs and services.

5. Effective managers are organized, delegate appropriately, set goals, monitor progress against predetermined objectives, expect timely feedback, demand excellence, take corrective action as needed, maintain objectivity, and use reason and judgment. They are thorough, maintain their focus on the client or customer, create diversity, recognize achievement, and coach and support others as needed.

6. Skilled communicators listen well, have good interpersonal skills, are effective negotiators, and encourage feedback and an open discussion of critical issues. They know how to share information in a timely manner and are sensitive to the needs of others. And they often are good public speakers.

7. Many leaders have strong personal characteristics, such as discipline, ethics, internal motivation, accountability, control of emotions, conflict management skills, and good organizational and community values. Such leaders are committed to professional and personal growth.

8. People's leadership becomes visible through their service as a mentor and role model. This inspires others to take the initiative and helps demonstrate their commitment to excellence. Motivating others connects the organization's broad vision to today's work. Effective leaders believe in teams and link individuals and groups, keeping the end results in mind when setting priorities.

9. Developers empower others through words and actions. They encourage planned risk taking, support professional development, and are not threatened by others' successes.

In conclusion, this chapter described the following six political, professional, and policy issues that will affect nonprofit organizations in the future:

1. Meeting the externally imposed requirements for accountability.
2. Preparing for backlashes against nonprofits for their advocacy efforts.
3. Working with colleges, universities, professional associations, and others to form a strong professional education process to train the next generation of nonprofit leaders.
4. Complying with the more stringent rules for nonprofit organizations to maintain their tax-exempt status.
5. Preparing to meet the challenges of forming successful partnerships, mergers, and consolidations.
6. Developing the appropriate competencies to be successful in the future as nonprofit managers and leaders.

For Discussion

1. What other trends do you think may shape nonprofit organizations in the future? How should the field deal with them?

2. How should a nonprofit organization position itself for success in dealing with future challenges?

3. Who are your role models? Are any of them in the nonprofit sector? What about them do you admire? Have you tried to adopt their perspectives and skills?

4. In light of the trends in the nonprofit field, what professional development needs should you work on?

The Oakwood Community Center's Articles of Incorporation

The articles of incorporation for the Oakwood Community Center state the organization's mission and purposes and its rules and limits on its activities and uses of assets. The articles have been approved by the undersigned, who are citizens of the United States desiring to form a nonprofit corporation under the laws of the federal government and the state of New York.

Article 1

The name of the corporation shall be the Oakwood Community Center.

Article 2

The place in this state where the principal office of the organization is located is the city of Dawsonville, county of Greene. The organization will maintain a registered office and a registered agent whose business office is identical with its registered office. It may have additional places to carry out its work as the Board of Directors may from time to time designate. Presently, the registered office is located at 151 Elm Street, Dawsonville, N.Y., and the registered agent is Ms. Martha Jones.

Article 3

Membership: This organization shall not have members.

Article 4

Board of Directors: The business and activities of this organization shall be governed by its board of directors. That board will have the powers and duties necessary to oversee the affairs and resources of the organization, including ensuring compliance with the provisions of section 501 (c) (3) of the Internal Revenue Tax Code and the laws of the state of New York.

Article 5

The purpose of this organization is restricted exclusively to public charitable and educational purposes. Its mission is to improve the quality of life for citizens of Greene County. It will provide programs for youth development and adult education for them. Additional services may be authorized by the Board of Directors. Any such programs or activities will be carried out in accordance with the provisions of section 501 (c) (3) of the federal tax code and relevant sections of the code of the state of New York.

Article 6

No part of the net income of this organization will go to benefit to its members, trustees, officers, or any other person, other than approved compensation for services rendered to the organization. The Board of Directors will not engage in any act of self-dealing, nor retain any excess business holdings, nor make any investments in ways that incur tax liability, nor make any taxable expenditure.

Article 7

No substantial part of the activities of the organization will be used for efforts to influence legislation or for participation in political campaigns for or against any candidate for public office. The organization will not, except in an insubstantial degree, engage in any activities or exercise any powers that are not in furtherance of its purposes or not permitted by section 501 (c) (3) of the Internal Revenue code.

Article 8

Upon the dissolution of this organization, its remaining assets will be distributed to other nonprofit organizations whose purposes are in compliance with the meaning of section 501 (c) (3) of the Internal Revenue Code, or those assets will be distributed to the federal government, the state of New York, or the local government of Dawsonville. Any assets not so distributed shall be disposed of by a court of competent jurisdiction in Greene County for such purposes or to such organizations as the court shall determine, consistent with that section of the federal code.

In witness whereof, we have subscribed our names on this day of March 3, 2000:

(signatures of officers)

APPENDIX B

The Oakwood Community Center's Bylaws

Section 1

The name of this organization is the Oakwood Community Center. Its principal office will be in Greene County. The board may designate other offices to carry out the organization's purposes. It is governed by the board and will carry out only those activities that comply with section 501 (c) (3) of the Internal Revenue Code and the laws of the state of New York.

Section 2

The purpose of this organization is restricted exclusively to public charitable and educational purposes. Its mission is to enhance the quality of life for all residents of Greene County, especially those in economically disadvantaged situations. It will provide programs for youth development and adult education, and additional services may be authorized by the Board of directors. All of the income of organization will be documented and used for activities of the organization, and none of the net resources of the organization will be given to the benefit of any individual, firm, or other corporation.

Section 3: Board of Directors

A: Powers and Duties: All aspects of this organization and its resources will be governed by the board of directors. The board will have all powers and duties necessary to oversee and supervise the affairs of the organization, including those specifically assigned by federal and state laws. The board will be the policy making body for the organization; hire, evaluate and terminate the Executive Director; and oversee the financial and corporate affairs of the organization. The board will ensure that accurate financial records are maintained.

B: Number and term of office: The number of members of the board will be 9 or such other number as the board may determine. The term of office for a member will be three years, with one-third of the board rotating off every year. Members will serve until their successors have been qualified and elected.

C: Election of board members: Persons may be nominated for election to the board by the nominating committee established by the board. They may also be nominated from the floor of the annual meeting each year. A majority of the voting members of the board is required for the election of a new member.

D: Removal, resignation or disqualification: Any member of the board may be removed from office with or without cause by a majority vote of the board. A board member may resign at any time by giving written notice to the Chairman. A vacancy created by these steps will be filled by a successor by a majority vote of the remaining members. A successor thus chosen will serve the remainder of the term of the person being replaced.

E: Place and time of meetings: The board will hold its meetings and keep the organization's accounting information at the principal office of the organization. The board may determine other sites for its meetings. The board will meet regularly on a designated day and time each month. Notice of fixing or changing time or place or purposes of a board meeting must be mailed to each board member at least 7 days prior to a meeting. The board may transact any business that comes before it at its regular meetings; however, it may by majority vote call special meetings to deal with urgent or unusual matters. Written notice must be sent to every member in case of such special meetings at least 7 days prior to the meeting, but such notice may be waived by any member. A meeting may be adjourned by a majority of those members present, whether or not a quorum is present.

F: Quorum: A majority of the members of the board will constitute a quorum for the transaction of any business before the board. A majority of the quorum in any meeting can act on behalf of the full board. Should less than a quorum be present at any meeting, a majority of those present may adjourn the meeting.

G: Compensation: Members of the board may not receive any salary for their services. Members may be reimbursed for expenses incurred by attending any regular or special meeting of the board. Such reimbursement shall be payable whether or not a meeting is adjourned because of the absence of a quorum.

H: Actions taken by the board: Every decision by a majority of board members in meetings where a quorum is present shall be regarded as an act of the board. Any action taken outside of such meetings shall be regarded as an act of the board provided that a majority of members provide written approval of the proposed action within seven days.

I: Committees: By resolution passed by a majority of the whole board, it may establish one or more committees to address matters designated by the board. Included among such committees will be an Executive Committee, composed of the officers of the board.

J: Conflicts of interest: To avoid an appearance or actual conflict of interest, any board member who engages in any remunerative activity related to the operations of the organization must declare that interest and refrain from participating in the deliberations and votes on such matters. The activity must be authorized by the board and recorded in its minutes.

Section 4: Officers

A. Elections: The officers of the board shall include Chairperson, Vice Chairperson, Secretary, and Treasurer. Persons holding these roles must have served at least one full year on the board. Nominations may be made by any member of the board.

Terms of office will be one year, renewable once during a member's three-year term on the board. Election to an office will be made by a majority of the votes at a meeting having a quorum. All officers of the board will perform the duties specified below and other such duties as the board shall from time to time assign. The board may appoint other officers as it deems necessary, and those officers shall hold their offices for such terms and perform such duties as specified by the board.

B. Removal: Any officer may be removed by the board whenever in its judgment the best interest of the organization will be served thereby. Any officer may resign at any time by giving written notice to the members of the board. Vacancies in offices for any reason may be filled by the board for the unexpired portion of the term.

C. Chairperson: The chairperson of the board will oversee all the business and affairs of the organization, supervise the Executive Director, serve as ex-officio member of all committees of the board, and preside at all meetings of the board.

D. Vice-Chairperson: The Vice-Chairperson of the board will perform the duties of the Chairman in case of that person's death, disqualification, resignation, inability or refusal to act.

E. Secretary: The Secretary of the board will attend and keep minutes of all meetings of the board, see that notices are given to members regarding meetings and other events, and serve as custodian of all board records.

F. Treasurer: The Treasurer of the board will oversee all funds, financial transactions and accounting records of the organization. The Treasurer will ensure that all accounting records conform to generally accepted accounting principles, and report regularly to the board about the financial condition of the organization. If any of these duties are delegated by the board to the Executive Director or managing agent or accountant, the Treasurer will be responsible for supervising that person and ensuring that accurate records and reports are maintained.

Section 5: The Executive Director

The board will employ an Executive Director who serves at the pleasure of the board. The Executive Director will direct the daily activities of the organization within the guidelines of the policies and procedures established by the board. The duties and compensation of the Executive Director will be consistent with these by-laws and prescribed in an employment contract with the board. The executive is responsible for preparing annual budgets for board consideration and approval, and may make minor changes in that budget only in circumstances where immediate action is required. Such changes must be presented to the board at its next meeting for review and acceptance. The Executive Director may negotiate and execute all contracts, including those related to grants, on behalf of the organization, and report such actions to the board at its next meeting. Except in extraordinary circumstances, the Executive Director will consult with the board prior to execution of any contract to obtain board approval. The Executive Director will have the authority to employ, supervise, and discharge all staff of the organization, within the policies and guidelines established by the board. The board will evaluate the performance of the Executive Director annually, and it may discharge this person at will.

Section 6: Finances

A. Fiscal Year: The fiscal year of this organization will begin and end with the calendar year unless the board sets another fiscal year.

B. Funds: The funds of the organization shall be divided into general operating funds and other specified funds. Specified funds will include all donations, gifts, legacies, and other contributions for which they have been designated by donors or by the board. Those funds will be used solely for the purposes designated. All income and funds of the organization will be deposited promptly to the credit of the organization in banks or other depositories as the board shall select. All checks, drafts, or orders for the payment of money shall be signed by the Executive, and when the amounts are over $500 also signed by the Treasurer.

C. Financial statements: No later than three months following the ending of each fiscal year, the Executive Director and the Treasurer will present to the board a balance sheet showing in reasonable detail the financial condition of the organization as of the close of that fiscal year. An audit will be conducted annually by an independent auditor who has no other relationship with the organization and shall ensure conformity with generally accepted accounting principles and applicable regulatory standards. The Executive Director and Treasurer will also prepare, sign, and submit all required tax reports, including IRS Form 990 and other required reports.

D. Disbursements: Checks will be issued for obligations of the organization in accordance with the budget adopted by the board. Checks will be signed by the Executive Director and when amounts exceed $500, also signed by the Treasurer.

E. Donated services: All members of the board volunteer their services to the organization without compensation.

Section 7: Dissolution

In the event that the organization is dissolved, the remaining assets will be given to one or more other organizations that are recognized as exempt under section 501 (c) (3) of the Internal Revenue Code, or to federal, state, or local government for exclusive use for public purposes.

Section 8: Amendment

These by-laws may be amended by the board at a meeting duly called and held for such purpose. The full text of all proposed amendments and the date and time of the meeting where they are to be considered must be given in writing to each member of the board at least one month in advance of such board action.

We hereby certify that these by-laws were duly adopted by the board of this organization on the ———— day of the year ————.

(signatures of officers)

APPENDIX C

Tufts University's Sexual Harassment Policies and Procedures

Tufts University provides an extensive process for handling complaints on its campus.[1]

What Is Sexual Harassment?
Who Are the Participants?
What Are the Consequences of Sexual Harassment to the Victim and the University?
What Can You Do If You Feel You Are Being Sexually Harassed?
University Procedures for Addressing Sexual Harassment
A. Where Should the Grievance Be Filed?
B. What Should Be Filed?
C. When Should the Grievance Be Filed?
D. How Will the Grievance Be Processed? Where to Find Help?

What Is Sexual Harassment?

Sexual harassment is a form of sex discrimination that violates federal and state laws and University policy. Tufts University, its agents, supervisory employees, employees, and students shall be held liable for their acts of sexual harassment and are subject to appropriate University disciplinary action and personal liability. Sexual harassment is prohibited at Tufts University.

Sexual harassment, whether between people of different sexes or the same sex, is defined to include but is not limited to, unwanted sexual advances, unwelcome requests for sexual favors, and other behavior of a sexual nature when:

1. Submission to such conduct is made either explicitly or implicitly a term and condition of an individual's academic status or employment; or
2. Submission to, or rejection of, such conduct by an individual is used as a basis for employment or academic decisions affecting him or her; or
3. Such conduct, whether verbal or physical, has the purpose or effect of unreasonably interfering with the individual's academic or work performance or of creating an intimidating, hostile, or offensive environment in which to work or to learn.

Who Are the Participants?

Sexual Harassment can involve:

Professor and student
Teaching assistant and student
Supervisor and employee
Instructor and instructor
Student and student
Staff member and student
Other relationships among colleagues, peers, and coworkers
Agents of the University whose activities come under University control

The Following Behavior May Constitute Sexual Harassment:

As stated by the Massachusetts Commission Against Discrimination (MCAD):

While it is not possible to list all those additional circumstances that outline sexual harassment, the following are some examples of conduct which if unwelcome, may constitute sexual harassment depending upon the totality of the circumstances including the severity of the conduct and its pervasiveness:

Lewd remarks, whistles, or personal reference to one's anatomy.

Unwanted physical contact such as patting, pinching, or constant brushing against a person's body.

Subtle or overt pressure for sexual favors.

Persistent and offensive sexual jokes and comments.

Persistent and unwanted requests for dates.

E-mail messages of an offensive sexual nature.

What Are the Consequences of Sexual Harassment to the Victim and the University?

Clearly, sexual harassment affects the victim of harassment. The student or employee may suffer a performance decline, disrupted education, disrupted relationships, etc. A student's educational goals may also be significantly affected if the student decides to avoid certain courses, change his or her area of study, or transfer to another institution.

In addition, sexual harassment impacts the University and the department(s) involved. The University and department may experience an atmosphere of fear, declining work productivity and office morale, a loss of reputation, divisiveness, rumors, etc.

The Consequences to a Person Responsible for Sexual Harassment Can Include:

Disciplinary action
Letter of reprimand
Denial of promotion
Suspension
Demotion
Termination

Retaliation Is Prohibited

It is unlawful to retaliate against an individual for filing a complaint of sexual harassment or for cooperating in an investigation of a complaint of sexual harassment. Any person who retaliates against an individual reporting sexual harassment or filing a sexual harassment complaint, is subject to University disciplinary procedures up to and including expulsion or termination by the University.

Confidentiality

The University recognizes that some individuals filing complaints may want their identity to remain confidential. In some instances, the alleged harasser can be spoken to without the complainant being identified. In other cases, issues of confidentiality must be balanced against the University's need to investigate and take other action.

What Can You Do If You Feel You Are Being Sexually Harassed?

If you are experiencing or have experienced some form of sexual harassment, you need to know that Tufts provides several options to assist you. If you believe you are being or have been sexually harassed, you should consider taking the following steps immediately:

1. You may want to keep track of dates, places, times, witnesses, and the nature of the harassment. Save any letters, cards, or notes in a safe place.
2. Don't be led into believing that if you wait a while the inappropriate behavior will stop. Seriously consider taking immediate and appropriate action under this policy.
3. Seek the advice of or report the incident to any of the individuals listed as Sexual Harassment Resource Persons (below). These members of the community provide information about University policies on sexual harassment, assist with the informal and formal mechanisms for resolving complaints, and are responsible for reporting all complaints to the university Title IX Coordinator.

University Procedures for Addressing Sexual Harassment:

There are two types of resolutions that can be implemented when resolving a complaint of sexual harassment. They are *Informal* and *Formal* processes:

Informal Resolution:

Any member of the Tufts community who believes that he/she has been sexually harassed may first attempt to resolve the problem through discussion with the other party. When discussing the problem with that person presents particular stress or difficulties, the complainant has the right to consult with management, a University Sexual Harassment Resource Persons listed on this Web site. The complainant should make contact with a Sexual Harassment Resource Person for consultation and assistance with resolution of the problem on a timely basis so that the time period for filing a grievance can be met if he or she chooses to do so. Conclusion of an informal complaint proceeding ordinarily should be sought within three weeks of the beginning of informal proceedings. The complainant has the right to institute formal proceedings at anytime during this process.

Formal Resolution: The Sexual Harassment Grievance Procedure

If the problem has not been resolved to the satisfaction of the complainant through informal discussion, she/he has the right to file a grievance in accordance with the following procedure.

A. WHERE SHOULD THE GRIEVANCE BE FILED?

If the person alleged to be responsible for the harassment is:

1. A *staff member* or an *administrator*. File with the Director of the Office of Equal Opportunity, the Vice President of Human Resources, or the Campus Human Resources Manager.
2. A *faculty member*. File with the appropriate Dean of college/school or the Provost.
3. A *student*. File with the Dean of Students or the Dean of the college/school.

B. WHAT SHOULD BE FILED?

The grievance should be in writing and should summarize the harassment complained of, the person alleged to be responsible, and the resolution sought. A Sexual Harassment Resource Person may assist in writing the formal grievance if the complainant wishes, with the exception of the Title IX Coordinator.

C. WHEN SHOULD THE GRIEVANCE BE FILED?

Students: The grievance should normally be filed within one year of the incident(s) giving rise to the complaint. The University may extend this period if it finds that there are extenuating circumstances.

Staff/Faculty: The grievance should normally be filed within (90) ninety days of the incident(s). The University may extend this period if it finds that there are extenuating circumstances.

D. HOW WILL THE GRIEVANCE BE PROCESSED?

Students: If the person alleged to be responsible for the harassment is a student, the grievance will be processed according to the student's specific school/college disciplinary procedure.

Staff/Faculty:

1. If the alleged harasser is a staff member, administrator, or faculty member, the person with whom the grievance is filed will notify the Director of the Office of Equal Opportunity/Affirmative Action of the complaint within five (5) working days of receiving the written grievance.

2. The Director of OEO, upon receiving the grievance, will immediately notify the charged party of the complaint and request that he/she submit a written response to the charges within ten (10) working days. Response to a complaint is required and will be pursued to see that it is obtained in a timely fashion.

3. Upon receiving the written response from the charged party, the OEO Director will attempt to resolve the situation through discussion, investigation, hearing or other steps that he/she feels is necessary. The complainant will be informed by the Director (or his/her designee) of any action to be taken.

4. Investigation by Panel: If a panel is utilized, the findings and recommendations of the panel will be sent to the President. A panel may include staff, faculty, or students (when involving a student complaint). The President or his/her designee will review the findings and recommendations of the panel and may review other facts relating to the grievance. A decision of the President is binding and shall not be subject to review under any other grievance procedure in effect at Tufts University.

Within the constraints of the academic schedule, the Director will strive to conclude the investigation within thirty (30) working days from the date the original grievance was filed.

Note: The time limits mentioned on this webpage are intended as reasonable amounts of time for specific activities to occur. The appropriate University officials may adjust the time lines for extenuating circumstances that will further ensure a fair and equitable process for all parties.

Central Reporting and Coordination

Title IX regulations of the Education Amendments of 1972 require all University personnel to report any case of sexual harassment whether resolved informally or formally through the grievance procedure to the University's Title IX coordinator. (The role and responsibilities of the Title IX coordinator are assigned to the Director of the Office of Equal Opportunity as noted under the section entitled *Where to Find Help* on this Web site.) *Such reports should not include the names or identities of the persons involved.* They should include, however, a description of the complaint and the schools or administrative units with which the participants are affiliated. Reports from decentralized areas will allow the Title IX coordinator to identify patterns of frequency in a particular area or location within the University and report these findings to the President as necessary.

Notes

Preface

1. L. M. Salamon, *The Resilient Sector: The State of the Nonprofit Sector* (Washington, D.C.: Brookings Institution Press, 2003).

2. D. Kolb, *Learning Style Inventory* (Boston: McBer, 1985).

3. R. Boyatzis, *The Competent Manager* (New York: Wiley, 1982).

4. Peter Vaill, "The Theory of Managing in the Managerial Competency Movement," *EXCHANGE: The Organizational Behavior Teaching Journal* 8, no. 2 (1983); available online at http://cobe.boisestate.edu/msr/jme8(2)/jme8(2)a.htm.

1. Nonprofit Organizations Today

1. Max Lerner, *America as a Civilization* (New York: Simon and Schuster, 1957).

2. http://www.hno.harvard.edu/guide/intro/ (accessed January 3, 2006).

3. L. M. Salamon, *The Resilient Sector: The State of Nonprofit America* (Washington, D.C.: Brookings Institution Press, 2002).

4. http://www.nationalservice.gov/pdf/VIA/VIA_summaryreport.pdf (accessed June 13, 2006).

5. J. S. Tucker, J. C. Cullen, R. R. Sinclair, and W. W. Wakeland, "Dynamic Systems and Organizational Decision-Making Processes in Nonprofits," *Journal of Applied Behavioral Sciences* 41, no. 2 (December 2005): 482–502.

6. http://national.unitedway.org/about/missvis.cfm (accessed December 28, 2005).

7. Excerpted from U.S. Office of Personnel Management's documents (http://www.opm.gov/insure/health/cbrr.htm), accessed January 27, 2006.

8. http://www.creditcards.com/credit-consumer-rights-article.php?a_aid = 1017 = 1204 (accessed January 27, 2006).

9. http://www.chevron.com/social_responsibility (accessed February 21, 2006).

10. http://www.starbucks.com/aboutus (accessed February 21, 2006).

11. For an in-depth review of issues related to conflicts of interest, see Roger A. Ritvo, Joel D. Ohlsen, and Thomas P. Holland, *Ethical Governance in Healthcare* (Chicago: Health Forum, AHA Press, 2004).

12. Robert K. Greenleaf, *The Servant Leader Within: A Transformative Path*, edited by Hamilton Beazley, Julie Beggs, and Larry C. Spears (Westfield, Ind.: Robert K. Greenleaf Center, 2003).

13. Greenleaf Center's Web site: http://www.greenleaf.org/leadership/servant-leadership/What-is-Servant-Leadership.html (accessed January 7, 2006).

14. Don Kennedy, "Clark Will Leave Legacy of Progress," *The Flagship* (Hampton Roads, Va.), June 22, 2000, available at http://www.chinfo.navy.mil/navpalib/cno/covenant.html (accessed March 8, 2006).

2. History and Theories of Nonprofit Organizations

1. L. M. Salamon, *The Resilient Sector: The State of Nonprofit America* (Washington, D.C.: Brookings Institution Press, 2002).

2. H. K. Anheier, *Nonprofit Organizations: Theory, Management, Policy* (New York: Routledge, 2005).

3. R. A. Lohmann, *The Commons: A New Perspective on Nonprofit Organizations* (San Francisco: Jossey-Bass, 1992).

4. R. A. Gross, "Giving in American: From Charity to Philanthropy," in *Charity, Philanthropy, and Civility in American History*, edited by L. J. Friedman (Cambridge: Cambridge University Press, 2003), 29–48.

5. B. A. Weisbrod, *The Voluntary Nonprofit Sector: An Economic Analysis* (Lexington, Mass.: Lexington, 1977).

6. Eric Foner, *Forever Free: The Story of Emancipation and Reconstruction* (New York: Knopf, 2005).

7. Andrew Carnegie, "The Gospel of Wealth," *North American Review,* 1889.

8. L. Coser, *The Functions of Social Conflict* (Glencoe, Ill.: Free Press, 1956).

9. B. Lanker and M. W. Edelman, *I Dream a World: Portraits of Black Women Who Changed America* (New York: Stewart, Taborie, and Chang, 1989), 121.

10. H. Bennett and T. Dilorenzo, *Unfair Competition: The Profits of Nonprofits* (Lanham, Md.: Hamilton Press, 1989).

11. K. L. Chinnock and L. M. Salamon, "Determinants of Nonprofit Impact: A Preliminary Analysis" (Baltimore: Johns Hopkins University). Paper presented at Transforming Civil Society, Citizenship and Governance: The Third Sector in an Era

of Global (Dis)Order," ISTR Fifth International Conference hosted by the Graduate School in Humanities, University of Cape Town, South Africa, July 2002.

12. Peter Drucker, *The Age of Social Transformation* (Glencoe, Ill.: Free Press, 1994).

13. Internal Revenue Service, *Exempt Organizations Business Master File* (January 2006), cited by Urban Institute, National Center for Charitable Statistics (http://nccsdataweb.urban.org).

14. http://www.whitehouse.gov/omb/budget/fy2007/pdf/hist.pdf.

3. Ethical Issues in Nonprofit Organizations

1. L. R. Burns, J. Cacciamani, J. Clement, and W. Aquino, "The Fall of the House of AHERF: The Allegheny Bankruptcy," *Health Affairs* 19, no. 1 (2000): 7–41.

2. E. Schwinn, "Senator Questions Operating Practices of Nonprofit Hospitals," *Chronicle of Philanthropy*, March 21, 2006, available at http://www.philanthropy.com/free/update/2006/03/2006032102.htm.

3. Lynn Neary, "Questions Hang Over Administration of Getty Trust," National Public Radio, March 27, 2006.

4. J. P. Thiroux, *Ethics: Theory and Practice*, 8th ed. (Upper Saddle River, N.J.: Prentice-Hall, 2004).

5. See the case of *Tarasoff v. Regents of the University of California*; *131 California Reporter 14*. See also J. R. Meloy, *The Psychology of Stalking* (San Diego: Academic Press, 1998).

6. J. Picoult, *My Sister's Keeper* (New York: Washington Square Press, 2004), 301.

7. R. A. Ritvo, J. D. Ohlsen, and T. P. Holland, *Ethical Governance in Health Care* (Chicago: American Hospital Association, 2004).

4. Creating Effective Nonprofit Organizations

1. S. Hutton and F. Phillips, *Nonprofit Kit for Dummies* (New York: Hungry Minds, 2001).

2. http://www.cvas-usa.org (accessed March 2, 2006).

3. For specific guidance, see http://www.irs.gov/charities/index.html (accessed June 16, 2007).

4. "Meeting Your Fiduciary Responsibilities," U.S. Department of Labor Web site, http://www.dol.gov/ebsa/publications/fiduciaryresponsibility.html (accessed January 16, 2006).

5. T. K. Hyatt, *The Nonprofit Legal Landscape* (Washington, D.C.: BoardSource, 2005).

6. B. Headd, "Redefining Business Success," *Small Business Economics* 21 (2003): 55.

7. Unfortunately, incubators provided by the federal Small Business Administration are open only to start-up for-profit businesses and are not available to nonprofits.

8. B. Headd, "Redefining Business Success: Distinguishing Between Closure and Failure," *Small Business Economics* 21 (2003): 51–61.

9. R. Holland, *Planning Against a Business Failure*, ADC Info no. 24 (Knoxville: Agricultural Development Center, University of Tennessee, October 1998), 1.

10. T. E. Deal and K. D. Peterson, *The Leadership Paradox* (San Francisco: Jossey-Bass, 1994), 47.

11. A. Grossman and V. K. Rangan, *Managing Multi-Site Nonprofits*, Harvard Business School Enterprise Series no. 8, 2000.

5. Understanding Nonprofit Organizations

1. Henri Fayol, *General and Industrial Management*, translated by C. Storrs (New York: Pittman and Sons, 1949).

2. Frederick W. Taylor, *Principles of Scientific Management* (New York: Harper Bros., 1941).

3. According to the Dartmouth College Web site, the Amos Tuck School of Business was "the first graduate school of management in the world" (www.dartmouth.edu/home/about.history.html).

4. D. McGregor, *The Human Side of Enterprise* (New York: McGraw-Hill, 2006).

5. Robert Tannenbaum and Warren H. Schmidt, "How to Choose a Leadership Pattern," *Harvard Business Review* 36 (March/April 1958): 95–101.

6. Peter Drucker, *The Practice of Management* (New York: HarperCollins, 1954).

7. E. Watkins, T. P. Holland, and R. A. Ritvo, "Improving the Effectiveness of Program Consultation," *Social Work in Health Care* 2, no. 1 (fall 1976): 43–54. Also see E. Watkins, T. P. Holland, and R. A. Ritvo, "Evaluating the Impact of Program Consultation in Health Settings," *Health Education Monographs* 3, no. 4 (winter 1975): 385–402.

6. Leading and Managing Nonprofit Organizations

1. Peter Drucker, "What Business Can Learn from Nonprofits," *Harvard Business Review*, July/August 1989, 88–93.

2. www.gsb.stanford.edu/news/headlines/ssir_mccormick.shtml (May 2003) (accessed June 16, 2007). The article noted that the Nature Conservancy's fund-raising results place it in the top ten in the United States.

3. Peter Drucker, *Managing for the Future: The 1990s and Beyond* (New York: Penguin Books, 1992).

4. Michael B. McCaskey, "The Hidden Messages That Managers Send," *Harvard Business Review* 57, no. 6 (November/December 1979): 135–148.

5. John Gardner, *Self-Renewal: The Individual and the Innovative Society* (New York: Norton, 1995).

6. T. J. Peters and R. H. Waterman, *In Search of Excellence: Lessons from America's Best Run Corporations* (New York: Warner Books, 1982).

7. Kenneth Blanchard, "Situational Leadership II," in *Managing in the Age of Change*, edited by R. A. Ritvo, A. H. Litwin, and L. Butler, 14–33 (Burr Ridge, Ill.: Irwin Professional Publishing, 1995).

8. P. Williams, "Managing Professionals," in *Managing in the Age of Change*, edited by R. A. Ritvo, A. H. Litwin, and L. Butler, 34–42 (Burr Ridge, Ill.: Irwin Professional Publishing, 1995).

7. Key Issues in Human Resources

1. R. A. Sundeen, S. A. Raskoff, and M. C. Garcia, "Differences in Perceived Barriers to Volunteering in Formal Organizations," *Nonprofit and Voluntary Sector Quarterly* 17, no. 3 (spring 2007): 279–300. See also L. A. Hartenian, " Nonprofit Agency Dependence on Direct Service and Indirect Support Volunteers," *Nonprofit and Voluntary Sector Quarterly* 17, no. 3 (spring 2007): 319–334.

2. Adapted from http://www.mmfa.org/information.cfm#volunteers (accessed December 27, 2005).

3. http://www.alcatel-Lucent.com/wps/portal/!ut/p/kcxml/04_Sj9SPykssyox-PLMnMzovMoY_QjzKLd4w3MfMESYGYRq6m-pEoYgbxjggRX4_83FT9IHiv_QD9gtzQiHJHR0UAw7uxiQ!!/delta/base64xml/L3dJdyEvd0ZNQUFzQUM-vNElVRS82X0FfNDZO (accessed June 17, 2007).

5. A public service offered by the Office of Disability Employment Policy of the U.S. Department of Labor (800-526-7234).

6. www.eeoc.gov/facts/accommodation.html (accessed January 25, 2006).

7. V. J. Ramsey and J. K. Latting, "A Typology of Inter-Group Competencies," *Journal of Applied Behavioral Sciences* 41, no. 3 (September 2005): 265–284.

8. http://www.officedepot.com/companyinfo/companyfacts/ethics.pdf (accessed June 17, 2007).

9. U.S. Bureau of the Census, "Family Type by Employment Status," *Census 2000 Supplementary Survey: Summary*, table 61, 2002 (http://factfinder.census.gov).

10. Betsy Robinson, "An Integrated Approach to Managing Absence Supports Greater Organizational Productivity," *Employee Benefits Journal* 27 (2002): 7–11.

11. Organization for Economic Co-operation and Development, *Balancing Work and Family Life: Helping Parents Into Paid Employment* (Paris: OECD, 2001), 130–133.

12. S. Bevan, S. Dench, P. Tamkin, and J. Cummings, "Family-Friendly Employment: The Business Case," DfEE Research Report no. RR136, Institute for Employment Studies, 1999 (ISBN 1 84185 063), available at http://www.employment-studies.co.uk/summary/summary.php?id=fambus.

13. Oklahoma Marriage Initiative Web site, www.okmarriage.org/ProgramHighlights/FamilyRelationships.asp.

14. Mary S. Doucet and Karen Hooks, "Toward an Equal Future," *Women and Family Issues* June 1999, www.aicpa.org/pubs/jofa/jun1999/women.htm.

15. Gina Hannah, "Moms Find Companies That Care," *Huntsville* (Ala.) *Times*, September 14, 2005, www.al.com/business/huntsvilletimes/index.ssf?/base/business/11266893114081.xml;=1=1.

16. A. L. Saltzstein, Y. Ting, and G. H. Saltzstein, 2001. "Work–Family Balance and Job Satisfaction: The Impact of Family-Friendly Policies on Attitudes of Federal Government Employees," *Public Administration Review* 61 (2001): 452–467.

17. Ibid.

18. T. Rasp, "Family Friendly Attitude Earns Local Firms Spirit Awards," *Enid* (Okla.) *News and Eagle*, September 29, 2005, www.Enidnews.com.

8. Governing Effectively

1. R. A. Ritvo, J. D. Olsen, and T. P. Holland, *Ethical Governance in Health Care* (Chicago: American Hospital Association, 2004).

2. T. P. Holland, "Board Accountability: Some Lessons from the Field," *Nonprofit Management and Leadership* 12, no. 4 (summer 2002): 409–428.

3. W. A. Brown, "Board Development Practices and Competent Board Members," *Nonprofit Management and Leadership* 17, no. 3 (spring 2007): 301–317.

4. B. E. Taylor, R. P. Chait, and T. P. Holland, "The New Work of the Nonprofit Board," *Harvard Business Review* 74, no. 5 (September–October 1996): 36–46.

5. R. P. Chait, T. P. Holland, and B. E. Taylor, *Improving the Performance of Governing Boards* (New York: Greenwood Press, 1996).

6. T. P. Holland, R. A. Ritvo, and A. R. Kovner, *Improving Board Effectiveness* (Chicago: American Hospital Association, 1997).

7. R. E. Quinn and J. A. Rohrbaugh, "A Spatial Model of Effectiveness Criteria: Toward a Competing Values Approach to Organizational Analysis," *Management Science* 29 (1983): 363–377.

9. Organizational Growth and Renewal

1. R. L. Daft, *Organizational Theory and Design* (St. Paul: West, 1992).

2. S. R. Block and S. Rosenberg, "Toward an Understanding of Founder's Syndrome: An Assessment of Power and Privilege Among Founders of Nonprofit Organizations," *Nonprofit Management and Leadership* 12, no. 4 (summer 2002): 353–368.

3. R. M. Kanter, *The Change Masters* (New York: Simon & Schuster, 1993), 18.

4. W. D. Eggers, *Unleashing Change* (Washington, D.C.: Brookings Institution Press, 2005).

5. J. Greenberg and R. A. Baron, *Behavior in Organizations*, 8th ed. (Upper Saddle River, N.J.: Prentice-Hall, 2003), 607.

6. J. L. Wirtenberg, L. Abrams, and C. Ott, "Assessing the Field of Organizational Development," *Journal of Applied Behavioral Science* 40, no. 4 (2004): 465–479.

7. W. E. Deming, *Out of the Crisis* (Cambridge, Mass.: Center for Advanced Engineering Study, Massachusetts Institute of Technology, 1982), 58.

8. For a helpful presentation of this approach, see J. M. Watkins and B. J. Mohr, *Appreciative Inquiry* (San Francisco: Jossey-Bass/Pfeiffer, 2001).

9. Deming, *Out of the Crisis*.

10. Kanter, *The Change Masters*.

11. Kenneth Thomas and Ralph Kilmann, *Thomas-Kilmann Conflict Mode Instrument* (Palo Alto, Calif.: Consulting Psychologists Press, 2003).

10. Strategic Planning

1. J. M. Bryson and F. K. Alston, *Creating and Implementing Your Strategic Plan* (San Francisco: Jossey-Bass, 1996).

2. R. McCambridge, "A Gateway to 21st Century Governance: Are We Ready? A Powerful Vision: Governance Suited to Purpose," *Nonprofit Quarterly* 10, no. 3 (fall 2003); available at http://www.nonprofitquarterly.org/section/462.html.

3. W. E. Deming, *Out of the Crisis* (Cambridge, Mass.: Center for Advanced Engineering Study, Massachusetts Institute of Technology, 1982).

4. T. J. Peters and R. H. Waterman, *In Search of Excellence* (New York: Harper and Row, 1982).

5. www.cityyear.org. City Year is an "action tank" for citizen service that works to demonstrate, improve, and promote the concept of voluntary citizen service as a means of building a stronger democracy.

6. www3.leigh.edu.

7. http://www.nadefa.org/aboutnadefa.html.

8. http://www.aid http://www.aidsquilt.org/squilt.org.

9. http://www.georgiaaquarium.org/aboutUs/index.aspx.

10. "Bill Gates' New Rules," *Time*, March 22, 1999; available at http://www.time.com/time/reports/gatesbook/gatesbook1.html.

11. Community Relations

1. R. B. Artman, president, Siena Heights University, in *Journal of College and Character*, http://www.collegevalues,org/diaries.cfm?id=325&a=1.

2. R. Putnam, "Bowling Alone: America's Declining Social Capital," *Journal of Democracy* 6 (1995): 65–78.

3. http://www.rotary.org/programs/com_serv/information/about.html.

4. J. S. Irons and G. Bass, *Trends in Nonprofit Employment, Earnings 1990–2004* (Washington, D.C.: OMBWatch, 2005), available at http://www.ombwatch.org/article/articleview/2347/1/2.

5. R. McCambridge, "A Gateway to 21st Century Governance," *Nonprofit Quarterly* 10, no. 3 (fall 2003); available at http://www.nonprofitquarterly.org/section/462.html.

6. W. Wymer, P. Knowles, and R. Gomes, *Nonprofit Marketing* (Thousand Oaks, Calif.: Sage, 2006).

7. J. Pine and J. Gilmore, *The Experience Economy* (Boston: Harvard Business School Press, 1999).

8. http://www.independentsector.org/mission_market/Rondinelli_London.htm.

12. Principles and Practices of Effective Fund-Raising

1. www.effectivephilanthropy.org (accessed January 1, 2006).

2. http://aafrc.org/gusa/GUSA05_Press_Release.pdf (accessed January 1, 2006).

3. P. G. Schervish, M. A. O'Herlihy, and R. Steinberg, *Charitable Giving: How Much, By Whom, To What, and How?* (New Haven, Conn.: Yale University Press, 2002). See also K. A. Froelich, "Diversification of Revenue Strategies," *Nonprofit and Voluntary Sector Quarterly* 28 (1999): 246–268.

4. S. Weinstein, *The Complete Guide to Fundraising Management* (San Francisco: Jossey-Bass, 2002).

5. H. J. Bryce, "Organizational and Tax Consequences of Business Ventures," chapter in *Financial and Strategic Management for Nonprofit Organizations*, edited by H. J. Bryce (San Francisco: Jossey-Bass, 2000), 310–46.

6. D. P. McIlnay, *How Foundations Work* (San Francisco: Jossey-Bass, 1998).

7. J. E. Austin, "Strategic Collaboration Between Nonprofits and Businesses," *Nonprofit and Voluntary Sector Quarterly* 29 (2000): 69–97.

8. J. C. Geever, *The Foundation Center's Guide to Proposal Writing* (Washington, D.C.: The Foundation Center, 2001). See also D. Ward, *Writing Grant Proposals That Win* (New York: Jones and Bartlett, 2003).

9. Schervish, O'Herlihy, and Steinberg, *Charitable Giving*.

10. J. Mount, "Why Donors Give," *Nonprofit Management and Leadership* 7, no. 1 (fall 1996): 3–14.

11. R. A. Prince, K. M. File, and J. E. Gillespie, "Philanthropic Styles," *Nonprofit Management and Leadership* 3, no. 3 (1993): 255–268.

12. J. R. Dee and A. B. Henkin, "Communication and Donor Relations: A Social Skills Perspective," *Nonprofit Management and Leadership* 8, no. 2 (1997): 107–119.

13. A. R. Andreason and P. Kotler, "The Growth and Development of Nonprofit Marketing," chapter in *Strategic Marketing for Nonprofit Organizations*, edited by A. R. Andreason and P. Kotler (Upper Saddle River, N.J.: Prentice-Hall, 2003), 3–36.

14. Developed by American Association of Fund Raising Counsel, Association for Healthcare Philanthropy, Council for Advancement and Support of Education, and Association of Fundraising Professionals.

15. A. Sargeant, "Relationship Fundraising: How to Keep Donors Loyal," *Nonprofit Management and Leadership* 12, no. 2 (2001): 177–192.

16. H. A. Rosso, *Achieving Excellence in Fundraising* (San Francisco: Jossey-Bass, 1991).

17. W. D. Diamond and S. Gooding-Williams, "Using Advertising Constructs and Methods to Understand Direct Mail Fundraising Appeals," *Nonprofit Management and Leadership* 12, no. 3 (2002): 225–242.

18. M. Warwick, *How to Write Successful Fundraising Letters* (San Francisco: Jossey-Bass, 2001).

19. Sargeant, "Relationship Fundraising." See also W. E. Lindahl, "The Major Donor Relationship: An Analysis of Donors and Contributions," *Nonprofit Management and Leadership* 5, no. 4 (1995): 411–432.

13. Program Evaluation

1. D. Peterson, *An Evaluation of an Elementary School Based Intergenerational Linkages Program: Mentoring for Academic Enrichment* (Philadelphia, Big Brothers / Big Sisters of America, 1994).

2. J. Boulmetis, *ABCs of Evaluation* (San Francisco: Jossey-Bass, 2005).

3. H. Hatry, T. Houten, M. Planaz, and M. T. Greenway, *Measuring Program Outcomes: A Practical Approach* (Washington, D.C.: United Way of America, 1996).

4. H. Chen, *Practical Program Evaluation* (Thousand Oaks, Calif.: Sage, 2005).

5. Hatry et al., *Measuring Program Outcomes.*

6. D. Royce, *Program Evaluation: An Introduction* (Belmont, Calif.: Thompson, Brooks, Cole, 2006).

7. J. C. McDavid and L. R. L. Hawthorne, *Program Evaluation and Performance Measurement* (Thousand Oaks, Calif.: Sage, 2006).

8. Ibid.

14. Accountability

1. http://hbswk.hbs.edu/archive/1452.html (accessed June 23, 2007).

2. *Update 1: Nonprofits Adopting a For-Profit Model* 07.28.2005, 10:11 p.m. (accessed February 28, 2006) http://www.forbes.com/associatedpress/feeds/ap/2005/07/28/ap2164003.html.

3. http://www.aei.org/events/eventID.329,filter./event_detail.asp (accessed January 7, 2006).

4. T. P. Holland, "Board Accountability: Some Lessons from the Field," *Nonprofit Management and Leadership* 12, no. 4 (summer 2002): 409–428.

5. M. Lagace, *When Society Is Everyone's Business: HBS Working Knowledge for Business Leaders* (Cambridge, Mass.: Harvard Business School, 2000).

6. Mark W. Everson, Remarks to the Greater Washington Society of CPAs by Commissioner of Internal Revenue in Washington, D.C., December 14, 2005, 4.

7. Elizabeth K. Keating and Peter Frumkin, "Reengineering Nonprofit Financial Accountability: Toward a More Reliable Foundation for Regulation," *Public Administration Review* 63, no. 1 (January/February 2003): 4.

8. Panel on the Nonprofit Sector, *Strengthening Transparency, Governance, Accountability of Charitable Organizations* (Washington, D.C.: Independent Sector, 2005).

15. Financial Accountability

1. R. E. Herzlinger and D. Nitterhouse, *Financial Accounting and Managerial Control for Nonprofit Organizations* (Cincinnati: South-Western Publishing, 1994).

16. Nonprofit Organizations Tomorrow

1. http://www.marylandnonprofits.org/html/standards/sfx_intro.asp (accessed June 21, 2007).

2. Panel on the Nonprofit Sector, *Strengthening Transparency, Governance, Accountability of Charitable Organizations* (Washington, D.C.: Independent Sector, 2005).

3. www.humanics.org.

4. http://www.servicelearning.umn.edu/students/What_is_Service_Learning.html (2006) (accessed June 21, 2007).

5. As per the NYSE Certificate of Incorporation, http://www.nyse.com/pdfs/certificateofincorporation.pdf (accessed June 21, 2007).

6. Proposed Rules 53599, PR (REG-111257-05), *Federal Register* 70, no. 174 (September 2005).

7. http://www.nyse.com/about/history/1089312755484.html (accessed January 10, 2006).

8. http://www.uschamber.com/issues/accomplishments/default (accessed January 10, 2006).

9. http://www.independentsector.org/programs/leadership/3sector_background.html (accessed January 30, 2006).

10. http://www.independentsector.org/about/ (accessed January 30, 2006).

11. http://www.cose.org/ (accessed June 21, 2007).

Appendix C. Tufts University's Sexual Harassment Policies and Procedures

1. http://www.tufts.edu/oeo/harasspolicies.html (accessed June 17, 2007).

Index

Foundations of Social Work Knowledge
Frederic G. Reamer, Series Editor

Carina McGeehin
345 Research Dr
Apt 72
Athens, GA 306052775 USA

TXTBOOKSNOW.COM-HALF
8950 W PALMER ST
RIVER GROVE, IL 60171

Order #: 9419943014

TXTBOOKSNOW.COM-HALF
8950 W PALMER ST
RIVER GROVE, IL 60171

(Attn: Returns)

Order #: 9419943014

DO37485

Date: 08/17/2011

SKU	Qty	Condition	Title	Price	Total
53225090U	1	Used	Nonprofit Organizations 9780231139755 Refund Eligible Through= 9/19/2011	$ 19.32	$ 19.32
5270376U	1	Used	How to Change the World 2 9780195334760 Refund Eligible Through= 9/19/2011	$ 9.25	$ 9.25

Order #: 9419943014

Sub Total	$ 28.57
Shipping & Handling	$ 5.38
Sales Tax	$ 0.00
Order Total	$ 33.95

Refund Policy: All items must be returned within 30 days of receipt. Pack your book securely, so it will arrive back to us in its original condition. To avoid delays, please use the return section and label provided with your original packing slip to identify your return. For your protection, we suggest using a traceable, insured shipping service (UPS or insured Parcel Post). We are not responsible for lost or damaged returns. Item(s) returned must be received in the original condition as sold and including all additional materials such as CDs, workbooks, etc. We will initiate a refund of your purchase price including applicable taxes within 5 business days of receipt. Shipping charges will not be refunded unless we have committed an error with your order. If there is an error with your order or the item is not received in the condition as purchased, please contact us immediately for return assistance.

Reason for Refund/Return:
Condition   Incorrect Item Received   Incorrect Item Ordered   Dropped Class   Purchased Elsewhere   Other

Contact Us: For customer service, email us at customerservice@textbooksnow.com.

Page 1 of 1